Godly Ordinary

Holy
Ordinary

Finding God
in the Everyday

Carol Mead

Scripture taken from the
HOLY BIBLE, NEW INTERNATIONAL VERSION®. NIV®.
Copyright ©1973, 1978, 1984 by International Bible Society.
Used by permission of Zondervan. All rights reserved.

Copyright ©2003, CaRa, LLC

ISBN 0-9746702-0-0
Printed in the United States of America
Second printing, September 2014

Design by Cynthia Clark

Carol Mead
www.holyordinary.com

This book is dedicated to
our good and gracious GOD,

and to the good and gracious friends
who point me to Him every day.

Table of Contents

Introduction 9

January 11

February 34

March 73

April 105

May 137

June 169

July 201

August 233

September 265

October 297

November 329

December 361

Index 395

Introduction

This book first appeared in 2003, about four years after a moment of epiphany in my spiritual life. The meditations in it were mostly taken from an online writing ministry, *Holy Ordinary*, which I undertook as an impassioned lay person.

The road has taken many interesting turns since those first powerful encounters with God. Nourished by a strong and faithful community at St. Peter's by-the-Lake Episcopal Church in Brandon, Mississippi, I went off to seminary in 2006. I returned in 2009 to be the Episcopal chaplain at Mississippi State University and assistant priest at the Episcopal Church of the Resurrection in Starkville. That community also nurtured me as a newly ordained deacon and then as a priest. In a move which might be labeled synchronicity (but which I label the Holy Spirit), I have now returned as priest-in-charge at St. Peter's, my original "home church" in the Episcopal tradition.

My online writing ministry continues, almost 14 years after its inception. In that ministry, I write a brief meditation each weekday, based on readings from the Daily Office in the *Book of Common Prayer*. That ministry has grown in numbers, but it has also continued to deepen my own spirituality as I think and write about Scripture each day.

I pray that all of the work I do in God's name—including my ordained ministry and my writing ministry—points toward the presence and power of God. I thank God for making me a "words person," for fueling my passion for the divine and my passion for the written word. I also thank God for all of the persons in my life who have supported me and encouraged me, especially Jennet Lacey, who has stood by me since our college days.

In recent years, I have begun writing and speaking on "The Word Resurrected," an effort to rekindle interest in the study of Scripture. That work has reminded me of the longing we all have for the transcendent, for the holy. In our day, exploration of the transcendent through the Christian tradition is increasingly dismissed as unnecessary or even foolish. I now focus a great deal of energy and attention on making the distinction between concrete (provable) knowledge and transcendent spiritual knowledge. Both of those types of knowledge are critical to the human experience, and I feel called to remind others that we need not try to fit both types of knowledge into one framework. Such work, I pray, will help revive interest in the Church and in the Christian tradition.

I hope that the meditations in this book, and in my online writing ministry, help people to see and appreciate, through ordinary symbols and metaphors, the presence of God. I hope that readers will see in this work not me, but a glimpse of the God who created us, redeemed us, and sustains us.

> May God bless you and keep you.
> *Carol Mead*
> April 2014

January

JANUARY 1

Resolutions

And I heard a loud voice from the throne saying, ". . . There will be no more death or mourning or crying or pain, for the old order of things has passed away." He who was seated on the throne said, "I am making everything new!"

REVELATION 21:3-5

The club where I exercise will be absolutely packed the next few weeks, both with resolute new members and with old ones determined to make memberships pay this year. Weight control programs burst at the seams. Destructive old habits are laid down, and constructive new ones are taken up, at least temporarily. The air rings with expectancy that we can renew ourselves as easily as we can tear a page from a calendar and make a resolution.

The flaw in that logic is not what can be done, but the identity of the one who will do it. In Revelation, the one seated on the throne declares that everything will be made new. It's the key lesson to hold in mind as the new year dawns: only God can truly reshape us.

But since God does the work, there is no limit on the change that can take place, in a year, a month, a day, a moment. A soul gone gray in the winter with transgression or indifference can be made to glisten like freshly fallen snow. A soul that never before acknowledged a higher power can be brought to its knees and lifted up into companionship with God.

The old order of things has passed away. The new order puts God first.

And He will make everything new.

JANUARY 2

The best presence

... *"How then were your eyes opened?" they demanded. He replied, "The man they call Jesus made some mud and put it on my eyes ... then I could see."* ...

JOHN 9:10-11

I have more time off work the few weeks around Christmas than any other time during the year. So why am I vaguely relieved now that the holidays are over? And why am I so tired?

Because, unlike the man in this story, I forgot to see the holiness of life. The root of the word "holiday," after all, is "holy." It would've been easy for the man in this story to be more worldly, to give a more mainstream explanation of his new vision, but he insisted on naming Jesus as his healer. For him, a day which began as ordinary and dark became the holy day he was allowed to see, and he acknowledged, for all to hear, the Son of God as the source of that vision.

So why can't I, like this newly sighted man, take the small but courageous step of stepping out of the world of man and into the presence of God? Why can't all Christians forget growth in retail sales and remember, remember, remember that "holy" days are all the ones we spend with God?

Once blinded by the glitz of man's commercial and cynical world, I now receive, every day, the gift of the sight of God. I will spend the rest of this year reminding myself that I am blessed with that sight, that God is present everywhere, that every day is holy. True, the so-called holidays are over.

But the holy days are only beginning.

JANUARY 3

Bible belt

"Jerusalem, Jerusalem, you who kill the prophets and stone those sent to you, how often I have longed to gather your children together, as a hen gathers her chicks under her wings, but you were not willing...."
MATTHEW 23:37

In the summer of 2002, Texas police arrested a church pastor for allegedly beating a boy for "not taking his Bible verses seriously enough." So a man who beats a child says the child doesn't understand God's Word? The *child* doesn't understand?

The Bible tells the story first of a people continually turning away from God, and God repeatedly forgiving and protecting and loving them. Then it offers the story of Jesus, who tells us the only rules that matter are to love God above all else and to love our neighbor. He illustrates His love by saying that He longs to gather us to Him, "as a hen gathers her chicks under her wings." He says nothing about beating us until we take Him seriously.

How many people heard the story of the beating and said, "I don't care to be associated with the God such people worship"? How many people turn away from God because the self-righteous try to—physically or emotionally—beat the Bible into them?

Ironically, the man who inflicts harm in the name of God is the one who doesn't take the Bible's message seriously enough. The Bible is God's story, and mine. It's not just a book of rules, and it certainly is not a weapon. It's a love story.

Seriously.

JANUARY 4

Right of way

Let no debt remain outstanding, except the continuing debt to love one another, for he who loves his fellow man has fulfilled the law ... whatever commandments there may be, are summed up in this one rule: "Love your neighbor as yourself." Love does no harm to its neighbor. Therefore love is the fulfillment of the law.

ROMANS 13:8-10

One morning as I turned into the parking garage at work, I almost hit a guy on a bicycle who was riding on the wrong side of the median. He made some gesture at me (I'm optimistic, so I like to think his gesture meant, "Have a nice day!"). I bristled immediately, knowing that I was in the right and he was the one who caused the problem.

But being right would've been small consolation for having inflicted pain on another person, especially when that pain could've been prevented by one glance to the left. I know I have hurt people, and continue to hurt people, by pointing fingers when I've been hurt. I know it's a human reaction, to want to lash back, but it's not a Christlike one. Christ didn't cause others pain; He healed them, no matter who was right.

Do I truly have a personal relationship with Christ? If I do, then how can I look Him in the eye and tell Him I'd rather prove I'm right than to be with Him? He has sacrificed everything for me, and in return He's asking one thing from me.

He's asking me to yield.

JANUARY 5

God's dollar

They brought him a denarius, and he asked them, "Whose portrait is this? And whose inscription?" "Caesar's," they replied. Then he said to them, "Give to Caesar what is Caesar's, and to God what is God's."
MATTHEW 22:19-21

As a kid, every year on my birthday I got a new five-dollar bill from my favorite aunt. (one of the reasons she was my favorite aunt.) I treasured that bill every year, keeping it wrinkle-free, admiring it, using a magnifying glass to find the states' names on the Lincoln Memorial on the back. My brother made fun of me because I doted so much over that bill that I hesitated to spend it.

The coin brought to Jesus, bearing Caesar's image, had value because Caesar said it had value. If I worship God, I bear the image of Jesus in my life, in my heart, in my actions, and so my value, too, is instilled by my Creator.

But like the five-dollar bill I used to get for my birthday, it does no one any good to simply admire how currency looks. The devout Christian life may look good and bring admiration from others, but its real value lies in how that life is used. How does such a life bring me, and others, closer to God? Whom will I help in His name?

As I walk out of the door today, whose image—whose inscription—will I bear? How will I spend the gifts God has so generously given me? Will I use them to buy something for myself?

Or will I get something for my Father?

JANUARY 6

Christ is present (tense)

This is how we know what love is: Jesus Christ laid down his life for us. ... This then is how we know that we belong to the truth, and how we set our hearts at rest in his presence whenever our hearts condemn us.
1 JOHN 3:16-20

"Christ has died; Christ is risen; Christ will come again." I read those words, found in the prayer book of the Episcopal Church, for months before I saw that they capture the essence and the beauty of the Christian faith. Now I know that the verb tenses used in those sentences are no accident.

Death is a one-time occurrence, for Jesus Christ and for each man that walks this earth. Christ was here in the form of a human being, and now that form is gone. Past tense. He has died.

The prayer book doesn't say, "Christ rose" or "Christ has risen." Christ enters our lives in present tense; He is risen. Every day of triumph or tragedy, Christ is risen, a constant and an anchor in this fast-forward earthly existence.

Saying Christ rose from the dead describes a one-time miracle that occurred millennia ago, possibly unrelated to life today. But knowing that He is risen and among us changes our lives every day, from the way we love our families and friends to trivial encounters at the grocery store.

Because Christ is risen and walks with us, lessons are *present* everywhere. Angels are *present* everywhere. God's gifts are *present* everywhere.

Living a joyful and hopeful Christian life boils down to one verb tense: He is risen.

Christ is present (tense).

JANUARY 7

Parthenon

I will make justice the measuring line and righteousness the plumb line. . .; hail will sweep away your refuge, the lie . . .

ISAIAH 28:17

The magnificent Parthenon, the Greek temple dedicated to the goddess Athena, is among the world classics of architecture. It is also a masterpiece of deception.

The Parthenon is carefully constructed to adjust for optical distortion. If the columns and steps were perfectly straight, they would look crooked to the human eye. To compensate for that illusion, each column leans slightly inward; if continued into the sky, they would ultimately meet in the shape of a teepee. The columns are also built with a bulge in the middle to make them appear straight. Steps leading into the temple curve upwards slightly at the center to make them appear level from a distance.

This human life, this culture of ours, too often uses such building techniques. We look at the narrow wording of a rule or law or guideline; anything not specifically forbidden can be rationalized as acceptable and right. From where we stand, the columns look straight, the steps appear level.

A plumb line is "a line to determine verticality," an absolute measure of straightness that does not depend on or adjust for the perspective of the human eye. The true measure of verticality—whether a word or an act leads directly to God—is determined by justice and righteousness. Our human eye can rationalize almost anything as legal or acceptable. But as God's people, we have to ask, "But is it just? Is it right? Is it a perfectly straight line to our God?"

Or does it only look that way from where I'm standing?

JANUARY 8

I'm going to Grace-Land

All these people were still living by faith when they died. They did not receive the things promised; they only saw them and welcomed them from a distance. And they admitted that they were aliens and strangers on earth . . . they were longing for a better country—a heavenly one. Therefore God is not ashamed to be called their God, for he has prepared a city for them.

HEBREWS 11:13-22

One day when I saw two cars with license plates from Nova Scotia, it really took me back to my childhood. When our family traveled, I listed all the different states' plates we saw; those Nova Scotian tags would've wowed me back then.

And I loved the mottoes used to make states sound exciting or special: Sunshine State, Land of Enchantment, Land of 10,000 Lakes. How could the people in those cars even feel comfortable in ordinary states like mine?

The most powerful and profoundly moving moments of my life have virtually all come since I found my way to God. But now in some of the old places, with some of the old friends, I'm an "alien and a stranger." I can barely relate now to people who have no spiritual initiative. We speak different languages.

I keep hoping to encourage old friends to start spiritual journeys, knowing how those first baby steps can change a life. At the very least, I want them to visit the home I found in the last few years, because it's a great place to live.

I live in the state of Grace.

JANUARY 9

Junk door

Accept him whose faith is weak, without passing judgment on disputable matters. . . .Who are you to judge someone else's servant? . . .
ROMANS 14:1, 4

While driving through rural Tennessee one fall, I passed a home place with a rusty, worn out old pickup truck door lying in the yard. The grass around it was cut, but it looked as if it had been there for years. I thought, "Why would someone keep such a thing?"

Easy for me to criticize, but I often do the same thing in my spiritual life. I'm continually judging other people, harboring resentment and anger and frustration against them because I don't care for the choices they have made and the way they have treated me.

But all of that negative emotion is of no more use to me than an old truck door is to anyone else. Not only will it never be of any use, it is in the way. It's unsightly and dangerous to work around. No telling what lies beneath it.

But I think I'm right, and I believe that I have been treated unfairly. That's my rationalization, but it doesn't really carry much weight. No matter how right I may be, hanging on to the junk of self-righteousness and judgment hurts me much more than it hurts "them."

And, as the Scripture says, who am I "to judge someone else's servant"? Why hang onto this junk that obstructs the way between me and my God? It's unsightly and dangerous to work around. No telling what lies beneath it.

Why would someone keep such a thing?

JANUARY 10

Priceless

So too, at the present time there is a remnant chosen by grace. And if by grace, then it is no longer by works; if it were, grace would no longer be grace. . . . What Israel sought so earnestly it did not obtain, but the elect did.

ROMANS 11:5-7

I remember the day that I learned about the meaning of the word, "priceless." It confused me, because I thought it must be synonymous with "worthless." No price, no worth.

Maybe that same mindset kept me from looking earnestly for God. I kept thinking that these people must be wrong; it can't simply be a matter of my accepting God's presence and light. There has to be a catch. There has to be a price. Until I earn my way, until I brush up my spiritual and moral resumé, I cannot accept such a commodity. I cannot have something of such brilliance and worth.

I'm still learning, through my relationship with God, the difference between a gift and a paycheck. The gift of grace comes freely, out of love, and it must be freely accepted. It's not compensation for a life well lived. In fact, in a sense, the opposite is true: we offer our lives and our service to God to thank Him for the gift, not to earn it.

And, of course, grace did come at incredible cost; it just wasn't a cost I bore. The price was paid when a Man sacrificed His life to save mine, who paid the price, so that, every day of my life, I receive a priceless gift of grace.

Priceless. No price. Infinite worth.

JANUARY 11

God speed

Peter said to Jesus, "Rabbi, it is good for us to be here. Let us put up three shelters—one for you, one for Moses, and one for Elijah." (He did not know what to say, they were so frightened.)

MARK 9:5-6

Right after college, when my nephew bought his first new car, he was concerned about getting speeding tickets. It was the first time he'd had a car capable of exceeding the speed limit.

The sudden acquisition of power can be disturbing. Peter was understandably frightened to see the power of God up close; who wouldn't be shaken when God's hand lights up the sky? I've seen His light flash brilliantly in darker skies, in nighttimes when my soul was so fragmented and off balance I feared I'd never be whole again. Yet when He came into my life—even though it's what I asked for—it was downright scary.

His power still stuns me in its timing, its precision. Many times He has sent a friend's words to chase away some minor demons I was fighting. It wasn't coincidence that those words came exactly when I needed them; it was nothing less than the love and the presence of God, striking deep in my heart and my soul.

Our God cannot be contained in a little tent on a mountainside, or even in a cathedral, but wants all the room we can give Him in our fearful human hearts. And we need to let that power of God in so that he can give us the fastest, most beautiful car in the world.

Because there are no limits on Godspeed.

JANUARY 12

Enough for Him

So if you faithfully obey the commands I am giving you today—to love the Lord your God and to serve him with all your heart and with all your soul—then I will send rain on your land in its season...

DEUTERONOMY 11:13-14

All my life I've wanted to be a writer, a dream my dad always helped me dream. I tried unsuccessfully many times to write novels, but could never finish one. Finally, I did complete a book, a history of Madison County, Mississippi.

When the book came out, I immediately sent my dad a copy. He phoned me to say that he hadn't read it yet; every time he saw my name on it, his eyes filled with tears of pride until he couldn't see at all.

I told him it wasn't the kind of book that would make me famous or rich, but he didn't care. He was holding a book in his hands, and I had written it. That was enough for him.

I know God wants to be close to me, but I often wonder why He would want someone who has made such ungodly mistakes. Sometimes I experience doubt, thinking, "It's not possible for one person's life to change so dramatically in such a short time." I keep thinking that I don't deserve what God offers me, that I should have to earn this gift.

I don't have to earn it; in fact, I couldn't. Now the tears are in my eyes. It staggers me to know that today God holds my life in His hands—simply because I finally asked Him to.

And that's enough for Him.

A warm house

I love the house where you live, O Lord, the place where your glory dwells.

PSALM 26:8

The movie *The Crucible* is a fictionalized account of the Salem witch trials. In it, Goody Proctor apologizes to her husband, an adulterer, for driving him into another woman's arms. "It were a cold house I kept," she tells him.

And while a cold house is better than no house at all, we humans seek the warmth and light. Small wonder, then, that many of today's spiritual seekers shy away from church, where they find human judgment, self-righteousness, and little evidence of the presence of God. They are driven away to other forms of love, of worship, of community—cold houses because God does not live there.

Too often we say that we want others to worship with us, yet we insist that the people we "let in" think and express themselves and look and judge just as we do. But such thinking pushes away the people who need community and God the most: people who know that what they seek is spiritual, but who are confused about where to find it. Such thinking means that I seek to make the church a place where my glory, not the glory of God, dwells. And a cold house that would be.

The true house of God welcomes all, loves all, accepts all, supports all. The true house of God leaves the judging to God. His true dwelling place overflows with warmth and Light.

That's how we know that Father is home.

Oil and water

[The Lord] will judge between the nations and will settle disputes for many peoples. They will beat their swords into plowshares and their spears into pruning hooks. Nation will not take up sword against nation, nor will they train for war anymore.

Isaiah 2:4

Oil from a sunken tanker entered the waters of Spanish coastal villages, making it impossible for fishermen there to pursue their livelihoods. The problem is one of misdirection; the millions of gallons of oil plaguing the fish habitat weren't intended for the sea, but for heating, lighting, transportation.

Religious zeal unfounded on love for others works like that thick oil polluting a coastline. Something which could be used for so much good, which could save lives if carried in healthy vessels and channeled to the proper place, has been misdirected. Those who use manmade church doctrine to beat others into submission take the oil that God has given them, a passion for Him, and turn it loose in places and ways that are deadly.

Many people stay away from church today because they need plowshares, not swords. They long for love, not for judgment. They value righteousness, not self-righteousness. And they will not put themselves in a place where that oil—a passion for God—is used to destroy. They long for the same things that we do. Warmth. Light.

And a way to get to our God.

JANUARY 15

One well-placed Word

The Lord replied, ". . . the priests and the people must not force their way through to come up to the Lord, or he will break out against them."

EXODUS 19:24

My high school English teacher once wrote on the board, "She kissed the man she loved," and then suggested that we insert the word "only" into the sentence at each possible place. The teacher wanted to show the importance of word order to meaning. "She kissed the only man she loved" isn't even close to "She kissed the man only she loved."

In life, as in English class, one word can change everything. One word, well placed, can change a life for the better, while one word, unwisely placed, can turn a life into the ditch.

Those of us who pursue a relationship with God know that every person in our lives needs Him. Unfortunately, we get so zealous about passing the Gospel along that we may wield it as a blunt instrument instead of as a compass to God. The Lord told Moses to warn the people of operating on their own schedules, their own agendas. He said that if the people—or the priests—forced the approach to God, "The Lord will break out against them."

Everyone needs God, so how do we know when and how to approach someone about Him? I'm trying to learn to ask God what He wants me to do and, just as importantly, when He wants me to do it.

Because when it comes to bringing people to God, I don't know how to do it on my own, but God knows.

Only God knows.

JANUARY 16

Stocks and bonds

" '. . . I will put my dwelling place among you . . . I will walk among you and be your God, and you will be my people. I am the Lord your God, who brought you out of Egypt so that you would no longer be slaves to the Egyptians; I broke the bars of your yoke and enabled you to walk with heads held high.' "

LEVITICUS 26:11-13

When I visited Rome one spring, I walked around the Roman forum, looking for a place where Peter and Paul had purportedly been imprisoned. I wanted to see the place from which our God had freed them, because I needed Him to free me. It comforts me somehow that the very best of God's people, those who became His dwelling places, those who lived their lives and died their deaths only for Him, faced every manner of human persecution, yet ultimately triumphed.

I don't expect to be sentenced to prison, but I constantly build cells or place myself in slavery, and I have to ask God's help every day to get out. Some days I'm imprisoned by money, some days by the lack of it. Some days I'm a slave to others' opinions, and some days to my need for a better image of myself. Walls and stocks, bricks and mortar, yokes and chains are not required; but I have walled myself into prison just the same.

When I breathe in the Holy Spirit, and ask God to free me, walls crumble. The yoke and chains fall away. Stocks open.

Yet God doesn't ask me to die for Him. He asks so much less. Only that I live for Him.

And live free.

JANUARY 17

You may never know

". . . anyone who gives you a cup of water in my name because you belong to Christ will certainly not lose his reward."

MARK 9:41

I read about a scientific community in Antarctica where they estimated that the ice they melted for water in 1999 had fallen as snow sometime in the 15th century. An ordinary snowfall at the South Pole would become sustaining and life-giving centuries later.

Have I affected another person positively today? I may never know. I do know how often a harsh word—even from someone I don't know or respect—has ruined my day. I have been deeply grateful to a friend or stranger who showed me kindness. I suspect we would be staggered to learn how much we've affected the quality of someone else's day, week—or even life.

If a snowflake that fell in the 15th century can quench the thirst of an Antarctic expedition five centuries later, isn't it possible that my influence extends far beyond my wildest estimation? Isn't it possible to hesitate one moment before getting angry, since my words could ruin or make the day?

My actions could turn someone towards—or away from—a relationship with God. I find that thought sobering—yet exhilarating: that something I do today could have impact a moment or a lifetime later. It should be enough to make me tend people unfailingly with love.

I may need that precious drop of water myself some day.

JANUARY 18

Word from home

I am like a desert owl, like an owl among the ruins. I lie awake; I have become like a bird alone on a roof.

PSALM 102:6-7

The nun who taught my first-grade class in Catholic school gave me the responsibility of walking about a half-block every morning to mail letters she had written home to her parents. I now realize how that young woman missed her family, and I'm touched that she trusted me to bear her precious messages home.

Each Christian who listens to God and tries to bring others to Him is given a sacred trust, a mission every bit as important as carrying letters that will go home to a loved one. And in a human sense, it can be a very lonely walk sometimes; doing the right thing and carrying the message of God may not win the approval of other people. The bearer of the Gospel may be ostracized, avoided, persecuted, feeling like "a desert owl among the ruins." While there is no work more sacred, listening for the will of God and trying to remain in that will can be a very lonely business indeed.

Being a child of God in a secularized and often petty human world can mean taking some steps down a lonely road and being separated from the comfortable crowd. But in our hands we carry the word, the will, the presence of God to a hurting and hungry and wounded world. So when the road stretches long and lonely, we can be sustained by one life-saving fact.

We bear the message that will connect a child to home.

JANUARY 19

Proxy

... they sang a new song: "You are worthy ... because you were slain, and with your blood you purchased men for God ... You have made them to be a kingdom and priests to serve our God ..."
REVELATION 5:9-10

I once heard a heart-rending story about a man who battled childhood memories of being tormented by bullies. Ultimately, he was only able to let go of his fear by picturing Jesus standing in front of the tormentors, saying, "Hit me instead."

The only bullying I've endured has been self-inflicted. I don't know why yet, but all of my adult life I have beaten myself up for not measuring up intellectually. A strange little cloud follows me and whispers, "You're not good enough." I don't hate myself, but I certainly struggle to love myself.

When I heard about Jesus taking the hits for the victimized boy—and for the fearful man—something clicked. I had long understood giving negative forces—fear, sadness, pain, doubt—to Jesus to handle for me. But I had never thought to give Him love that I can't handle. Jesus stands for me in any circumstance, good or bad.

So when I think I'm not worthy to accept love, I can offer it to the Son of God in my place. I can love Him, and eventually I'll remember that I am in Him, so it's okay to love myself. Jesus wants me to let go of my fear of being loved, to love myself as He loves me. But until I can get there, I hear His healing words, whispered in the depths of my soul.

"Love Me instead."

Faithful and true

Jesus replied, ". . . have you not read what God said to you, 'I am the God of Abraham, the God of Isaac, and the God of Jacob'? . . ."
MATTHEW 22:23-33

Going through a desk drawer one day, I found my Dad's old wallet containing his social security card, his driver's license, my business card, and a couple of two-dollar bills. I decided to carry his driver's license in my wallet to acknowledge how much he remains in my heart and my life.

Since the moment I let God into my life, I have felt His presence within me, just as I know my dad will always be part of me. But some days I wish I had something that I could look at, a tangible reminder that He is there. Sometimes I can't hear His voice amid the noise of my ego, my fear, the voices of others who think they know what He wants me to do. Why can they hear His will for me more clearly than I can?

One contemplative said that in her conversion, she saw in her soul two words: "God only." I need to keep those words before me today to remind me that the God who was there for Abraham and Isaac and Jacob is also there for me. I know He is, because my heart and soul tell me that my God is faithful, even when I am not.

Along with my father's driver's license, maybe I should carry those two words with me to focus on the Father's presence even when I can't see or hear Him. "God only." There's no "I" in those words. There's no "u." God only.

Everything else is noise.

JANUARY 21

Now

Therefore, there is now no condemnation for those who are in Christ Jesus, because through Christ Jesus the law of the Spirit of life set me free from the law of sin and death.

ROMANS 8:1-2

Periodically I will cancel an appointment to get my cholesterol checked because my eating habits have been bad and I don't want to get "caught." I figure I'll wait a couple of weeks until I can get the number down.

I once (and sometimes still) take that same approach to my spiritual health. I don't want to give God a life that is weak, sinful, vengeful, petty, insecure, but one that is whole and pure and healthy. So I postpone going to Him until I can clean up my act. But as the doctor is the one who can help me lower my cholesterol, God is the only one who can make me whole and pure and healthy.

"There is now no condemnation for those who are in Christ Jesus," according to Romans. The text does not say anything about waiting awhile or that this offer is void if you have made, or continue to make, mistakes. "There is now no condemnation for those who are in Christ Jesus." *Now.*

My forgiveness was bought long ago, not by my willing myself to "be good," but by the grace and mercy of God and the sacrifice of His Son. So now is the time to ask God to give me the wholeness and strength I lack. Now is the time to accept the gift, and to express gratitude for what God has done for me.

Now.

JANUARY 22

Write about now

I write to you, dear children, because your sins have been forgiven on account of his name. I write to you, fathers, because you have known him who is from the beginning. I write to you, young men, because you have overcome the evil one. I write to you, dear children, because you have known the Father.

1 JOHN 2:12-13

One of my first college journalism professors told me to consider majoring in something other than journalism. "You learn to write by writing," he said. "Major in something to write about."

Life with God is not just a matter of religion—about learning how to write to God—but in learning what to write about. Life with God means hearing Him in every stage of emotional maturity, as His children, as parents, as weak humans, as humans strengthened by His presence.

Yet often I hesitate to "write God back," thinking some worry I have is unworthy of a conversation with the most powerful Being in the universe. But God speaks every day, and He wants us to speak to Him every day, on everything from the tawdry details we wish He didn't know to the victories we'd like to keep for our own.

The form we use for prayer is unimportant; all that matters is that we communicate now with the One who gives us our innocence and our wisdom, the One who speaks to us in our strength and our need. All that matters is that we hear the voice of God and respond. We learn to write by writing.

And we learn to pray by praying

HOLY ORDINARY

JANUARY 23

Baggage check

Since everything will be destroyed in this way, what kind of people ought you to be? You ought to live holy and godly lives as you look forward to the day of God and speed its coming . . .

2 PETER 3:11-12

"I gave you empty stomachs in every city and lack of bread in every town, yet you have not returned to me," declares the Lord.

AMOS 4:6

When I traveled abroad, I was determined to fit all of my clothes into one piece of luggage, so I bought a canvas thing so enormous it could have its own zip code. "The Big Ugly," as I dubbed it, was so heavy and unbalanced that it would barely roll. The longer I dragged it around, the less I cared about the contents, and the more I began to wonder, "Do I really need this stuff? Why not just drop it and get home?"

I have always carried the maximum in emotional baggage, too. Yet how can I embrace God if my arms are filled with that junk? How can I reach for His mercy if I lug around unforgiveness and resentment, if I criticize others or deride them so I look smarter or more important? God, I protest, I have grown so fond of those old things. But if you want me to, I will tell them goodbye.

The journey has shown me how empty a judgmental life is, and how heavy the burden of self-righteousness and rationalization. The journey has proven that God is my only Justifier. And so the baggage stays behind. After all, I'm trying to get home to my Father.

I need to be traveling Light.

Good fish, bad fish

... the kingdom of heaven is like a net that was let down into the lake and caught all kinds of fish. When it was full, the fishermen pulled it up on the shore. Then they sat down and collected the good fish in baskets, but threw the bad away.

MATTHEW 13:47-48

In the movie *Pretty Woman,* a call girl named Vivian is turned away from an exclusive Rodeo Drive store when a salesclerk declares her unfit to shop there. Later, after an expensive shopping spree elsewhere, Vivian returns, beautifully dressed. "Do you work on commission?" she asks the salesclerk. When the woman nods, Vivian says of her earlier rejection, "Big mistake. Huge."

With this mess I've made of my life, I keep thinking that I can't even dress well enough to go looking in God's store, a dangerous assumption. How many people thought they would work on their spiritual lives when their career was on track or their children grown, but then had no opportunity to go to God?

Every moment we live goes—like a fish—into God's net. He takes in the bad fish and the good—the moment you courageously did the right thing, the moment you let someone down, the moments in between. It's His job—not ours—to go through the net and cast out the "bad fish."

You could start enjoying His unbounded forgiveness, His unlimited, unconditional love, right now, no matter what you have done. Do you really think you should wait until you're all cleaned up?

Big mistake. Huge.

JANUARY 25

Prison in disguise

Listen to my cry, for I am in desperate need; rescue me from those who pursue me, for they are too strong for me. Set me free from my prison, that I may praise your name.

PSALM 142:6-7

One morning, on an unfamiliar highway, I drove past an attractive, understated building, and was surprised to see that it was a correctional facility. Skillful architecture served to disguise the facility's real purpose of keeping people behind bars.

I once thought all prisons looked the same: forbidding, unattractive, overtly frightening. But that day I learned the lesson that some prisons don't look like prisons at all. In fact, some places of imprisonment, like this one, look quite pleasant from the outside and even from inside.

I have been in such places, separated from God by walls made of paychecks, of career success, of ego, of unhealthy relationships. I didn't even know it at the time, but I was "in desperate need," pursued by strong foes that overwhelmed me and prevented my wanting to seek God. After all, who can fight back when someone makes such offers to a mere mortal? Who can fight such foes?

I know now that only God can fight those fights. Only God can win me true freedom from this world, and in it. I fooled myself into thinking I was free because the walls that imprisoned me were so seductively attractive, inside and out. Attractive, yes.

But a prison nonetheless.

JANUARY 26

In the mourning

In the morning, O Lord, you hear my voice; in the morning I lay my requests before you and wait in expectation . . .

PSALM 5:3

O Lord, heal me, for my bones are in agony. My soul is in anguish. How long, O Lord, how long? . . .

PSALM 6:2-3

I think I must have a flat learning curve, because God has to give me the same message over and over. "If you give all up to me, I will give back to you a life with unimaginable depth and grace and beauty. I can do more with your life than you could ever dream of doing on your own."

First I got that message about the direction of my life. It took over four decades, but I yielded to Him, and life took a brilliant, energizing turn upwards. Then I learned the message again about gifts. He took my love for words and finally, finally I found that I had something to write about.

And then I began to understand the need to let go of the people in my life. I still mourn losses in my family years ago, and until recently I never realized that I need to let them go to God. I have clung to them, to their memories, perhaps to prove how much I love them. But continuing to mourn them has kept me from seeing them in God's arms, the only consolation in their no longer being here with me.

Like my life's direction and my gifts, the people in my life belong to God. And they belong with Him.

Some things, it seems, can only be seen in the mourning.

JANUARY 27

Life savings

Once when we were going to the place of prayer, we were met by a slave girl who had a spirit by which she predicted the future. She earned a great deal of money for her owners by fortune-telling. This girl followed Paul and the rest of us, shouting, "These men are servants of the Most High God, who are telling you the way to be saved."
... Finally Paul became so troubled that he turned around and said to the spirit, "In the name of Jesus Christ I command you to come out of her!" At that moment the spirit left her.

ACTS 16:16-18

In a fast-growing neighboring county a new bank was under construction. The raw wooden walls were up, but though the windows, doors, and exterior weren't complete, a banner on the building proclaimed it, "Open." Personally, I thought it an unwise place to put my money, since it is literally open to the world and the elements.

For over 40 years, though, I banked in such a place spiritually, pursuing things that have no meaning in eternity. A great job and family members—the currency I worked so hard to save—were stolen from me because that bank was open, too. It was wide open to the vagaries of our transient world.

Like the slave girl, I cannot serve two masters. I have to make a decision of whether to pursue the god of material things or the Most High God. Besides, do I really want a god who is small enough to fit in a pocket, a god small enough to be saved in a vault?

Or the one God who is big enough to save me?

JANUARY 28

The book and its cover

... "God, who knows the heart, showed that he accepted them by giving the Holy Spirit to them.... He made no distinction between us and them, for he purified their hearts by faith ... it is through the grace of our Lord Jesus that we are saved...."

ACTS 15:8-9, 11

One afternoon in a bookstore I overheard a man buying a Bible as a gift. He didn't know which translation of the Bible to get, or whether it should include other reference tools. He knew for certain only that he wanted it to have a personalized cover and tabs to locate the books of the Bible.

Magnificent church ritual may draw people to God initially the way that man was attracted to a beautifully packaged Bible. He doesn't care yet what's inside the book, but just his appreciation of the elegant package may eventually encourage him to peek inside.

God, on the other hand, knows what's inside every package. He knew my heart all along, that despite the bluster and bravado on my "cover," inside I ached with emptiness, starved for His presence.

I love the trappings of church and religion; I was initially so mesmerized by the church's splendor that I stayed long enough to start seeing God. Now, words in the Bible resonate so deeply in my heart that I think they are permanently written there, or even that I helped write them in another lifetime. Before I knew it, that book had my name written on it.

And instead of going to church, I found myself going to God.

HOLY ORDINARY

JANUARY 29

Pompeii

The kings of the earth take their stand and the rulers gather together against the Lord and against his Anointed One. "Let us break their chains," they say, "and throw off their fetters." The One enthroned in heaven laughs ...

PSALM 2:2-4

When Pompeii was destroyed, images of the 2000 victims were preserved by a mixture of ashes and rainwater which molded around the bodies. Among the victims were slaves—identified by their iron chains—as well as the wealthy. The inferno played no favorites. Survivors who escaped the disaster later tunneled into the ruins and removed "valuable" objects, then fled.

God's power will surely enter your life. You can open your arms to accept His treasure of peace and richness, or you can stop to gather the physical goods that will weigh you down as you flee the fire. In my case, disaster came, but I later tunneled back into the ruins to find a relationship with God, the only treasure in my life with any meaning. When I found Him, I found my heart.

What will those who follow find among the archaeological digs of my life? Will they find a woman enslaved by this world—bound in chains of fear, of greed? Or will they find a Christian smiling at finally, finally becoming part of the fire and the power that is our God?

When God's fire comes into your life, what treasures will you carry with you—the ones in your cart?

Or the ones in your heart?

Apprehension

The angel swung his sickle on the earth, gathered its grapes and threw them into the great winepress of God's wrath. They were trampled in the winepress outside the city, and blood flowed out of the press . . .
REVELATION 14:19-20

I read about a nine-year-old Afghan girl who survived a rocket attack on her school, an attack aimed at keeping women from being educated. She said simply, "I am afraid. But I will continue."

The word "apprehension" can mean two vastly different things: a fear of future evil or the power of perceiving or understanding. Strangely, the two can go together: when I get past a fear, I often open myself up to much deeper understanding of God. Does it mean my faith is weak if I combat fear? I know, deep in my heart, that God loves and protects me, yet I become anxious about what He will ask me to do. I know that to speak His name openly in the world could prompt attacks on me, and sometimes my fear keeps me from doing what I know to be right.

But wine cannot be produced until grapes have been pressed. The fruit of righteousness cannot be offered to the world until it has become mingled with the blood of Christ. Apprehension figures into the formula. Christ was a human, like me. Was He apprehensive, as I am—afraid, and yet beginning to understand? Perhaps. But like the young Afghan girl, He made a decision, as I have.

I am afraid. But I will continue.

JANUARY 31

What you wish for

...Joshua tore his clothes and fell face down to the ground...and said, "Ah, Sovereign Lord, why did you ever bring this people across the Jordan to deliver us into the hands of the Amorites to destroy us?..."
JOSHUA 7:1-15

The Lewis and Clark expedition went originally in search of the Northwest Passage, the fabled "missing link" between the Atlantic and Pacific oceans. The link did not exist, but in their exploration, the men opened up vast reaches of the continent for the expansion of a new nation.

The search for God in our lives often takes similar turns. We go out, seeking a God who will give us more power in our lives, more peace, and we have a very carefully articulated idea of what that life with Him will look like. But then, like Joshua and his people, we find ourselves humbled, often driven to the wilderness, and we throw ourselves face down before God. "This is not what I asked for!" we rail at Him.

Like Lewis and Clark, I went exploring, thinking I knew what I would find, thinking I knew what I needed. That narrow passage I imagined didn't exist, but the journey has opened up expanses of myself and of my gifts that I could not imagine. And it's all happening because I have placed my life—albeit sporadically—in the hands of God.

This life with Him—it is simply not what I asked for. Not what I asked for at all.

Thanks be to God.

February

FEBRUARY 1

Pay it forward

They replied, "Let one of us sit at your right and the other at your left in your glory." "You don't know what you're asking," Jesus said. "Can you drink the cup I drink or be baptized with the baptism I am baptized with?" ...

MARK 10:37-38

A friend of mine experienced the nightmare of "identity theft." Someone pirated her social security number, then opened new credit accounts in her name, drained her bank account, and maxed out her credit cards. A thief was able to live the high life because someone else spent years building a good credit rating.

We expect instant gratification today, and often think someone else should pay the price. The people who stole my friend's name are there when the doors open to pick up the new computer, the new furniture, the new jewelry, because someone else will be forced to pick up the tab.

Most people say they want to "be more spiritual," as long as God doesn't get in the way of schedules, hobbies, jobs. "Change my heart, O God," I used to say. Inside I whispered, "But not my schedule. Not my address. Not my tee time."

And we'd all like to "play God:" to save the day, triumph over death, heal the sick, still the waters. Yet not one of us is interested in being on trial for the simple offense of loving unconditionally. Not one of us is interested in paying up on the day a cross with our name on it goes up.

But we don't have to, do we? That bill's been paid.

The river of God

Do you not know? Have you not heard? Has it not been told you from the beginning? Have you not understood since the earth was founded?
ISAIAH 40:21

Authorities in control of the Colorado River continually face disputes over who gets how much of the river; they're forced to ration out its life-giving waters.

When we pretend that we can completely understand God in our limited human minds and language, we try to ration the river of God. We speak as if He is transparent to us, trying to put Him in manmade vessels of religious doctrine and theology. We parcel Him out in manageable amounts rather than letting His mystery and power overwhelm us. When we accept God's presence but fail to accept His immensity, we ration the life-giving waters of the river out in a teacup.

What can the river of God accomplish if we let Him flow freely in our lives? What change can He bring to our hearts if we admit that we long only for Him? What can He fill us with if we let down the wall and accept His will rather than trying to capture Him in our own? What gifts can He bring if we admit that He is beyond our imagination—if we allow the mysterious river of God to pour in, to empower us, to cleanse us, to end our thirst? When will we realize that nothing but God will fill us?

"Do you not know? Have you not heard? Has it not been told you from the beginning? Have you not understood since the earth was founded?"

Will you keep trying to hold back the River?

FEBRUARY 3

The God of second chances

Light is sweet, and it pleases the eyes to see the sun.
ECCLESIASTES 11:7

A few years ago a local golf club held an event to determine the state's worst golfer. One of the terrible golfers playing in it said that he liked golf because, no matter how badly he played one hole, he still might make a par on the next hole. He saw every round as 18 opportunities to make a par.

Our God is the God of second chances, and third, and fourth, and literally, of chances into eternity. No matter how much darkness I seem to gather around myself one day, God offers me the opportunity, in the next day or even the next moment, to move close to Him and feel His presence. Sometimes it's painful to move close to Him, knowing how I have let Him down. Sometimes I feel as I do when I've spent a torturous, sleepless night: the light of day hurts my eyes, but I know I'm about to have another chance to get up and move on.

"Light is sweet, and it pleases the eyes to see the sun." No matter how weary my eyes are from lack of rest, from weeping, from looking too hard at myself, it is indeed sweet to know that the light of God awaits me one more time.

I frequently let God down. I continually bruise my relationship with Him. I routinely focus so much on myself that I neglect His people.

Yet I see the most remarkable sight when I awaken each morning. God is still here. He's still here.

And so, the Light goes on.

FEBRUARY 4

The shape of the universe

But Jesus would not entrust himself to them, for he knew all men. He did not need man's testimony about man, for he knew what was in a man.
JOHN 2:24-25

A new theory on the universe suggests that it may be donut-shaped rather than infinite in all directions. As one cosmologist said, "There's a hint in the data that if you traveled far and fast in the direction of the constellation Virgo, you'd return to Earth from the opposite direction."

Certainly the shape of an individual life has circularity, as Jesus knew, "for He knew what was in a man." Anxious to be autonomous and self-reliant, we travel as far and as fast away from Him as we can some days. Then when our own little cosmos falls apart, we appear before Him again, seeking forgiveness and comfort.

It's a case of human sameness versus divine sameness. Man is predictable, in his failing and returning, and God remains constant, always ready to forgive. He knows "what is in a man," yet He continues to love.

So each day I spend as a Christian convinces me of the circularity of my orbit, and the infinitude of God's universe. I travel away. I land in this dark spot. And if I can avoid despair, and simply keep moving, soon I find myself right back in the center of the universe, face to face with my unimaginably loving God. I am forgiven. Again. And I am loved. Still. The irrefutable fact? God is infinite in all directions.

Especially mine.

FEBRUARY 5

Future tents

. . . Jesus . . . sent them out to preach the kingdom of God and to heal the sick. He told them: "Take nothing for the journey—no staff, no bag, no bread, no money, no extra tunic . . ." So they set out and went from village to village, preaching the gospel and healing people everywhere.

LUKE 9:2-3, 6

My apartment complex is bounded along the back by woods and a small creek. One day I noticed a tent pitched between a building and the creek. I smiled to think that some kids wanted an adventure, but not too much of one.

In my work for God, I have been just about as adventuresome as those kids—willing to get out of my comfort zone, but desperate to keep it within sight. I tell myself that I'm doing His work, but I choose comfortable places, safe places, and say, "That is what I will do for God." Too often I haven't even asked Him if He wants me to do that job, or if He wants it done at all. Is it the greatest presumption, for me to think that I know what God wants without asking Him? Or is it that I'm so afraid of the answers—of where I will be asked to pitch my tent—that I won't even ask an open-ended question?

It becomes an issue of prayer, of trust, to go where God asks me to go, without hedging, with no staff, no money, no "extra tunic." If I do as He asks, God will honor my obedience with His constant and comforting presence. God will hold me close, there in my wilderness tent.

God is my comfort zone.

Nothing but the Truth

May those who say to me, "Aha! Aha!" be appalled at their own shame. But may all who seek you rejoice and be glad in you . . .
PSALM 40:15-16

How can we thank God enough for you in return for all the joy we have in the presence of our God . . . ?
1 THESSALONIANS 3:9

The movie *Apollo 13* is the story of a crippled space mission in which many of the navigation systems the crew relies on are inaccessible. But the commander knows that if he keeps the image of the earth constant and unchanging in the window, that their course will be true.

I'm a fact-gatherer—always have been—relying on manmade systems for navigation. But focusing too much initially on the "facts" of religion kept me from seeing the Truth about God, and now I see others caught in that same place. They ask things like, "Where did the wives of Cain and Abel come from?" Or they point out how archaeological finds or historical records dispute a "fact" of the Christian story.

People who "shoot down" Christianity using such questions seek facts but miss the Truth. I'm not smart enough to answer such questions, but I know the profound and unutterably beautiful Truth: that the presence of God in my life steadies me.

I know the Truth: that because of one Man's death, I have life, not just eternal life, but rich and abundant and joyful life today.

I know the Truth: that God loved me so much He sent His Son to die for me. I love God, and He loves me.

I know the Truth.

FEBRUARY 7

Walking crucifixes

... I tell you the truth, anyone who has faith in me will do what I have been doing. He will do even greater things than these ...
JOHN 14:12

Assisi, Italy, whether seen with physical vision or spiritual vision, is one of the most beautiful places I have ever visited. It's no wonder that it was home to passionate lovers of God like St. Francis.

Francis adopted the tau cross as his crest; the tau, which looks like a T, was the last letter of the Hebrew alphabet. It represents fulfillment of the entire revealed word of God in the cross of Jesus. Francis told his brothers that—with their arms outstretched in religious habits—they resembled the tau. He urged them to become "walking crucifixes," living examples of God's compassion and faithfulness.

Jesus asks the same of us, for us to reach out to others, to do what He did. He led others toward the Father. He healed. He taught. He soothed. But above all, He loved.

He loved those who followed Him, those who used Him, those who misrepresented Him, those who feared Him. (And still does.) He even loved those who killed Him. Wounded and dying, He still asked for others to be healed.

He asks us to do the same, to love so intensely and so unconditionally that we disappear, so the people in our world see only God. He asks us to take every opportunity to bring people to Him, even when it means unbearable pain for us. He asks us to welcome those who seek Him, as He did.

With open arms.

FEBRUARY 8

The bluest blue of heaven

. . . But as for me, I trust in you.

PSALM 55:23

Some places can be reached only by way of trust.

Near the end of a trip to Italy our tour group visited the island of Capri, one of those rock-carved-out-of-blue places so magnificent in that part of the world. We took a large hydrofoil out into the sea, then transferred to a small launch and finally to a tiny rowboat, to enter a place called the "Blue Grotto."

The grotto entrance is so small we had to lie down in the rowboat to get inside. The man piloting the boat couldn't even stay upright, so he pulled the boat into the cave on a rope. As we made that frightening little move into the cave, I panicked momentarily, worrying that my head would scrape rock. But the pilot knew what he was doing, and I found myself in a place that took my breath immediately away.

The light inside the grotto glows the bluest blue you can imagine, deep, bright, ethereal. It felt as if we were in heaven.

I see heaven often these days, finding the blue light of God shining in the loved ones and experiences of my life. I can reach that deep blue place by giving up my self and seeking only the light of God. But I have to put myself completely in His hands to get there.

Call it a cave entrance, or loss of self, or the narrow door. But whatever you call it, if you can make yourself small enough to enter, you will find the bluest blue of heaven. Here. Now.

Some places can be reached only by way of trust.

"Theory of mine"

But the Jews ... dragged Jason and some other brothers before the city officials, shouting: "These men who have caused trouble all over the world have now come here ... They are all defying Caesar's decrees, saying that there is another king, one called Jesus."

ACTS 17:5, 6-7

Research suggests that autistic people lack something called a "theory of mind." In other words, an autistic child may think that what is going on in his mind is also going on in the minds of others. He cannot learn well or interact with others because he fails to understand that their thoughts and feelings differ from his own.

As a new Christian, I, too, struggle with a theory of mind, or more accurately, a "theory of mine." I get so focused on gifts and tools that I think of as mine—my schedule, my talents, my needs, my wishes, my thoughts—that I catch myself feeling as if I should be congratulated for what I give to God.

Probably, though, it's a battle fought by new and experienced Christians alike: the battle to remember that all comes from God, all belongs to God, and all should return to God. It's not easy; that realization caused riots in Jesus' time, the thought that there is someone else out there, that there is "another king, one called Jesus." Yet this new King who turned their priorities upside-down, who "caused trouble all over the world," brings such peace to this world of mine.

This world of His.

Life redeemed

... Jesus himself came up and walked along with them; but they were kept from recognizing him ... "The chief priests and our rulers ... crucified him; but we had hoped that he was the one who was going to redeem Israel."

LUKE 24:15, 20-21

More often than not, I have to listen to someone else's music at traffic lights. The music from the next car is often so loud that I have to either close my window, listen to their music, or turn mine up.

Today's culture and the Gospel mix about as easily. The culture clangs so loudly and insistently around us that most people cannot hear, and probably wouldn't believe, that it could be redeemed, that it could live in the constant knowledge of God's presence.

But that inability to see God isn't new; two of Christ's own disciples "were kept from recognizing" Him right beside them. "We had hoped that he was the one who was going to redeem Israel," they tell the risen Christ. The unspoken addendum: "Yet here we are walking the same old road, living the same old life."

Life redeemed, though, isn't life lived in a different sphere, safely conducted and kept in the church building on Sunday. Life redeemed continues down that dusty road Monday morning, yet with God as companion. Life redeemed is telling this world that God walks right beside us, that He longs for us to turn and recognize Him. Life redeemed isn't a different road after all.

It's a different way of walking this one.

HOLY ORDINARY

FEBRUARY 11

The out-of-towners

The Lord is near . . . I am not saying this because I am in need, for I have learned to be content whatever the circumstances. . . . I can do everything through him who gives me strength.

PHILIPPIANS 4:5, 13

Often when I drive to work, I see cars from distant places. Those out-of-towners are likely to wander into my lane or to stop or turn without warning. But I try to be more patient with them; for some reason, I always picture that they're here for an early morning medical test or to consult a specialist about a scary diagnosis.

When my sister died, I started the morning of the funeral thinking, "I cannot survive this day." I was lost, sure that I hadn't the strength or the courage to endure the experience. Like those lost drivers, I strayed, hesitated, went the long way around, eventually realizing that my soul hungered for God. All the while, those comfortably at home with God—centered in a relationship with Him—gave me room and gently helped me find my way.

God first gave me the strength to get through a day, and then He showed me how to get through the pain. Finally, He began instilling Himself in my heart so that I would be ready to "do all things through Him who strengthens me." I once was lost, too, and now that I'm found, I need to remember that those lost souls are not in the way.

They're *on* the way—to the same God who healed me.

FEBRUARY 12

Detour

Before your very eyes Jesus Christ was clearly portrayed as crucified. I would like to learn just one thing from you: Did you receive the Spirit by observing the law, or by believing what you heard? Are you so foolish? After beginning with the Spirit, are you now trying to attain your goal by human effort?

GALATIANS 3:1-5

Driving to Dallas one day by interstate, I came upon a traffic snarl so serious that people turned off their engines and got out to visit and stretch. Conveniently near an exit, I pulled off, turned around, and decided to find an alternate route. When the numbered highway I chose turned into a narrowing dirt road in a wildlife refuge, I reluctantly returned to the interstate. This time, though, I was a couple of miles farther back. I went through all of that headache for nothing.

The Galatians thought they needed to follow strict guidelines in order to win God's approval. The law had not brought the Spirit of God upon them in the past, but they chose to try that alternate route anyway. And Paul knew it wouldn't work, He had once fervently obeyed the Jewish law, but found no God there.

But insisting that we earn our way only devalues Christ, and devalues His sacrifice. And Paul and every Christian who has had a personal experience of knowing God can tell the sobering truth. That road of "I'll do it myself" narrows quickly.

And eventually, it leads nowhere.

HOLY ORDINARY

FEBRUARY 13

Alchemy

Furthermore, since they did not think it worthwhile to retain the knowledge of God, he gave them over to a depraved mind, to do what ought not to be done. They have become filled with every kind of wickedness, evil, greed and depravity.

ROMANS 1:28-29

In the Dark Ages, alchemists fervently sought something called the philosopher's stone, a mysterious substance capable of transforming base metals into gold. This unknown substance, according to one source, was, "said to be . . . found everywhere but unrecognized and unappreciated." With gold, after all, one can buy anything of value in the world.

As spiritual alchemists today, we seek the magic formula to transform iron into gold, mundane existence into rich and vibrant life. The magical ingredient is not liturgy, or a certain type of music; it is not prayer or worship of a certain form. "Retaining the knowledge of God" is that magical ingredient that transforms the everyday into the priceless. Without Him, our lives tend to turn to the wicked, the evil, the greedy. With Him, every moment holds brilliance and value.

Like the stone the alchemists sought, God is "found everywhere, but unrecognized and unappreciated." Like the stone, He allows us to have anything of value in this world, or in the next, because all of life can be transformed. But not into gold.

Into God.

The color of love

. . . Delight yourself in the Lord and he will give you the desires of your heart.

PSALM 37:4

. . . Now this is eternal life: that they may know you, the only true God, and Jesus Christ, whom you have sent.

JOHN 17:3

So it's Valentine's Day, the day we celebrate love, the day of hearts and flowers. The "seasonal" aisle at the grocery store is filled with red, the color of love.

Probably Valentine's Day is associated with the color red because the heart, which pumps the body's lifeblood, symbolizes the emotions. Today people are sending red greeting cards, boxes of candy, flowers, everything you can imagine (and may choose not to) to express how true their love really is, this time.

But in the truest and longest-lasting love story of all, red is the color of ultimate love because it is the color of the blood God's Son shed for me. This is not a God who sends flowers, or jewelry, or heart-shaped boxes of chocolate. This God sends His Son, the being most precious to Him, as a message to His people who previously couldn't understand the depth of His love. The message is now clear; there's no need to agonize between, "He loves me . . ." and "He loves me not . . ."

A Man who doesn't even have to lower himself to be a man gives up His life and dies in humility, in servitude, in love. He does it for me. There's no question in my mind on Valentine's Day.

He loves me.

FEBRUARY 15

Vision

Are not all angels ministering spirits sent to serve those who will inherit salvation?

HEBREWS 1:14

. . . From the fullness of his grace we have all received one blessing after another. . . . No one has ever seen God, but God the One and Only, who is at the Father's side, has made him known.

JOHN 1:16, 18

For one solid month, I struggled with my vision, and I had trouble giving my anxiety about it to God. It scared me so much I couldn't find peace.

What I really lost sight of, it seems, was the presence of God. And just when I got so low I couldn't see Him, His angels stepped in to help point me to Him. I felt their hands lifting me up to get a closer look. I saw hearts opening wide to take on my pain. I saw the spirit of God in His people, all ministering to me in His name. In that sense, God was very visible, very tangible. I could see Him.

The people we think of as angels on earth only hint at the love embodied in Jesus Christ. He brought the ambiguous notion of God's love into focus, showing what it really looks like to human eyes. He sacrificed for—and tended to—the wounded bodies and souls of the world. Like mine and yours.

In this experience about blindness and sight, one lesson became clear. I will not find peace by "handling" worry or conflict, but only by giving it to God. He alone can bring me peace, because real peace is not just the absence of conflict.

It's the presence of God.

FEBRUARY 16

Like-minded

Then Jesus asked, "What is the kingdom of God like?" . . . He said to them, ". . . you will stand outside knocking and pleading, 'Sir, open the door for us.' But he will answer, 'I don't know you or where you come from.'"

LUKE 13:18, 25

I'm not a stickler for proper language, as I can be pretty casual with it myself. But one abuse of words bothers me so much I want to scream: use of the words "I'm like" in place of "I said." As "Valley Girl" as it sounds in print, it's quite common, as in: "She's like, 'What is your problem?' and I'm like, 'If you can't figure it out, I'm not going to tell you.'" It, like, drives me up the wall.

"Like" should paint a verbal picture or portray action, but "said" is a record of speech. Jesus warned against confusing lip-service to religion with real love of God. He tried to describe what the kingdom of God was "like." He tried to warn people that talk without action would never allow them to know God, and eventually the Master would no longer recognize them.

In Hebrew, one expression means both *word* and *deed*. God's Word, God incarnate in Jesus, isn't about talk, but about actively loving every living person. He spoke to us with His life, His sacrifice, His love and inclusion of all. He didn't just ask us to do as He said, but to do as He did. As He does.

So if I want to be in God's kingdom, I'm like, what do I do?

Well, I'm, like . . . Him.

FEBRUARY 17

The pot and the kettle

"But if I say to the boy, 'Look, the arrows are beyond you,' then you must go, because the Lord has sent you away."

1 SAMUEL 20:22

I hate for people to finish my sentences as I talk, as if trying to guess what's on my mind. I detest having conversations with people who don't ever really listen, but spend the time I'm talking trying to think of what they will say next. I even have a reprimand in my personnel file for yelling at an employee. I was trying to help him and he wouldn't listen to me, so I got angry.

I can't remember how the saying goes—does that make me the pot or the kettle for seeing my faults more clearly when others exhibit them? I am constantly running around, trying to do exactly the things God must want me to do. I ask Him, fairly often, what He wants me to do. But before I hear the answer, I'm doing something else, or asking more questions.

My life goes through spells when it feels incredibly agitated; friends think I try to do too much. But I feel agitated because I can't do enough to thank God for all the gifts He gives me. I have no peace, because I'm deciding what to do for God without asking Him what He wants of me. I constantly catch myself guessing at what God is thinking instead of asking. Even now.

Why guess when you could just ask? Why won't she listen instead of always thinking of what she will say to me next? Doesn't she see I'm trying to help? Why doesn't she see?

Why doesn't she listen?

FEBRUARY 18

Follow me up

Now faith is being sure of what we hope for and certain of what we do not see. This is what the ancients were commended for.

HEBREWS 11:1

Years ago, I hiked with friends to the site of a "ghost town." We began walking through the woods, knowing the general direction to head but unsure of the best route to take. As we bore south, we began noticing small pieces of colored fabric on trees, maybe 75 yards apart. We finally realized that they marked the easiest trail to the ghost town, so as we reached one marker, we scanned ahead to find the next one. We had no idea who had left the markers, but understood instinctively that they would help guide our steps.

My journey towards God travels a road seen by many Christians before me; I learn from their experiences and their wisdom. I don't know all of these Christians personally, but know of them—people named Abraham and Abel, Enoch and Noah. It's enough to know that they valued what I value—an intimate, loving relationship with God—and that they have seen more of the path than I.

God leaves me these people as gifts—spiritual markers along the road to help me find my way to Him. Many of them are the "ancients" found in the Good Book. Still others are found in my daybook. Whoever they are, it truly makes my journey easier and deeper to learn about and appreciate the spiritual guides who have gone before me.

Now I know it's my turn to leave a sign that reads, "Follow me up."

FEBRUARY 19

Tentmakers

. . . Paul went to see them, and because he was a tentmaker as they were, he stayed and worked with them.

ACTS 18:2

Of all I've read about Paul, the words that comfort me most are that, "he was a tentmaker as they were." I need that inspiration; otherwise, it's too easy to think I can't be working fervently for God because I have to "make a living."

Yet most of us who bring God to the world also work as tentmakers, doctors, lawyers, teachers, parents. Paul made tents for a living, but he also brought the good news of God's unending and unbounded love to people right there where they lived and loved, where they celebrated and grieved, where they fed and hungered. Where they worked.

As joyous as it is to spend time around other Christians, that is not where God's work waits. We have to go outside our "comfort zones," showing people how we Christians live in the "real world." Eventually, one—or more—will see what we have and start wondering if they can have it, too. Eventually one—or more—will ask how to find it. And as we make our tents, we will show them how to find our God.

We will show them, right where they live and breathe, how the God of Jesus Christ lives, how He breathes, in the real world. But we won't have to do it to make a living.

We'll do it to make a life.

FEBRUARY 20

witness

"You are witnesses of these things. I am going to send you what my Father has promised; but stay in the city until you have been clothed with power from on high."

LUKE 24:48-49

I may have watched too many crime dramas and lawyer shows growing up, because the word "witness" makes me extremely nervous. In those shows, witnesses were always made to look inept or unsure. Even if they clearly remembered what they saw, the opposing lawyer found a way to twist the truth.

Very few people in the world met Jesus Christ face to face. I never met Him in person, and yet I feel equipped to serve as His witness, without question, without hesitation. I have seen direct evidence of His handiwork.

I have been at the scene, in the depths of spiritual poverty. I have seen firsthand the love that God, in His infinite patience, continued to offer me. I saw firsthand the way a Christian reaches down to support another human being who is incapable of getting up and negotiating even one day unassisted. I have seen firsthand the color, the clarity, the power that clothe a person who finally accepts the presence of God.

I know firsthand, because my life is one life He touched, one life He changed, one life He saved. I know firsthand. So yes, I witness. And I tell nothing but the Truth.

So help me, God.

Someone touched me

But Jesus said, "Someone touched me; I know that power has gone out from me."

LUKE 8:46

A friend of mine once went through turmoil in so many areas of his life at once that he was somewhat depressed. He asked us, "Please pray for me. I'm so down that I can't even pray for myself."

My friend knew intuitively the same truth that the woman in this passage knew. Even when you can't go to God directly, when you're too angry or hurt, too tired or depressed, you stay close to the body of Christ to get the help you need. The power of healing faith flowed towards this woman just because she remained close to Christ.

When I first started coming to church, it was months before I even took communion because I felt so out of place. Still, every week I sat there among God's people, allowing the body of worshipers to help cleanse my soul. While I wasn't taking the bread and wine of communion, I was being nourished by the simple beauty of people reaching up to touch their God and then reaching out to touch me.

Somehow, as I sat nervously in that pew, the power had gone out from Christ, through the transformer of His people, and flowed into my life.

I had no idea what faith in Christ could do for me. Just like the woman in Luke's story, I was desperate, and thought that, somehow, if I could get close enough to God, He might help me. And ultimately I realized that I didn't need to know how to heal.

I just needed to know where to look.

Big G, little g

When the people saw that Moses was so long in coming down from the mountain, they gathered around Aaron and said, "Come, make us gods who will go before us. As for this fellow Moses who brought us up out of Egypt, we don't know what has happened to him."

EXODUS 32:1

When crisis comes, we too often throw aside God (with a big G) and try to fill our lives with other gods (little g).

Work becomes our god, and we worship it with an impossible schedule to convince ourselves that our lives matter. Pleasure becomes our god, and we pursue activity after activity until we realize that we still feel inexpressibly empty and alone. Even pain or sorrow can become our god; we wallow in it and show it like an old war wound, eventually losing all sense of equilibrium, all sense of joy. And still we feel so empty.

Ultimately we realize that those "little g's" are not gods at all, but simply feeble attempts to give meaning to our lives by filling every hour with activity. But our God does not give "busy work;" He gives comfort. Our God doesn't fill schedules; He fills hearts and souls. Our God waits patiently until we find him, then He immediately wipes our slate clean and forgets we ever looked anywhere else for Him.

Those gods with the little g's fill your daybook. The God with the big G fills your life.

FEBRUARY 23

Drawing the big circle

> . . . *let us stop passing judgment on one another. Instead, make up your mind not to put any stumbling block or obstacle in your brother's way. . . .*
>
> ROMANS 14:17-18

In the 10th grade I hated geometry, as I saw no connection between geometry and the real world. Now, I think that much of life is geometry; it involves drawing and measuring and filling circles.

The fullness of my life is a function of the circles I draw in it: big circles to include others, or small circles to exclude them. Healthy relationships allow me to draw big circles to include—and to love—more people in my life. Relationships that push people away—in ignorance or jealousy, in fear or shame or doubt—often implode, like a black hole that folds inside itself and disappears. If a relationship—even one formed in the name of religion—encourages me to relate to fewer people, I can't believe it is of God.

Some people, in the name of God, draw circles to exclude others who don't hold the "right" beliefs or pursue "acceptable" forms of worship. But Christ urges us to love one another, not just those who agree with us or those most like us. Nothing in the Bible says to love only Episcopalians, or Baptists, or even Christians. All of the verses I find about love tell us to love other people—no qualifiers, no exclusions, because the God that I love draws the big circles.

In fact, the God that I love *is* the big circle.

Looking back

Thus he overthrew those cities and the entire plain, including all those living in the cities—and also the vegetation in the land. But Lot's wife looked back, and she became a pillar of salt.

GENESIS 19:25-26

Every so often I become especially conscious, for some reason, that I need to divest myself of many of the material things that I own. I give away bags full of clothing and household items, throw away boxes full of paper, and give myself more space in the bargain.

I think I also occasionally need to take time, very intentionally, to clear out some of the emotional clutter in my heart. One of the biggest obstacles to my spiritual growth in my Christian life has been regret, regret over anger voiced, love unvoiced. It is so hard to let those regrets go; I suppose I cling to them in hopes that somehow, someday I can undo them. But I can't.

A life with God requires cleaning out the regrets and the attachments that keep me looking back over my shoulder instead of forward to the future He holds for me. I have to let the regrets go.

Only God can heal the past. Only God can love the ones I failed to love enough, and only God can convince me that I did the best I could. Only God can help me get rid of the junk.

Ultimately, it's not about deprivation. It's not about giving things up. It's about making room.

For the love of God.

FEBRUARY 25

me and Him

> *... Saul was still breathing out murderous threats against the Lord's disciples ... As he neared Damascus on his journey, suddenly a light from heaven flashed around him. He ... heard a voice say to him, "Saul, Saul, why do you persecute me?" "Who are you, Lord?" Saul asked. "I am Jesus, whom you are persecuting," he replied.*
>
> ACTS 9:1, 3-5

Ever since I have been writing about God, I have struggled with capitalization. I want to capitalize all pronouns and nouns dealing with God, to recognize Him above myself. But now I have gotten so used to typing "Him" with an uppercase H that I often catch myself capitalizing the word when it refers to a person (some not very God-like).

It is, perhaps, a small reminder of what the Christian life should be. When I love another person, I love God. When I strike out at another person, I strike out at a child of God, and at God Himself. So the words could be capitalized in every case, because every action I take affects and personifies my relationship with God.

Certain days, I get tremendously angry, resentful, depressed, and frustrated. When someone who is supposed to love me attacks me, I want desperately to strike back. But even if I successfully fight back, the one I have really attacked is Jesus Christ. He's the one who took abuse, humiliation, torture, and death, and He did it for me. So maybe it's time for me to endure some things for Him.

For him.

The worldwide web

... Let us not become weary in doing good, for at the proper time we will reap a harvest if we do not give up.

GALATIANS 6:9

One summer night, a streetlight illuminated for me the delicate lines of a spider's web arching across from a house to a garage. I wondered how the first strand of that web made it across the walkway.

Those tiny silken lines seemed incapable of withstanding a breeze; think of the impossible odds against survival of the first strand of that web, launched from one precarious point to another to anchor the whole design.

A few friends sent out such fragile threads to me years ago. They probably thought then that nothing in me could anchor one of God's designs. But their Father asked them to send a line my way, and so they did. Somehow, miraculously, one of those lines took hold to become a powerful and life-changing faith that would not find its form and expression until decades later.

As Christians, it's our job to send out lines to others in our lives, no matter how shaky the foundation may seem, no matter how improbable the survival of those threads. After all, every shimmering web drawn like artwork against the nighttime sky began with a single strand sent hurtling against all odds into the dark. The small task you perform faithfully today may become someone's relationship with God tomorrow.

So send your tiny thread out into the night.

FEBRUARY 27

God's house

In him the whole building is joined together and rises to become a holy temple in the Lord. And in him you too are being built together to become a dwelling in which God lives by his Spirit.

EPHESIANS 2:21-22

Years ago, when a mall was under construction, one man resisted selling his property to developers, despite skyrocketing land prices that would give him a profit of over a million dollars. Finally he agreed to sell, but only if the buyers moved his tiny, worn old house to a new piece of land. He was comfortable in it, and he wanted to keep living in it.

God's infinite love builds us a mansion that we cannot even imagine. To prepare us for it, He shows us His kingdom in small pieces—loving us through friends and family, giving us modest but comfortable cottages to inhabit until we're ready for the mansion.

God uses human ears to listen to our cries, human arms to enfold us, human voices to tell us that He loves us and that we are forgiven. He knows that sometimes human love is as much as we can fathom, so He puts another human being nearby to cling to our hand, to calm our fears, to hold us as we cry.

When a friend loves unconditionally or helps heal, we glimpse the kingdom of heaven, because it is truly God who holds and God who soothes and God who makes us whole.

For now, I think, He'll let us find comfort in our worn and tiny houses.

Leading the blind

As Jesus approached Jericho, a blind man was sitting by the roadside begging. When he heard the crowd going by, he asked what was happening. They told him, "Jesus of Nazareth is passing by." He called out, "Jesus, Son of David, have mercy on me!"

LUKE 18:35-38

All of God's creatures hold within them an instinct to journey safely home. Birds kept in captivity even struggle, during migration time, against the sides of their cages in the direction they would migrate if free.

I was drawn for years toward God, even though I could not identify the source of my longing. Like the blind beggar by the road, I heard the believers moving past, and ultimately learned the reason for the excitement. "Jesus of Nazareth is passing by."

Those of us who have found God are asked to pause along the road for others—those who cannot yet see but have that powerful yearning for God. I am asked simply to point to Christ, to explain that He centers my life and pours His mercy and peace out on me. God asks me to try to give a person blinded by tragedy, confusion, or doubt the chance that I had: the chance to stop Jesus and seek His mercy.

Why would a God—a *God*—stop long enough to help me see? Why would a God allow me to point the way the next time a blind man seeks Him? Incredibly, inexplicably, Jesus of Nazareth didn't just pass by, but allowed me to see Him. And then asked me to walk with Him.

Lord, have mercy.

March

MARCH 1

Breaking news

Then Saul said to Samuel, "I have sinned. I violated the Lord's command and your instructions. I was afraid of the people and so I gave in to them."

1 SAMUEL 15:24

Frequently news channels, particularly local ones, seem more concerned with getting a story first than with getting it right. Reporters say things like, "In a story first reported by our news team . . ." to emphasize that they got there ahead of the other guys. Meanwhile, so much valuable time is spent talking about news coverage that the real news goes untold.

Religious denominations and churches today seem so preoccupied with determining the absolute "right" position on an issue that we seem to have forgotten why churches and denominations exist in the first place. We anxiously search Scripture to find the right stance on an issue, and forget that we're talking about people's lives. We become so intent on proving we have the favored place in God's heart that we forget His heart is entirely about loving.

Like Saul, we become "afraid of the people" and worry more about what the world thinks than we do about loving others as God loves us. Like the news teams, we become desperate to prove our own worth, to say that we told the story first, or that we told the story best. Meanwhile, the people most in need of God's love go without.

And the real News goes untold.

MARCH 2

"I am"

Believe me when I say that I am in the Father and the Father is in me; or at least believe on the evidence of the miracles themselves. I tell you the truth, anyone who has faith in me will do what I have been doing.
JOHN 14:11-12

"I think, therefore I am." With those words, philosopher René Déscartes felt he had proven his own existence, in a time when skeptics questioned whether man truly existed. The human mind is easily fooled, so how do we even know for certain that we exist?

Today we're very sure of our own existence and importance, but many question the existence of God. We wonder where God has gone when grief and pain arrive. We know we're made in God's image, but we look at people like Ted Bundy, Osama bin Laden, Adolf Hitler, John Wayne Gacey and wonder what this God must look like.

How do I know God exists? I know God exists because I now find myself trying to love people who seem very unlovable. When someone hurts me, my human instinct is to lash out and hurt back. But when I have instead a deep sense that I should love rather than defend, it's nothing less than God working in me, and on me.

Through it all, amid all the world's human failing, I know unequivocally that I am made to love others and to be loved. Man alone could not create such a powerful force. Only our God could do it.

I think, therefore I am. But I also love.

And therefore, *He* is.

MARCH 3

Moving pictures

But the Lord said to Samuel, ". . . The Lord does not look at the things man looks at. Man looks at the outward appearance, but the Lord looks at the heart."

1 SAMUEL 16:7

I saw a cartoon once that mocked some yuppies filming the Rocky Mountains with a camcorder. The caption read, "Pet peeve: people who take moving pictures of things that don't move."

If I didn't know God, I would probably do something similar, always staring at mountains, at beaches, at constellations, at friends, and wondering how they could be so breathtakingly beautiful. Often, seemingly with impossibly perfect timing, a friend sends along a message that I desperately need. If I don't remember to look for the hand of God at work, I would have to continually examine that message to see why it moves me so much.

But I know that it moves me for the same reason the sound of waves crashing on the beach and the brilliance of sunset and the depth of solitude and the touch of a friend's hand move me. They move me because they come directly from God.

I look with great sadness on people, some of them close friends, whose "lives" seem so dead. They seek entertainment and busy-ness, because in quiet time doubt rattles around in hollow souls. They desperately cling to every positive, happy moment, thinking they may never see such moments again.

But I know the beauty will be there later today, and tomorrow, and always, because my God will be with me always. He never changes.

And so everything moves.

MARCH 4

Things left undone

We took such a violent battering from the storm that the next day they began to throw the cargo overboard. On the third day, they threw the ship's tackle overboard . . . When neither sun nor stars appeared for many days and the storm continued raging, we finally gave up all hope of being saved. . . .

ACTS 27:18-20

In our Episcopal service, we ask forgiveness for "things we have done, and things we have left undone." Some days, I can barely utter the words.

I knew nothing of faith when my dad and my sister could've been helped by it. I didn't find God until it was too late to help them, and it was the biggest thing I left undone. I ache to have one more chance to talk to them, to say I love you. Go to God. I'll see you later.

I used to see religion as decoration, like a ship in a bottle—beautiful but incapable of bearing weight. But faith is different; it isn't just built for calm seas, but to weather the roughest waters, the fiercest storms, the most violent winds. There is no need to throw cargo overboard. There is no need to cast pieces of my life, of my heart, into the sea to lighten God's load. There is no need to give up all hope of my being saved. Of their being saved.

God is capable of carrying me with my load of grief, and He will eventually convince me that I cannot beat myself up for something I simply did not know in time. I am so sorry. I just didn't know in time.

I didn't know.

HOLY ORDINARY

MARCH 5

Whose fault?

For we do not have a high priest who is unable to sympathize with our weaknesses, but we have one who has been tempted in every way, just as we are—yet was without sin.

HEBREWS 4:15

Earthquakes occur when massive tectonic plates beneath the earth's surface shift. Near San Andreas, California, two plates—the Pacific plate and the North American plate—meet, making the area very prone to earthquakes.

Spiritual unsteadiness, too, seems to strike where life's priorities conflict. At the intersections of money and family, religion and politics, friends and career, spirit and flesh lie dangerous "faults" with tremendous energy which can move us toward God or away from Him.

God knows, literally, how difficult this life can be when priorities clash. He has visited this place as a mortal human being and encountered the same pressures and conflicts we face. "For we do not have a high priest who is unable to sympathize with our weaknesses." In Jesus, Spirit prevailed over flesh because His only focus was His Father's will.

Not one of our other priorities can stand the pressures of this world. Money will go away, as will loved ones, jobs, status, religion. All of those things, which may seem so important to us today, will change, and only God will remain. So if we're separated from Him, it will be because we allowed something to move us away.

And it's our own fault.

MARCH 6

Diamonds and pearls

"For I know the plans I have for you," declares the Lord, "plans to prosper you and not to harm you, plans to give you hope and a future."
JEREMIAH 29:11-12

I don't wear much jewelry; I consider myself highly accessorized if I wear a watch. But that's my physical being. In my spirit, I wear diamonds and pearls.

Pearls develop when a small piece of foreign matter enters an oyster, and it covers the irritant with layers of nacre to create the gem. Geologists don't agree on the exact process that creates diamonds, but they do know that it requires tremendous heat and pressure.

Irritation. Heat. Pressure. All are molding my soul right now.

A coworker annoys me so mightily that I cringe every time she comes near. When I noticed that irritation, I realized that I make snap judgments about people, and take things personally instead of considering what the other person is battling.

A few years ago, heat and pressure in a job made me realize that I was spending 50 or 60 hours a week doing something I hated for money and prestige.

God wishes me prosperity, so my spirit will grow with each irritant and perceived threat, if I allow Him to cover them with love and grace. If I learn from all these weak spots in my life, I'll be clothed in His righteousness, and I'll be wearing diamonds and pearls. I hope they look good on me.

They're from my Father.

MARCH 7

My bodyguard

I rise before dawn and cry for help; I have put my hope in your word. My eyes stay open through the watches of the night, that I may meditate on your promises. . . . Those who devise wicked schemes are near . . .
PSALM 119:147-148

One night years ago, I came home from a friend's house about 2:30 a.m. Through my open window, I heard heavy footsteps outside—someone in boots walking by, then stopping at my window. I called 911 and soon heard him run away, but it terrified me. I closed and locked the windows and left the air conditioner off, afraid I wouldn't hear the man if he returned. I lay awake all night and faced the next day totally exhausted.

We're so jaded by man's ways that we stay awake—too frightened to rest, never at peace. We spend untold energy and anxiety worrying about the pain or sorrow waiting outside our window. But God wants us to listen for His comforting, guiding voice. He wants us to trust Him, and to rest.

Now that I've found God, I assign a new identity to the Man outside my window. He is the bodyguard who shields me from people with "wicked schemes" to humiliate me, hurt me, haunt me. He stands watch so I can meditate on His promises. He stations himself close by so He can hear my voice—and I can hear His—when I cry out in fear or exhilaration, sorrow or exuberance.

Knowing how I love Him, He stays awake and listens for me. And because He watches, I can rest.

I know the Lord my soul will keep.

MARCH 8

Access

While all the people were listening, Jesus said to his disciples, "Beware of the teachers of the law. They like to walk around in flowing robes and love to be greeted in the marketplaces and have the most important seats in the synagogues and the places of honor at banquets."

LUKE 20:45-46

A New Jersey architect who recently became confined to a wheelchair has been forced into an entirely new way of looking at the world. The altered perspective has given him a different view of buildings he has designed; features he once thought marvelous and easily functional are no longer within reach.

Jesus saw hypocritical "teachers of the law" as architects of a temporal building, a place where the pursuit of God was easily within their own reach but beyond the realm of possibilities for the "little people." They wanted God to be about exclusivity, only reachable from their high places. In valuing religion above God, they designed an esoteric place that suited their own needs for the moment, their own desire for adulation and status. But ultimately they loved their important positions so much that they forgot to love God.

Conspicuous piety feels good in the moment. It's a building that looks great from the outside. But can I live in it forever?

Can He?

MARCH 9

"Us against them"

At this, she bowed down with her face to the ground. She exclaimed, "Why have I found such favor in your eyes that you notice me—a foreigner?"

RUTH 2:10

I am such a picky eater that I dislike things I haven't even tasted. A friend recently assumed that I wouldn't like coconut; her faulty "logic" was that picky people often don't like coconut, so I must not like it. I hate for people to make assumptions about me, even on something as minor as food preferences.

My dad made sweeping assumptions; he was a racist, not in a cross-burning, invective-spouting way, but in a quieter, more ingrained "us and them" kind of way. He frequently talked about what "they" do, based on prejudices which apparently had festered for decades.

If I make a statement about "them," I'm almost certainly harboring prejudice— extrapolating one experience into a broad statement about people I've never even met. If one person treats me badly, I shouldn't ask, "Why do they do that?" I should ask, "Why did he do that?"

It's not that I shouldn't judge people on the basis of race; I'm not supposed to judge others at all. I learned the hard way that judging others constantly makes my days negative, unsettled, unrewarding. Life becomes a battleground of "me against you" or "us against them."

Anyway, if I'm truly interested in being one of God's people, it simply cannot be a story of "us and them."

It's a story of "us and us."

MARCH 10

Room for rent

I have hidden your word in my heart . . .

PSALM 119:11

As you come to him, the living Stone—rejected by men but chosen by God and precious to him—you also, like living stones, are being built into a spiritual house . . .

1 PETER 2:4

In Boston is an odd little place called "Spite House." A rich man there owned a piece of property which was only five feet wide and 100 feet long. His neighbors, thinking he couldn't use the lot, tried to buy it for an unfair price. To "spite" them, he built a long, narrow house in the space; the only problem was that he had to live there, in a series of rooms barely wide enough for furniture.

I lived in spite house for years. I held a grudge—very justifiably, I thought—in my heart, which left little room for compassion and kindness and gentleness. And, as one of my favorite quotes says, "The size of your world is the size of your heart." My heart—and my world—both felt very small.

Then I wrote the person who prompted the grudge, someone who hurt me very deeply, to ask forgiveness for the jagged edge of resentment I carried so long in my heart. I didn't do it for her; I did it for me, and for my God. I did it because I tired of living in the five-foot-wide space of self-righteousness and unforgiveness.

I want my heart to be God's heart, where there is room even for people who have hurt me deeply. He wants them healed. Surprisingly, so do I.

So I'll lock the door on my way out.

Spite house is closed.

HOLY ORDINARY 83

MARCH 11

Work of heart

He who was seated on the throne said, "I am making everything new!"
REVELATION 21:5

[Jesus replied] "I tell you the truth, if you have faith as small as a mustard seed . . . Nothing will be impossible for you."
MATTHEW 17:20

Michelangelo sculpted with the idea that he was not creating a figure, but releasing one imprisoned by the stone. He looked deeply into the stone and saw David, magnificent. He saw Mary, grieving. He saw Moses, strong and resolute.

A friend helped me realize one day that God thinks of me as His work of art waiting to be released. I had chosen to remain imprisoned in a block of unattractive, unwieldy stone, mostly because I feared the hammer and chisel. I looked at myself and saw a rectangular block of stone, nothing much to look at, nothing much to envy, nothing much at all.

But God looks at the stone and sees what it could be. He looks at me and knows that nothing is impossible for me to accomplish once He releases me. He looks within the block of stone and sees fullness, energy, light, compassion, limitless love, limitless life, desperate to escape. He sees those things because He put them there.

I sense that it is now my time to emerge from the stone. A few blows of the hammer can free me if I will let them. A few blows of a hammer, pounding nails into the hands and feet of a precious Son, all so that I can be released.

So that I can be His work of art.

MARCH 12

God bless me!

But you, O Sovereign Lord, deal well with me for your name's sake; out of the goodness of your love, deliver me. For I am poor and needy, and my heart is wounded within me.

PSALM 109:21-22

My sister Marsha used the English language in some very creative ways, constantly mixing metaphors and scrambling sayings. For instance, she would confuse the phrase, "We're in a bad way" with "We're all in the same boat," which resulted in "We're all in a bad boat." She was also the only person I've ever heard say, "God bless me!" to herself when she sneezed.

She overflowed with joy, despite a life filled with difficulty. She raised three boys into three fine young men, and she mostly did it alone. She endured tough financial times, and suffered from many health maladies. Yet she smiled and laughed through it all because she knew in her bones how to let herself be loved and how to love another person.

You couldn't tell by looking at her bank account, but of all my family, she was our "richest relative." God did bless her with enormous capacity to love, and through her, He blessed all of us. I realize now that the lesson of how to accept love and give it to others is the greatest gift my sister ever gave me.

So now I ask God to bless me, too, to teach me that money fills only bank accounts, but that love fills hearts and changes—even saves—lives.

Without that lesson, we'd all be in a bad boat.

HOLY ORDINARY

MARCH 13

Lift me up

So many gathered that there was no room left, not even outside the door. Some men came, bringing him a paralytic . . . Since they could not get him to Jesus . . . they made an opening in the roof above Jesus and, after digging through it, lowered the mat the paralytic was lying on.

MARK 2:2-4

Someone pointed out to me how often in conversation we unnecessarily add the word "up" to a verb. We fill the tank up, when it would be enough just to fill it. We take up tickets, make up beds, figure up costs. We call people up on the telephone. Perhaps an instinct to put everything in God's hands makes us emphasize the "up."

Once, when a spiritual buddy hit some rough waters and I asked how I could help, she said simply, "Lift me up." She knew that getting closer to God would equip her to rise (up) above the problem. The men in these verses didn't do any healing, but just lifted up a friend to bring him to Christ. They offered no instructions, no specific requests on how they thought the problem should be solved. They knew the Son of God could figure out what to do once they brought their friend near.

How well could our world work if we operated solely to connect other people to the true power of the universe? God (literally) knows that extraordinary power could be unleashed if we more often forgot ourselves and lifted others in prayer. God knows.

So we can leave the rest (up) to Him.

MARCH 14

Fully redeemable

"As for you, go your way till the end. You will rest, and then at the end of the days you will rise to receive your allotted inheritance."
DANIEL 12:1-4, 13

"I have much more to say to you, more than you can now bear."
JOHN 16:12

One day while I waited in the doctor's office, another patient searching through an enormous purse for something kept pulling strange objects out. She looked up sheepishly and said, "I save everything."

As does God. Every gift we have, as well as every bit of grief, doubt, fear, and every experience we have can be redeemed by God to make us stronger and bring us closer to Him. If we will just persist in reaching toward Him, in "going our way till the end," we will find Him, or a message about Him, in every ordinary thing we do.

The gifts God holds for us, and the truth He offers, are "more than we can now bear," so He speaks to us in these indirect ways— through our relationships with other people, through the liturgy of our faith, and through the deepest wounds and most gut-wrenching crises of our lives.

God doesn't cause the pain, but He can use every bit of it to make us empathetic to others and to make us begin to trust Him with everything. My grief today will become someone else's strength tomorrow. My doubt today will become someone else's hope tomorrow. My brokenness today may open someone else's door to faith tomorrow. That's the way our God works.

He saves everything.

HOLY ORDINARY

Ineffable

Half of the wood he burns in the fire; over it he prepares his meal . . . From the rest he makes a god, his idol . . . No one stops to think, no one has the knowledge or understanding to say, "Half of it I used for fuel; I even baked bread over its coals . . . Shall I bow down to a block of wood?"

ISAIAH 44:16, 17, 19

"Ineffable" is one of my favorite words because it is a paradox. It means, "incapable of being described in words," and yet it is itself a word to describe the indescribable.

For me, "God" is also such a word, woefully inadequate to describe the presence of love and light in a life. After all, God created us—our minds, our language, our ability to think, our imaginations. For us to assign finite characteristics to Him is like Hamlet trying to decide what Shakespeare will be like. The creation cannot define the Creator.

People who worshiped wooden idols sought to have an icon before them to remind them of God's presence. But soon the idol became the god, and they worshiped something that could just as easily be used to build a fire or cook a meal. "Bowing down to a block of wood," they thought that the creation could carve out the Creator.

The word "God," though, is the best our limited minds and imaginations can muster. If we didn't use that inadequate human word, how could we describe what His presence means in a moment, a day, a life?

What does God mean to me? Words fail.

Ineffable.

Empty space

Even though I was once a blasphemer and a persecutor and a violent man, I was shown mercy because I acted in ignorance and unbelief. The grace of our Lord was poured out on me abundantly, along with the faith and love that are in Christ Jesus.

1 Timothy 1:13-14

Cosmologist John Wheeler, who first developed the theory of black holes in space, wrote, "No point is more central than this, that empty space is not empty. It is the seat of the most violent physics."

While it's a statement made in the realm of science, it resonates deeply with me, and with other Christians who found God only by coming to the absolute end of self. Space in the mind, or heart, or soul that roils with activity is not the kind of space in which great spiritual growth occurs.

I used to keep things stirred up within myself, thinking that I could make it on my own if I could just become a little stronger, a little smarter, a little more resilient. Finally, everything in my life went so wrong that I gave up. I knew I couldn't do it, whatever "it" might be. I had wandered so far in the wilderness that I thought I would never see vibrant life again.

Amid the desolation, I began to see God because I was finally open to Him, because I had emptied myself of myself. And I learned that, in the spiritual version of Wheeler's statement, empty space is not empty.

It is simply room for God to work.

Written in stone

At that time Jesus, full of joy through the Holy Spirit, said, "I praise you, Father, Lord of heaven and earth, because you have hidden these things from the wise and learned, and revealed them to little children."

LUKE 10:21

A stone found near Jerusalem appears to be the earliest known documentation of Jesus' existence other than the Bible. The ossuary, or burial box, which presumably once contained the bones of James, is inscribed, "James, son of Joseph, brother of Jesus." What a relief to the "wise and learned" seekers who long for proof of Jesus' existence: something, literally set in stone, which says that Jesus existed.

But like most Christians, I didn't really need archaeological proof of Christ's existence, because I have dug deep within myself and found too much spiritual truth to be refuted. I know Christ exists because I have seen the deepest sorrow become a fulfilling relationship with God. I know Christ exists because I have seen one person—profoundly wounded—forgive only because God asks it. I know Christ exists because I have seen strangers reach out to one another and stand strong in Christ to help shoulder grief, pain, loss, fear.

I have the faith of a child—a child of God—so I don't require physical proof that Christ exists. I simply know that He does.

I can feel it in my bones.

MARCH 18

What we worship

"What fault did your fathers find in me, that they strayed so far from me? They followed worthless idols and became worthless themselves."
JEREMIAH 2:5

In high school I read a little paperback called *Alas, Babylon,* a novel about the aftermath of nuclear war. In the book, one man thought he had outsmarted the system by scouring deserted houses and stores for gold and hoarding it in his home. He envisioned that, when the world returned to normal, he would be incredibly wealthy, with his stored-up "precious" metal. In deadly irony, he dies from exposure to radiation; the metal is radioactive, contaminated by the nuclear blast.

We become what we worship, in a sense. If we follow worthless idols, we become worthless. The man who worshiped gold—something with no intrinsic value—lived a life with no substance and died utterly empty. If we worship things that can be bought, then we, too, can eventually be bought.

But the Good News is that the other side of the "coin" is also true. When I worship the one true God, I become truly one with Him. When I worship this God who has proven loving and merciful, strong and wise, I grow in love and mercy, strength and wisdom. When I worship this God who loves me in all of my weakness, I become capable of loving myself and others, despite our weakness. God lets me choose what I worship.

God lets me choose what I will become.

HOLY ORDINARY 91

MARCH 19

Necessary losses

Though you have made me see troubles, many and bitter, you will restore my life again; from the depths of the earth you will again bring me up.

PSALM 71:20

In World War II, the Allies had broken the Germans' code, but needed to hide that knowledge so they could later determine what the enemy knew about D-Day invasion plans. In the meantime, codebreakers determined that Coventry, England would be the target of an air raid; the Allies declined to warn the city so they would not give away their knowledge of the code. The city was virtually destroyed for a greater good—victory in World War II.

A few years ago, I was incredibly arrogant, thinking I had it all, with a good job, great family, a seemingly full life. Then came two deaths in my family within four months; in the blink of an eye, my life had changed forever.

What I didn't realize at the time was that God didn't just change the circumstances of my life; He changed *me* with those deaths. Until then, I was so confident of my ability to "control" my life that I never would have sought God without those tragedies. Since that time, I've learned to look to God for strength that doesn't exist within me when I'm without Him.

My little city of hubris was leveled by seemingly inconsolable loss—a loss that ultimately turned the tide of the spiritual war in me.

Now it's my turn to fight.

MARCH 20

Where to draw the line

Not that I have already obtained all this, or have already been made perfect, but I press on to take hold of that for which Christ Jesus took hold of me.

PHILIPPIANS 3:12

Using techniques in a book called *Drawing on the Right Side of the Brain,* I found to my amazement that I could draw recognizable sketches. At first, I would look at an example and think, "I could never draw that!" But when I focused on imitating one line at a time, I was startled to see that my final product very much resembled the one in the book. I didn't know what to call it, but I was drawing using the right side of my brain.

I know that I'm supposed to model myself after Jesus Christ. But when I dwell too much on the unreachable perfection of the goal, I'm unable to take the smallest step toward it.

But Christ drew his own portrait line by simple line. He fed someone—and drew a line. Healing a person drew another line. Forgiving people—even those who would have Him killed—completed the picture of a perfect Christian life.

I can't be a perfect person. But I am perfectly capable of loving one other person. I am perfectly capable of healing one wound—emotional, physical, spiritual. I am perfectly capable of forgiving one person.

Today I'll concentrate on drawing one small line. Tomorrow I'll draw another. Before long, perhaps a recognizable image will emerge.

Then I'll know I'm drawing from the right side.

HOLY ORDINARY 93

MARCH 21

Repairer of souls

Jesus answered him, ". . . Two men owed money to a certain moneylender. One owed him five hundred denarii, and the other fifty. Neither of them had the money to pay him back, so he canceled the debts of both. Now which of them will love him more?" Simon replied, "I suppose the one who had the bigger debt canceled." "You have judged correctly," Jesus said.

LUKE 7:41-43

I once saw a small sign tacked up on a utility pole; the sign gave a phone number and said, "We buy cars, working or not." Apparently the person who posted the sign has so much confidence in his repair skills that he knows he can get any car running again.

I wish I had realized earlier that God accepts all of us, "working or not." I wanted to get myself in presentable condition before I even thought about a relationship with Him. I thought my soul didn't work well enough to approach God, because I didn't know about the Bible or the church, because I didn't know how to worship, how to pray, how to relate to God.

But God can repair any soul, and often the most un-Godly human lives can be turned to the greatest good. And like the man with the great debt in Jesus' parable, sometimes the person who was once farthest from Him will love Him more when the immense debt is forgiven.

I finally saw the sign, and finally understood, that God longs for—and can repair and use—the most devastated of hearts, the darkest of souls.

Working or not.

MARCH 22

Deafening silence

... there was loud wailing in Egypt, for there was not a house without someone dead ...

EXODUS 12:30

But Christ has indeed been raised from the dead ... For since death came through a man, the resurrection of the dead comes also through a man.

1 CORINTHIANS 15:20-21

While in Italy, I heard the sounds of the death and life of ancient Rome. We stood in the Colosseum, once filled with thousands of empty people, screaming for more and more and more of nothing. Only days later, we walked the catacombs, where Christians prayed and worshiped and took comfort in their loving and powerful God. The noise of death, of decadence, of excess, echoes in the emptiness of one place. The silence of the peace and fullness of the Christian heart reigns in the other.

The lesson remains for me and you today, the lesson that—on our own—we can do nothing that will make us feel full. The lesson remains that all the noise and busy-ness in the world do not fill a life, because the emptiness we feel is hunger for the presence of God.

In the Colosseum, thousands died to entertain people who believed only in themselves. Thousands died. And it was not enough.

But the silence in the catacombs continues to whisper to us about what is really important in this life. That one Man died so that all who believe in Him could live into eternity. One Man died. And it was enough.

It will always be enough.

HOLY ORDINARY

Distance

When the water . . . was gone, Hagar put the boy under one of the bushes. Then she went off and sat down nearby, about a bowshot away, for she thought, "I cannot watch the boy die." And as she sat there nearby, she began to sob. God heard the boy crying . . .

GENESIS 21:15-17

In the years since I began earnestly seeking God, my life has changed so much that some people who have known me for years almost don't recognize me. And while I don't second-guess the decisions and changes I've made, it's hard to leave people behind.

Like Hagar, in some cases I have just distanced myself from other people rather than watch them starve to death spiritually. Some friends I call much less often than I used to. Only one of my family members is on the distribution list to get my e-mails that I send willingly to strangers.

Hagar's boy was saved, ultimately, when she closed her eyes and gave up all hope. God heard, not a direct plea from her, but simply the boy's sobs of fear. Although the passage doesn't specifically say, I sense that Hagar wept not over the impending loss of her own life, but over her inability to help someone she loved.

It's hard sometimes to be forthright about God with "nonbelievers," but it is work that has to be done. I think God is telling me to take the "chance" with my old crowd. When I do hold back, I seem to hear someone sobbing. Is it me? Or them?

Or is it God?

MARCH 24

Letting go

"For God so loved the world that he gave his one and only Son, that whoever believes in him shall not perish but have eternal life. . . . Whoever believes in him is not condemned, but whoever does not believe stands condemned already because he has not believed in the name of God's one and only Son . . . whoever lives by the truth comes into the light, so that it may be seen plainly that what he has done has been done through God."

JOHN 3:16, 18, 21

The film *Into the Arms of Strangers* tells about German Jewish children sent away to escape the Nazis in WWII. One woman recalls her doting father, who clung to her hands so tightly that he pulled her from the train that would've taken her to safety. Because he couldn't bear to let her go, she later ended up in Auschwitz.

Not so many years ago, I held my dad's hand tightly, loving him so much that I wanted him to stay with me forever. Intellectually, I knew he needed to go in peace. But it would be years before I truly let him go.

I couldn't give my grief to God, to ask His help with it; I felt small and ungrateful that I wasn't rejoicing over the gifts He gives me. I may have even felt that God couldn't understand the raw hurt and guilt that can invade a tiny human heart. The pain was excruciating.

But now I know God does understand—-perfectly—-how much I have been hurting. The word "excruciating," it turns out, comes from a Latin word meaning, "to crucify." So yes, God knows how it hurts to let go of Someone you love.

God knows.

MARCH 25

Now, do you understand?

This was to fulfill what was spoken through the prophet Isaiah: "Here is my servant whom I have chosen, the one I love, in whom I delight; I will put my Spirit on him, and he will proclaim justice to the nations."

MATTHEW 12:17-18

Once I tried to give a friend a favorite material thing in an attempt to express the inexpressible, the joy that her friendship brings me. She said, when I made the offer, "It nearly broke my heart."

Sometimes it's so hard to describe how deeply we care that we seek another way to convey the message. I was saying, "This is one of my favorite things, but I am willing to give it to you." The gift itself was not important in this case; the real truth lay in the willingness to offer it.

And yet, our deepest, most selfless human love cannot even approach the way that God our Father loves us. When His children simply could not fathom how much He loved them, He offered a gift to somehow express the inexpressible. This is my Son. I love Him more than anything, more than anyone. And I want you to have Him. Now, do you understand?

We see what He offers us, and on the rare occasions when we understand the depth of divine love, it does break our hearts. It absolutely breaks our hearts that a Father could love a child so much.

It breaks a heart. And then stretches it, and fills it, however briefly, with understanding.

With the love of God.

MARCH 26

Remnants

Elijah . . . prayed that he might die. "I have had enough, Lord," he said. "Take my life . . . "

1 KINGS 19:3-4

[Jesus] said to his disciples, "Gather the pieces that are left over. Let nothing be wasted."

JOHN 6:12

Driving on a Mississippi highway one morning, I followed a trailer filled with newly harvested cotton. Bits of the fluff were everywhere—still in the field, on the roadside, flying from the trailer. How many more yards of cloth could have been made, how many more garments woven, if every piece of that cotton were put to use?

God accomplishes His purposes in the world by putting to work every bit of raw material in every human who seeks Him. Circumstances I cannot understand are sometimes the only way He can get my attention focused on Him. Experiences that looked like absolute losses became lessons I could not have learned any other way. Painful separation from loved ones brought me to God. Seemingly horrible timing turned out to be the only timing I would respect.

I will never see the entire pattern, but I see enough already to know that God uses every scrap of a life to complete His vision for the world. Every bit of material, every moment of my life, God has woven into an everlasting and dazzling piece of fabric. I see that nothing in the Christian life is left alongside the road; nothing is lost.

And lives are saved.

HOLY ORDINARY

MARCH 27

Essential things

Do not fret because of evil men or be envious of those who do wrong; for like the grass they will soon wither, like green plants they will soon die away. Trust in the Lord and do good; dwell in the land and enjoy safe pasture.

PSALM 37:1-3

Once in the doctor's office I couldn't resist looking at a magazine whose cover promised, "81 Essential Things to Do Before the World Ends." A few suggestions had lasting value ("Talk to a stranger"), but most were vacuous experiences like "Go kite-boarding" and "Trademark your own name like Billy Joel did." The most tragically telling one? "Just once experience general anesthesia so you'll know what those irreversibly closing freight-elevator doors of death will feel like."

When I get to the end of my life, I would be heartbroken to realize that I had spent the majority of my time and energy pursuing "coolness" while sacrificing warmth with other human beings, that I casually traded the transcendent away for the transitory. So personally, I think the list of "Essential Things" needs not two pages to describe, but two lines. 1. Love God, now and forever. 2. Love the people in your life, now and forever.

And when you do those things, for the first time or for the millionth time, you approach one more item on the list of essentials: You will see what those irresistibly opening doors of eternity feel like.

And there, you will see God.

MARCH 28

Judgment

The Word became flesh and made his dwelling among us. We have seen his glory, the glory of the One and Only, who came from the Father, full of grace and truth.

JOHN 1:14

The Last Judgment is a massive fresco that covers the altar wall of the Sistine Chapel, showing Christ judging sinners and saints, striking down the damned and beckoning the saved to Him. As the story goes, when the work was unveiled by Michelangelo for the pope, the pope fell to his knees and begged God's forgiveness for his sins. Was it the fear of judgment that humbled the pope, or the stunning realization of how little his life reflected the life of Christ?

Very often, I will be in one of my self-righteous and defensive modes, and someone will offer a forgiving act or make a healing statement that makes me realize how petty and shallow I am acting. Like the pope, perhaps, I see suddenly, undeniably, that I am not the center of the universe. I see suddenly, undeniably, that living for myself will be a living hell. It's not the last judgment; it's a very present one.

Christ dwells in other people, in the flesh, right here in the middle of my world, in the middle of my day. The "judgment" takes place when I see Him clearly—when the face of God, through Christ, and through other Christians, is unveiled. But in the final picture, it will not matter that I have fallen so short.

As long as I have fallen to my knees.

MARCH 29

Walk on by

Now there was a man named Joseph . . . a good and upright man who had not consented to their decision and action . . . he was waiting for the kingdom of God. Going to Pilate, he asked for Jesus' body.

LUKE 23:50-52

Once when I was little, as my family returned home late at night, my dad stopped the car when he saw something along the road that looked like it could've been a body. In the headlights, we watched him move the bundle with his foot, then pick up the burlap over it. It was nothing, but he didn't know that when he stopped.

Later I realized how scary it must've been for him to do it; he could have just driven on and rationalized that it wasn't his business. I didn't make that mess, we say of a life, or house, or roadside, or soul, and we feel no obligation to bring it healing and wholeness. So many times in my life, I have walked past someone I knew to be in need, out of pure fear that if I stopped, I would find something I couldn't handle.

Sometimes the right thing to do is simply to refuse to add to our world's ungodliness. Sometimes it requires getting past debilitating fear. For another person's problem is my problem if I intend to be part of the body of Christ. That life, that house, that roadside, that soul is mine, and if I'm looking for the kingdom of God, I have to stop. I have to stop when I see pain in someone's eyes, partly because it is my pain, mostly because it is His pain.

And because He stopped for me.

MARCH 30

Those who trespass

. . . continue to work out your salvation with fear and trembling, for it is God who works in you to will and to act according to his good purpose. Do everything without complaining or arguing, so that you may become blameless and pure, children of God without fault in a crooked and depraved generation, in which you shine like stars in the universe as you hold out the word of life. . .

PHILIPPIANS 2:12-16

I talk a good game of Christianity, but I often struggle with what God asks of me. I ask Him to forgive me my trespasses, as I forgive those who trespass against me. But when I speak the words, I keep seeing planes plunging into buildings, death camps, the hollow eyes of a child's lost innocence, senseless violence. *Those who trespass.*

God, don't ask me to forgive them. I beg you, do not ask me to look at concentration camps, at Twin Towers, at Oklahoma City, at inferno and dust and rubble and bodies and forgive those who would destroy us all and call it holy. I pray for the victims and can even superficially pray for those responsible. I'll help in disaster relief. I'll relinquish my convenience and portions of my rights to ensure that such a tragedy isn't repeated.

But I can't imagine forgiving someone who used planeloads of innocents as missiles to bring down buildings, lives, economies, governments. I can't imagine forgiving a child molester, or a torturer, or an economic predator. Would you really ask me to forgive *them*, to forgive *this?*

I am not a God, but only a person, and a person cannot do it. It's too hard.

Hard as nails.

HOLY ORDINARY 103

MARCH 31

"The map is not the territory"

Sacrifice and offering you did not desire . . . Then I said, "Here I am, I have come . . . I desire to do your will, O my God; your law is within my heart."

PSALM 40:6-8

Every day, as a committed Christian, I try to remember that, as Alfred Korzbyski said, "The map is not the territory." I do the things I'm "supposed" to do: attend church, take communion, go to Sunday school, sign up for committees. But if I'm not careful, I can get so involved in "churchy" activities that I forget where they're supposed to take me.

Before I travel, I pick a destination first, then I find a map to tell me the best route. In the same way, the psalmist first identifies his destination—living in the will of God—before writing the law—or map—in his heart to guide him.

I want my journey to take me to a living, breathing, intimate relationship with God. Becoming self-satisfied with my Christian activities would be like standing on a map of Europe and saying I've been to the Louvre. Having a map in hand doesn't allow me to experience a place deeply or even accurately; the road atlas itself is not a destination, and it's not a mode of transportation. It just points the way.

A good map helps me travel more efficiently, but I'm not really headed for a personal relationship with God until I get on the road and go.

After all, the map is not the territory.

April

APRIL 1

Backburn

Then Peter came to Jesus and asked, "Lord, how many times shall I forgive my brother when he sins against me? Up to seven times?" Jesus answered, "I tell you, not seven times, but seventy-seven times."
MATTHEW 18:21-22

When wildfires in Colorado in 2002 burned over 100,000 acres, firefighters set "backburns" to try to keep the disaster from spreading further. A backburn is a small fire set ahead of the main fire to reduce available fuel and control the burn.

Forgiveness is such a difficult task for us humans that we're constantly looking for ways around it. Peter wanted a limit to the number of times he would have to forgive, but Jesus told him to forgive and forgive and forgive without limit. And He asks me to forgive and move on, even in those circumstances when I know I'm in the right.

In a sense, Jesus asks me to set a "backburn," a small fire to keep the larger inferno from destroying me. I sacrifice a small part of myself—my ego and my insistence on proving that I was wronged by someone else—and that small bit of controlled "destruction" quells the larger fire.

While I have hung onto some of these grudges like familiar old friends, I know I have to let them go, for my sake and everyone else's. Then I stop feeding the fires of destruction and begin to feed the healing process instead.

I become a fuel for Christ.

APRIL 2

Two eagles

. . . Paul said, ". . . Under Gamaliel I was thoroughly trained in the law of our fathers and was just as zealous for God as any of you are today . . . suddenly a bright light from heaven flashed around me. I fell to the ground and heard a voice say to me, 'Saul! Saul! Why do you persecute me?' "

ACTS 22:3, 6-7

When I visited Delphi, Greece, I heard the story of why the oracle was located there. According to myth, Zeus released two eagles which flew around the earth, and where they met was determined to be the center of the world. There, the Delphic oracle dispensed the wisdom of the gods.

Years ago, I released two eagles—my intellect and my heart—to find God and my place in His universe. My heart flew through failed relationships, grief, inadequacy; my mind learned that the one thing I needed most to know lay just beyond the realm of proof. My heart told me that there has to be more to existence than getting by. My mind shouted that something powerful created, and works behind, the beauty and symmetry of this world.

Eventually I saw that I'm here to humanize the face of God, the incredibly powerful God who created our elegant universe as a backdrop for expressing His love for us. Of course, it is the Truth, so it made sense. It felt right.

Where the eagles of heart and head came together, I found my soul. My God was there, waiting for me to join Him.

Precisely at the center of the universe.

APRIL 3

The darkest rooms

Be not far from me, O God; come quickly, O my God, to help me.
PSALM 71:12

When I first became a committed Christian, my instinct was to block out and forget all of the pain that had gone before. But soon I realized I could not live a full life until I ventured into some dark and frightening places that I desperately wanted to avoid.

To make my new life healthy and whole, I had to relive the pain of a phone call that told me my sister was gone. I went again into a hospital room to tell my dad for the last time that I loved him.

I completely avoided those places, but the same walls which block out grief also block out joy. It had been too painful for me to think about my sister or my dad at all, so I couldn't even let myself think of the blessings they brought into my life. For the longest time, if I thought of my dad's lightning wit, I also had to think about how much I missed him. If I let myself remember how my sister laughed at herself until we all cried, I found myself dredging up regrets for things I had left undone with her.

I realize now, though, that I never have to go into those rooms alone. I can ask God to "be not far from me." He can hold me in His arms as I sift through memories, sweet and painful, as I cry all the tears of regret and joy, as I remember those people I loved so very much.

My soul finally found liberation from its suffocating grief. Now I'm free to come and go in the rooms of memories once too painful to confront.

Because now I go with God.

APRIL 4

Stairway to heaven

Taking one of the stones there, [Jacob] put it under his head and lay down to sleep. He had a dream in which he saw a stairway resting on the earth, with its top reaching to heaven, and the angels of God were ascending and descending on it.

GENESIS 28:11-12

Years ago I had to drive in winter "white-out" conditions in Illinois; fine snow flew so fiercely in the wind that visibility was nil. I would have missed the turn to my family's house if another car hadn't turned ahead of me. I was so close to being home, yet I could not see.

Jacob dreamed of a stairway, a place where heaven and earth intersect. But every place in this earthly life is such an intersection. When a baby laughs at my silliness, I place one foot on the ladder between heaven and earth. When two people comfort each other in unimaginable grief or pain, each begins to ascend. Yet it often takes another traveler to point the way, to say that this is where heaven and earth come together in our lives.

God asks those of us who can see Him and His heaven, in any given moment, to stop another, to say, "Look, this is about God." And on days when we cannot see, others will hold us up, reminding us of the nearness of God, pointing the way to Him.

In every breath we take, we have the opportunity to live on Jacob's ladder, to take a step on the stairway to heaven, to see our God. In every moment, we are so close to being home.

If we could only see.

APRIL 5

God's little acre

The Lord is my shepherd, I shall not be in want. He makes me lie down in green pastures, he leads me beside quiet waters, he restores my soul.
PSALM 23:1-3A

A 2002 NPR story talked of the Central Valley area of California, "home to the greatest garden in the world" and an area that grows a fourth of our nation's food. But because it's also a great place to live, many of the Central Valley's fields have been turned into subdivisions. As one man said, "A couple of houses on an acre of land are worth much more than an acre of tomatoes." Sadly, later generations will never know the richness of the land beneath them, as it will all be paved over in the name of "progress."

Nothing can grow in an area completely covered with manmade things, just as a relationship with God cannot deepen and grow if every moment is busy with manmade concerns. If we stay on the move in a noisy world, we cannot find the still waters of God. He cannot restore souls that don't stop long enough to listen to Him and to connect deeply with Him. He cannot grow us in love, in patience, in depth, if we have covered over every acre of our land. Everything remains on the surface, with nowhere to go deeper, with no roots, no stability, no growth.

If we let Him lead, He will give us still waters, and He will restore our souls. But if we pave over all of the gardens, He will have nowhere to grow our food, and we will go hungry.

God is not to be found among our manmade things.

110   HOLY ORDINARY

APRIL 6

Paying the premium

I said to the Lord, "You are my Lord; apart from you I have no good thing." As for the saints who are in the land, they are the glorious ones in whom is all my delight. The sorrows of those will increase who run after other gods.

PSALM 16:2-4

One rainy spring Mississippi night, floodwaters swept in and totaled my beloved little car. The insurance company took days to call, then gave me the runaround. So I yelled into the phone and hung up on them. It's not like me, but my treasured possession was gone and they wouldn't help me get it back.

Since my conversion, I have railed against people who value material things too highly, who "run after other gods." I have clucked in disapproval to see them cling so tightly to possessions that they cannot open themselves to God's embrace or express His love. But in the past few weeks, "they" have become "we."

When I treat people harshly, I let my concern for a material thing get in the way of my love for God. I try to explain to Him that they accepted all those premiums I paid, and when it came time to pay, they wouldn't even talk to me. God can't understand how frustrating that can feel.

Or can He? He sacrificed His beloved Son, and yet I will not do the smallest thing—like have patience with a bureaucrat—to bring Jesus to life again in our world. So yes, God understands how it feels to be ignored after paying the premium.

Because that's exactly how I've treated Him.

April 7

Future perfect

"I have swept away your offenses like a cloud, your sins like the morning mist. Return to me, for I have redeemed you."

Isaiah 44:22

Nobody's perfect. Limited warranty. The manufacturer is not liable.

Our world is filled with disclaimers, with confessions of imperfection, with admonitions not to expect anything or anyone to be perfect.

But then we encounter God. In this passage of Isaiah, commentary describes God as using the "perfect" tense, describing something in the future and speaking of it as if it were already an accomplished fact. Though Israel had not yet admitted its offenses and sought God's forgiveness, He has forgiven them.

And He does the same for us. Unfortunately, it's not an aspect of God I am anxious to imitate. When someone hurts me, I want to be sure that everyone notices, that others admit my "rightness," before I forgive. I dwell on the past too much, on times when someone I love has let me down, or when I have let them down so profoundly that I cannot yet admit the fault.

I'm unable to operate in the "perfect" tense, largely because my own past, present, and future, are so far from perfect. Yet I still want to hold grudges, to "be right." I still want to judge them in a way I cannot afford to be judged myself. Before I forgive, I want to pronounce sentences. Yet, to be like my God, and with Him, there is only one sentence I should pronounce.

I will forgive, as my God forgives.

APRIL 8

Waiting on Jesus

A few days later, when Jesus again entered Capernaum, the people heard that he had come home.... Some men came, bringing to him a paralytic, carried by four of them. Since they could not get him to Jesus because of the crowd, they made an opening in the roof above Jesus and, after digging through it, lowered the mat the paralyzed man was lying on.

MARK 2:1, 3-4

For the word "mitzvah," *Webster's Dictionary* lists two definitions: "a commandment of the Jewish law" and "a meritorious or charitable act." The two definitions seem vastly different, but are they really?

When Jesus said that the most important commandments were to love God and to love one another, He made it clear that each time I serve another person, I also serve God. I fulfill the divine law.

In the same way, the men who found a way to get the paralytic to Jesus were serving both their friend and their God. And because the presence of Jesus had "come home" to live in the hearts of men, the crowd saw the divine law living and breathing that day.

Divinity shines through each time we bring someone to Jesus who could not get there alone. God asks us to let His Son "come home" to live in our hearts, to sacrifice our time, our resources, our lives for someone else. And the bottom line is that, like the men bringing their friend to God, when we serve another, we aren't just passively waiting for Jesus.

We're waiting *on* Him.

HOLY ORDINARY

APRIL 9

Sacrifice

But their swords will pierce their own hearts, and their bows will be broken.

PSALM 37:15

"... God has numbered the days of your reign and brought it to an end. ... You have been weighed on the scales and found wanting.... Your kingdom is divided and given to the Medes and Persians."

DANIEL 5:26-28

The *New York Times* once lamented that the Mets baseball team "made errors and accumulated strikeouts in bulk, a curious habit for a team with a $120 million payroll." Baseball, where players once stayed with one team for a career, has become a collection of overpaid stars who won't sacrifice for the team because personal statistics determine the salary figure in their next contract.

We become what we worship. When a player seeks the highest salary based on his individual performance, sooner or later another player comes along who is younger, stronger, more dedicated . . . and paid more. "Their swords pierce their own hearts." Those who live by the stat die by the stat.

God urges us constantly to value Him and His kingdom over the things and successes of this world. Like the narcissistic baseball player, we focus on what we can gain for ourselves, on our status, and soon the game moves on without us. The days of our reign are numbered; our little kingdom soon is divided, gone. Weighed on eternal scales, we are found wanting.

Wanting God.

APRIL 10

God's vessel

. . . if our hearts do not condemn us, we have confidence before God and receive from him anything we ask, because we obey his commands and do what pleases him. And this is his command: to believe in the name of his Son, Jesus Christ, and to love one another as he commanded us. Those who obey his commands live in him, and he in them.
1 JOHN 3:16, 19-20

I once had a favorite coffee cup that I used every morning until I dropped it and broke it into pieces. I glued it back together, but it never again was usable. Tiny pieces were still missing, and the cup leaked.

I am a vessel, a cup in which God's message goes out to the world. If any piece of the vessel is missing or damaged, then the presence of God cannot be carried effectively. So many seemingly small things can damage the vessel, even a casual thoughtless word. If I repeat a rumor, I damage another person's reputation and poison the listener against him. When I judge others, they get the message that Christians are self-righteous and unloving. When I insist on proving my viewpoint, I may inhibit someone from expressing themselves freely.

Every word I speak should strengthen the vessel of faith. Every action I take should make me more capable and more credible in carrying God to others.

I watch my words, to ensure that the vessel—my heart—is loving, strong, healed, whole. After all, it carries precious cargo.

The body and blood of Christ.

APRIL 11

Remember

Israel was a spreading vine; he brought forth fruit for himself. As his fruit increased, he built more altars; as his land prospered, he adorned his sacred stones.

HOSEA 10:1

I once read a study entitled, "Why People Sue," which concluded that often people bring malpractice lawsuits because no one will listen to them, because no one hears and acknowledges their pain. So they seek validation of their loss in the court system.

Like Israel, we listen to the voice of God and then fail to listen to our fellow men, as if these voices are unrelated. We proclaim our faith, wearing it like a badge, and then ignore the pain and fear our fellow human beings face. We talk about God's love, but don't take time to hold someone's hand who is experiencing loss. We busy ourselves at our "altars and sacred stones," yet we fail to listen to others' needs in the real world.

But every time I ignore or marginalize another person, I ignore the body of Christ. And every time I seek out another, listen to him, help him, I help the body of Christ. I have the opportunity to bring the members of the body of Christ back together—to "re-member" Him—with each loving gesture I make.

Jesus Christ gave everything up for me, sacrificing His body for my soul. So yes, as difficult as it may be today, I will listen to someone, Lord. I will hold someone's hand. I will love another person, as You love me.

I will re-member You.

Won in the Spirit

Be still before the Lord and wait patiently for him; do not fret when men succeed in their ways, when they carry out their wicked schemes. Refrain from anger and turn from wrath; do not fret—it leads only to evil.

PSALM 37:7-8

Certain people in my life are determined to make me look small, and I seem determined to help them in that mission. Intellectually, I can catalogue my gifts and accept my weaknesses, but when someone points those weaknesses out, I get defensive, attacking anyone who makes me feel small. The only result is that we all end up being small together.

I am a very competitive person, and a very defensive person, so when someone hurts me, I want to hit back quickly and win. Winning is so highly valued in our society that, if I don't have the last and most stinging word, my human instinct is to feel as if I'm less of a person.

But I am less of a person when I am "still before the Lord," when I sacrifice my ego to someone else's needs. I am less of a person, and more a part of God. And while it's fine to want to win, it's deadly to try to win at the cost of my humanity or someone else's, or at the cost of that whisper of divinity that God offers. I wish I could remember that, in these petty word battles, I don't have to win.

I am won, by Christ. I am one, with Him.

APRIL 13

The empty tomb

There was a violent earthquake, for an angel of the Lord came down from heaven and, going to the tomb, rolled back the stone and sat on it. His appearance was like lightning, and his clothes were white as snow. The guards were so afraid of him that they shook and became like dead men.

MATTHEW 28:2-4

One day in Rome we stopped for lunch in a cafeteria where few of the workers spoke English. I couldn't figure out how the system worked. I finally ended up with something on my plate, wondering if I could pay with American money instead of Eurodollars. I was hungry, but my currency was useless.

Is that how the guards at Jesus' tomb felt? Their jobs, suddenly, were meaningless. Their weapons, which once made them feel self-important and powerful, were useless. The system by which their world was measured changed one Sunday morning, and it scared them so that they "shook and became like dead men."

I once stood watch, vigilantly, over such emptiness—self-important, proud of my job and material success. When the earth shook violently, I peered inside and saw the reality of life, that none of it means a thing in eternity. All I had to spend had no value.

Now I know that the tomb is empty, but it no longer makes me shake or feel dead inside. It makes me want to celebrate. Yes, God told me, the tomb is empty.

But you don't have to be.

My "X"

We pray this so that the name of our Lord Jesus may be glorified in you, and you in him, according to the grace of our God and the Lord Jesus Christ.

2 THESSALONIANS 1:12

I have never liked the prefix "ex-." I just don't like the sound of having an ex-boss, ex-friend, ex-husband. (I should have anticipated that one when he introduced me as his first wife and we were still married.) Words that begin with "ex-" so often mean that important relationships, important chapters in our lives, have ended, usually with little possibility of going back.

But the same sound—in the letter "X"—also stands for the Greek letter chi, the first letter of "Christ" in Greek. In the 16th century, Europeans began using the "X" in place of the word Christ as shorthand. So now, in my life, "X" signifies a beautiful and growing force, the beginning of my life rather than the end of one chapter.

The X, in man's world, can mean many things. The X can mean, "I make my mark and agree to this contract." The X can mean, "Look here for the treasure." The X can mean "You are here."

But in my life with God, marking myself with X shows that I belong to Christ, and my world changes dramatically. This X means that I honor His Word. This X guides me to the most precious treasure of all: the certainty that I am loved. This X means, not that I am here, but that He is.

I hope you've met my X.

APRIL 15

The high way

[God] rained down manna for the people to eat, he gave them the grain of heaven. Men ate the bread of angels; he sent them all the food they could eat.

PSALM 78:24-25

Whenever I get frustrated about paying taxes, I try to be more attentive to the road between my place and work. I think about what it would take for me to build such a road: the expense, the time, the expertise. Then I become less resentful of my taxes, because I know that, if I had to build my own road, I would go nowhere.

I wonder what decision—large or small—God will ask me to make for Him today. I wonder if He will ask me to change my life, my schedule, my mind, my perspective. Certainly if the past is any indication, I will question much of what He asks of me. And if what I must pay today is something uncomfortable or frightening or unpleasant, I will probably balk. In fact, sometimes it seems I will do almost anything to avoid paying what I owe to God.

And then I look down at the road. I remember how He held me when I thought the world was ending. I remember that He rained down food from heaven and fed me when I had no strength to go on. I remember that He offers me the bread of angels in the form of a life that finally means something, and finally goes somewhere worth going. I remember that, without God, I could not have gotten where I am in this moment, that I could not go where I need to go tomorrow.

If I had to build my own road, I would go nowhere.

APRIL 16

Terms of endearment

And a voice came from heaven: "You are my Son, whom I love; with you I am well pleased."

MARK 1:11

Several years back, I volunteered to teach a first-grade Junior Achievement class once a week. When one of the little guys in the class helped me pass out some papers, I told him, "Thank you, dear." He whispered to me, "I like it when you call me 'dear.' "

It knocks me over to think that God our Father calls me dear, but the evidence is indisputable. He gave me the life of His Son, and through that Man, He gave me my own life, a life so beautiful and so rich I never could have imagined it was for me. I can never thank Him for the grace He showers on me, but I would like to know that something I do, at least occasionally, pleases Him.

While the sacrifice His Son made, and the life He lived on earth, prompted God to say that He was "well pleased," I think we can make much smaller gestures that also delight Him. Simple obedience, childlike faith, passion for His Son—these are gestures that can warm the heart of God.

I haven't done one thing—and could never do enough—to deserve the gifts God gives me, in the life of His precious Son and in my life, every day. Yet the gifts continue to appear, simply because God loves me. Simply because He wants me near Him. I hope that, today, I will do some small thing that makes God think of me as His servant, with whom He is "well pleased."

I love it that He calls me dear.

APRIL 17

Life is short

They are darkened in their understanding and separated from the life of God because of the ignorance that is in them. . . . Therefore each of you must put off falsehood and speak truthfully to his neighbor, for we are all members of one body.

EPHESIANS 4:18, 25

I went several weeks one time looking at a silver convertible car, a sporty little mid-life crisis. I kept expressing that it was too flashy for me, but friends told me to get it. Their philosophy? "Life is too short."

During that same time, I made my first visit to a hospice facility, where I saw a friend with pancreatic cancer. Diagnosed less than six months earlier, she told me, "I won't be getting out of here." Life is short.

I could never bring myself to talk with her openly about God. We prayed with her and talked around Him, but I knew I should offer a gentle question, a door opening wide, for her to express her thoughts about God. And then, the day I decided I had the courage to do it, she wasn't receiving visitors. Soon after, she was gone.

Something is wrong with my priorities when I am anxious to maximize this short life and too fearful to help someone enter the next eternal one. I'm not being faithful to God if I'm not willing to speak to a friend facing imminent death, about the preciousness of life with God. I'm not loving God and my neighbor if I don't offer His presence in crisis.

Who else did I expect to help this friend find God? Who else but me?

Life is too short.

APRIL 18

Fissures of men

"It is not by strength that one prevails; those who oppose the Lord will be shattered. He will thunder against them from heaven . . ."

1 SAMUEL 2:9-10

A fissure was formed in the roof of the Apocalipsis Cave on the island of Patmos, volcanic rock splitting, when the voice of God boomed to tell John of what the future holds.

For some of us, it takes an earth-shattering event to focus our attention on God. For John the Divine, it was a voice so powerful that it could rend volcanic rock. For other Christians, it may be the loss of someone important, even of the self, or of some*thing*—health, position, autonomy.

I've always thought that "apocalyptic" was used only to describe things involved in the end of the world, but "apocalypse" comes from the Greek word meaning "to uncover." God will uncover so much truth, so much light, so much power for us if we will only let Him in.

In the bad old days I sealed myself in a homemade cave of denial, self-absorption, fear until one day in AD 1999 when the voice of God boomed as loudly for me as it had for John in AD 95. It truly sounded like the end of the world. Certainly my own life had fallen apart. I heard the rock split above me; it terrified me.

But that was how the Light got in.

APRIL 19

Bigger than rules

Before your very eyes Jesus Christ was clearly portrayed as crucified. I would like to learn just one thing from you: Did you receive the Spirit by observing the law, or by believing what you heard?

GALATIANS 3:1A-2

In the movie *Babe*, Ferdinand the duck tries to convince Babe the pig to help in a nefarious mission that involves sneaking into the house while the boss is gone. But Babe protests, saying that there's a rule against farm animals going into the house. Ferdinand replies, "I like that rule. It's a good rule. But this is bigger than rules." After all, the duck feels his life is at stake.

And while breaking the rules—God's law—is not justified, I'm afraid too often we glorify the law. We forget that what Christ really gave us on the cross was the freedom to stop thinking about rules and to start thinking about love.

Living like Christ means focusing on unconditional love. God loves us that way; knowing how it changes our lives, we seek to love others the same way, in the name of Jesus Christ. People who get hung up on the "rules"—as if they're a method of scorekeeping, are missing the best part—that God loves us, period. No conditions have to be met. No report cards have to be signed. He loves us purely, and purely because we ask Him to do it. That pure love is what we seek, what we accept. Our lives are at stake here.

This is bigger than rules.

APRIL 20

Wish you were here

You will call and I will answer you; you will long for the creature your hands have made.

JOB 14:15

My first semester in college, my mother sent me a brief handwritten note almost every day. Since I went to school 600 miles from home, I assumed that she was looking out for me, trying to keep the child she loved from being lonely and homesick. Until very recently, it never occurred to me that it also made her feel better to connect with me. Now I look back and realize she was telling me, "I miss you, dear. Keep in touch."

God writes me letters every day, sending me messages of comfort, of joy, of insight, and I have thought all along that He is simply trying to make life easier for the child He loves. But I also think that God "longs for the creature His hands have made." He is all-powerful, but He created us for some reason. And I believe He made us "creatures" not only to lavish His love on us, but also to remain connected to us.

Prayer is not just an entreaty or a monologue, but a two-way conversation. It is a series of letters in which God holds us and tends to us, in which we share with Him every detail of our days. It is a channel to share the most intimate and mundane details of our lives with the One whose hands have made us. Prayer is God's way of telling us what my mother told me with her letters every day.

"I miss you, dear. Keep in touch."

APRIL 21

Small beginnings

"Your beginnings will seem humble, so prosperous will your future be."
JOB 8:7

Twenty-five years after graduating from college, I revisited my alma mater and went inside a dormitory where I had lived as a senior. I was struck by the tiny size of the room, and I thought, "I can't believe I lived in a space this size with another person."

My spiritual life has taken such a turn upwards that I constantly marvel at the small spaces I used to inhabit. It used to be enough that I had a God to pray to in a panic. It used to be enough to see and worship God only within the walls of a church. It used to be enough to see others radiant with the presence of God, and to feel victimized because I didn't understand.

But those small rooms are no longer enough for me. Now I talk to God every day, conversing comfortably with the most powerful being in the universe. Now I find God everywhere: in my job, in my recreation, in my friends, in my life, and deeply in my heart. Now God glows around me and through me, in the wide open spaces of the world.

Not that long ago, those cramped rooms were enough, because I didn't allow myself to think or dream of anything larger or more important than getting through the day. But now that I have become more spiritually "prosperous," worldly success no longer seduces me. I'm so grateful to be out of that small space, that cramped old life of worshiping small gods.

Like myself.

APRIL 22

Save the world

Set your minds on things above, not on earthly things. For you died, and your life is now hidden with Christ in God.

COLOSSIANS 3:2-3

Finally, after years of resisting, I began to recycle: plastic, aluminum cans, and paper. I once thought my contribution to cleaning up the environment was too small to matter. But then I realized that, with little effort on my part, there could be one less piece of trash in the world.

Frequently I get incredibly angry—justifiably, I tell myself—over stupid, insignificant issues. I try to make someone else feel worthless and wrong. A few hours later, I regret it deeply, knowing I have hurt both the target and myself, and usually not even over an issue of substance.

I instinctually "set my mind on earthly things:" on my reputation, my ego, my convenience. And so, without thinking, I add more junk to a world already hurting, already angry, already labeling the Christian life as self-righteously hypocritical and meaningless.

Yet if I could somehow "set my mind on things above," on the presence and power of God, I could make a difference in this wounded world. Lives, souls, worlds can be saved by one person doing one righteous thing. An angry word is held, left unsaid, until the anger and self-righteousness pass. Respect for others remains. Minds are set on things above.

And there's one less piece of trash in the world.

Unknowable

Into your hands I commit my spirit; redeem me, O Lord, the God of truth.

PSALM 31:5

You think so hard about it all, don't you? You gather evidence and think that someday, you will find the piece of proof that will convince you that believing in Me is "reasonable." That proof, my beloved, does not exist. It's not going to make you happy when I tell you that much of what you seek to know about Me is unknowable.

No matter how hard you look, you can see neither the beginnings of life nor its ultimate worth. Some truths, you see, are only for Me. You can begin seeking Me with your mind, if that makes you feel better. But you cannot get here from there.

You can look at the order of the universe, that magnificence of the human being, the instinct of that human being to love. Yet these things will only point you to a gentle precipice. I know they like to call it a "leap," but I like to think of it as more of a backward fall, a surrender into my arms.

No energy is required. No forward movement. No great act of intellect. Simple trust is the question. Simple trust is the answer.

Certainly you can begin to see Me with your mind, and in your mind. But just give Me your spirit, and I will show you all of the truth you can handle. Because you can only love Me with your heart. With your soul. With your life. When you offer those gifts to Me, we will have all the proof we need. Trust Me. I am here.

And I will still be here when you're ready to fall.

One up

But he answered one of them, "Friend, I am not being unfair to you. Didn't you agree to work for a denarius? . . . I want to give the man who was hired last the same as I gave you."

MATTHEW 20:13-14

Students in New Bedford, Massachusetts plotted an attack on their high school, saying it would be "bigger than Columbine." They didn't want to make an important point, bring an issue to light, or even exact revenge. They just wanted more headlines than the last guys.

This deadly game of "one up" doesn't just happen among the dysfunctional or the disturbed. It happens in healthy classrooms, healthy families, healthy churches. Be sure you notice that I'm doing the right thing. I'm only doing it for God. But be sure you notice.

We can't resist comparing ourselves to others; we want so desperately to look better than our neighbors. The vineyard workers were happy with their wages until they found out what the next guy made. It isn't fair! We've been here longer. We worked harder.

What if Christ had held that attitude? You mean I'm going to pay this awful price and you're going to let just anybody in? Even this thief? He sneaked in at the last minute, and I gave my whole life! It isn't fair!

Only on the cross did Christ place himself above others. Just that once. Because He loved His Father, He sacrificed His life. Not His Sunday morning, but his life.

Suddenly no one wants to play one up anymore.

APRIL 25

Reflections

There is a river whose streams make glad the city of God, the holy place where the Most High dwells. God is within her, she will not fall; God will help her at break of day. . . . "Be still, and know that I am God . . ."

PSALM 46:4-5, 10

I often drive along a manmade lake, a reservoir near my apartment. On one rare occasion, the surface of the water was so still and peaceful that it reflected the sky like a mirror. Every cloud, every bird that flew over, every tree on the shore was reflected almost perfectly in the stillness of the lake.

As a Christian committed to bringing God to other people, I am an earthbound reservoir of His love, His power, His peace, His comfort. I continue to hear God gently urging me to calm down, to listen carefully not only to His voice, but to His silence. Too often, I get all stirred up and busy, supposedly on God's behalf, and I probably end up missing many signals He sends me about what to do. And, as importantly, I miss signals about what not to do.

If I'm a reservoir, though, the best possible state I can achieve in God's presence is stillness. The more I am at peace, resting in God's care, the more connected I am to His will. And when I know His will, I can help "make glad the city of God," because God is within me.

Only by listening carefully to God can I reflect His image. Only by constant prayer can I reflect the image of the One above.

in stillness. only in stillness.

APRIL 26

Everyday miracles

... the Lord ... passed in front of Moses, proclaiming, "The Lord, the Lord, the compassionate and gracious God, slow to anger, abounding in love and faithfulness, maintaining love to thousands, and forgiving wickedness, rebellion and sin. . . ."

Exodus 34:6-7

When I was in college, I received a Peanuts greeting card, signed simply, "Your oldest admirer." My dad hadn't signed his name, and nowhere in the card were the words, "I love you." But it had my father's love written all over it.

When Moses wanted evidence of God's power, God didn't send a "miracle" like a parted sea as reassurance. He sent love, reminding Moses that, despite His people's continual indifference and sin, God remained "abounding in love and faithfulness, maintaining love to thousands, and forgiving . . . "

I see evidence of God's existence and might in everyday miracles. People love me who have no business loving me, after the way I have neglected and hurt them. Blessings shower into my life every day, despite my having wasted so many years, opportunities, gifts. I have disappointed, and ignored, and turned away from God. I have taken the easy way more often than His way.

But God stays with me. Despite all I have done, He stays with me. Merciful in His power, and powerful in His mercy, He loves me still. And that's the only miracle I need to see to know God exists.

He's my oldest admirer.

HOLY ORDINARY

April 27

Counting sheep

Jesus replied: " 'Love the Lord your God with all your heart and with all your soul and with all your mind. . . . Love your neighbor as yourself.' All the Law and the Prophets hang on these two commandments."
Matthew 22:36-40

I once read that counting sheep brings sleep because it occupies the mind enough to soothe its agitation. The counting activity occupies the analytical side of the brain, and imagining the sheep occupies the creative side. The brain quiets, and sleep comes.

Sometimes I wonder if God gave us specific commandments to allow us to imagine and count something so that we can rest in Him. Loving God and loving neighbors is hard to measure, an assignment that is never complete. We humans may find the Ten Commandments comforting because we can go down a list and have the wonderful validation of checking items off. We read about false witness, or stealing, or adultery, and we can count and articulate the things we have done—or not done—to honor God.

But then God tells us it is most important to love Him and to love our neighbors, and we are stumped. No matter how much we love God, we cannot thank Him for His presence. And no matter how many people we love, there will be another person in need, another day of need, waiting.

So to make our minds rest, perhaps we can simply imagine the possibilities, and understand that it's okay to count less.

Because our lives will count more.

APRIL 28

Don't you see?

So what shall I do? I will pray with my spirit, but I will also pray with my mind. . . .

1 CORINTHIANS 13:15

A teacher friend once told me that a student talked to her about God and said, "I just don't believe in anything I can't see."

I can't see gravity, but I know it exists. I drop a golf ball; it hits the ground. I drop another, and it hits the ground. When all of my golf balls end up on the ground, I eventually catch on that there's a force at work that I cannot see.

Without provocation, people fly airplanes into office buildings to bring fear to 300 million Americans. Students assassinate their classmates. Predators sell images of pornography of children, and to children. I can't see evil and hatred and resentment, but I see their chilling effects. I know they exist.

A life changes, literally overnight, from desolation to fullness, and I believe—I know—that God is here. Once I was so stooped over by grief that I could barely stand up straight. Now I connect with a love so powerful that I am able to soar, free of gravity, free of hate, free of resentment.

What else but a loving God could explain tears of emotion, tender care, broad smiles of joy—on behalf of absolute strangers? What else could explain the peace now settling in my once troubled heart? What else could account for my forgiving someone who hurt me so deeply I wanted to withdraw from the world?

God is here. I feel His work in my spirit. I recognize His work with my mind. I can't see Him, but I know He is here.

I know He *is*.

APRIL 29

Opportunity cost

Then the high priest and all his associates ... arrested the apostles and put them in the public jail. But during the night an angel of the Lord opened the doors of the jail.... "Go, stand in the temple courts," he said, "and tell the people the full message of this new life."

ACTS 5:17-20

In economics, the term "opportunity cost" describes what we give up when we choose to spend time or money on an alternative. In other words, if you forgo working a part-time job in favor of playing golf, the direct cost is the fee for golf, and the opportunity cost is the money you might have made working in that time.

God continually tries to save us from opportunity costs we incur from failing to love or failing to forgive. The direct cost of unforgiveness is the venomous resentment that lives in our hearts. The opportunity cost is the soul of another person who might have been reached if we could have stepped outside the walls of our own self-righteous ego.

God did not save me from my miserable homemade prison for my own sake. He opened my prison doors so I can enter the temple courts and teach others the meaning of living free, so that I can "give the people the full message of this new life."

God must weep at the sight of so many of His children, trapped in prisons made by their own hands, unable to forgive, unable to live the life He has for them. He must weep, not only at the opportunity cost.

But at the opportunity lost.

APRIL 30

There's no present like the time

. . . the sun stood still, and the moon stopped, till the nation avenged itself on its enemies. . . . There has never been a day like it before or since, a day when the Lord listened to a man. . . . Surely the Lord was fighting for Israel!

JOSHUA 10:13, 14

When my mom died, I received a beautiful old chime clock, a family treasure. It seldom worked, but when it did, I valued it much more for the music it made than for timekeeping. When it recently started working again, I had the sensation that time had stopped, then restarted.

Time belongs to God, not to us, and He may stop it or accelerate it to accomplish His purposes. Sometimes time appears to speed up, and I realize that I am trying to govern it myself rather than asking God how He would have me spend it. At other times, it feels as if God has stepped through a narrow place on the face of the clock and opened up a vast room where His work can be done. The sun stands still. The moon stops.

Why can't I remember this lesson—that God will give me the time to do whatever He asks me to do, and that I can let the rest of it go? Time after time, He teaches me. And time after time, I return to my own agenda, my own anxiety about not having enough time.

Someday I hope to remember the lesson that time, in the hands of God—spent according to His will—is a gift from God, a treasure. Then maybe I can stop being distracted by the ticking.

And start listening to the music.

HOLY ORDINARY

May

MAY 1

Mayday

Awaken your might; come and save us. Restore us, O God; make your face shine upon us, that we may be saved.

PSALM 80:2-3

The international distress signal word comes from the French *m'aidez,* pronounced "mayday." It means "Help me."

We use the words "Crash and burn" so casually in our world. The phrase has come to mean abject failure. I took the job I wasn't qualified for. It would be only a matter of time before I would crash and burn. And when I did, I called out to God for rescue, for validation. "Restore me, O God. Make your face shine upon me." Implicit in that last sentence was the word "again," as if my failure had been God's. Still, I cried, "M'aidez. Help me. I am afraid."

The time to ask God for strength, though, is before I fly, to minimize the chance of crashing and burning. If I ask God about a course of action, and remain in His will but fail by earthly standards, at least I will have the knowledge that I have done the right thing. In God's eyes, if not in the world's. Or even in my own.

I'm about to take off, God, on a new route. I am so afraid. Rescue me, restore me, smile upon me. I am so weak that I court disaster. M'aidez. Mayday.

My prayers for guidance and deliverance so seldom come when I am on the way up, because I always credit my own skills with the rise. But on the way down, I am quick to pray.

Help me, God. I might save some of the others. Merciful and powerful God, I am on the way down again. Help me, my God.

Mayday. *M'aidez.*

MAY 2

The ABCs of Christianity

The commandments . . . are summed up in this one rule: "Love your neighbor as yourself." . . . love is the fulfillment of the law.
ROMANS 13:9-10

By my first day in school, I had made my older brother teach me every word in the entire first-grade reading primer. I thought I knew how to read, when really I could just recognize a few words by sight and parrot them back. I wondered how in the world you could learn enough words to communicate about more important matters than, "See Spot run."

Then we learned the alphabet, 26 little building blocks of language. Suddenly I understood that its foundation allowed us to build words instead of memorizing them. The door to all of the English language opened up to me with the acquisition of that simple key called the alphabet.

Don't some people make Christianity too complicated, trying to memorize all the rules about how to operate in this world? With every new person they meet, in every new situation, they panic, thinking they can't handle something they've never seen before. "I met a new person today, God. What am I supposed to do?"

The fundamentals of Christian life are as basic as our ABCs, because all of God's language makes sense when we understand Christianity's three-letter alphabet.

A: I love God. B: God loves every person. C: I love everyone He loves. It's not easy, but it is simple.

As simple as A-B-C.

MAY 3

On fire

How can I curse those whom God has not cursed? How can I denounce those whom the Lord has not denounced?

NUMBERS 23:8

One contract firefighter was accused of setting a fire in Arizona that destroyed hundreds of thousands of acres of timber, and another firefighter was charged with starting similar fires in Colorado. It makes no sense to me that a person who devotes a career to protecting forests would set fires.

Like those two firefighters, people who call themselves Christians have certainly done their share to hurt God's people, to keep others from seeking Him. They're destroying the very gift they have committed their lives to protect.

God is love—absolute and unconditional. Yet people supposedly speaking on His behalf are often only interested in judgment—usually their own. They denounce, criticize, become self-righteous, and quibble over styles instead of focusing on loving one another. Firefighters are setting the fires.

Balaam asked how he could curse someone God has not cursed, and how he could denounce someone God has not denounced. If I truly seek God and want others to find Him, it's not my job to judge at all, because then I destroy what I have pledged to protect.

I speak clearly for God when I love the ones He loves—every single one, without exception, without condition.

No more firefighters setting fires.

MAY 4

Study heart

Now that you have purified yourselves by obeying the truth so that you have sincere love for your brothers, love one another deeply, from the heart.

1 PETER 1:22

When I took American history in college, I was totally unprepared at final exam time. A friend had had the same professor and had kept her final exam, 150 multiple-choice questions. In desperation, hoping to see the same exam, I studied it, reading only the correct answers so the others wouldn't even sound familiar. I aced the exam, but I knew nothing about American history.

I wonder how many people sit in church week after week but still have no clue about how deeply God loves them, no clue about how to love someone else deeply. Before I understood, I thought religion was all about obeying rules. I thought religion was just a matter of reading the right answers, learning them by rote. I thought rules were all that religion had to offer. I had no idea that following the rules results from a love of God, rather than the other way around.

It's so hard not to lament all those lost and hollow years without God, those years before I learned to love deeply, from the heart. But I have learned my lesson: that memorizing the right words just to pass a test is a way to get by, but it's no way to learn—or to live.

And it's certainly no way to love.

MAY 5

Kourion

Sustain me according to your promise, and I will live; do not let my hopes be dashed. Uphold me, and I will be delivered . . .
PSALM 119:116-117

In about 365 AD, an earthquake devastated a place called Kourion on the island of Cyprus. The site of the quake, preserved almost intact, allowed archaeologists to reconstruct the city's dying moments. In one building, apparently a young man tried to shield his wife and baby from falling limestone; all three were found together in a tableau of death.

Self-preservation is probably our most basic instinct until we find God. Once we become Christians, though, we begin to think of Him first, and we begin, more often at least, to think of others rather than focusing on ourselves.

When Christ enters our lives, our first instinct is to bring Him to those we love. We agonize over friends and family members who haven't found God or, worse yet, who don't even seem to be seeking Him. When crisis comes, we rush, as that young man did sixteen centuries ago, to cover those we care about with the love and strength we've found in God.

As the young man at Kourion raced to his wife and baby, he held up his hand. The hand that reached desperately to protect those he loved bore a ring inscribed with the Greek letters chi and rho, known as "Christ's monogram." That young man knew where he would go.

But he wanted those he loved to be there, too.

MAY 6

The divine aria

Be still, and know that I am God!

PSALM 46:10

In a scene from the movie *The Shawshank Redemption,* a prison's residents stop for a moment when fellow inmate Andy Dufresne plays beautiful, uplifting opera music over the loudspeaker system. It's an amazing scene: scores of convicted criminals, standing stock-still in a prison yard, deeply touched, strangely moved — by opera, of all things.

I know, it's just a movie, but it could be a scene in our lives, too. Prisons don't have to be concrete and steel; we can be penned in by overwork or low self-image, by abuse or unresolved grief. The "real world" rails at us, attacking us with noise and busyness and stress almost 24/7. Yet opera music plays over the loudspeaker if we will only still ourselves long enough to listen.

A friend tells you to be careful on a business trip. Your sister tells you "Call me when you get home so I know you're safe." Someone at church holds your hand when you lose your equilibrium. A stranger in the mall smiles at you without any idea of how much you needed it. All are notes in which God is singing to you, through the people and experiences of your life, the most beautiful music of all. The piece is called "You are loved."

Today, take the time to be still — to listen to the divine aria.

And when you know it by heart, don't forget to sing it to someone else.

MAY 7

Beach scene

Then Jesus said to them, "Don't you understand this parable? ... The farmer sows the word.... Others, like seed sown on good soil, hear the word, accept it, and produce a crop—thirty, sixty or even a hundred times what was sown."

MARK 4:14-20

Local ads urge me to visit a portrait studio to take advantage of "new backgrounds" available. One ad showed a child with a pail and a shovel, a beach ball nearby, and a fake beach scene behind him. Still, the simple truth is that having a photo that makes it look like he has been to the beach doesn't mean the child got to run in the edge of the water, or make a sand castle, or see what cool things washed ashore.

When Jesus told the parable of the seed, He talked about the difference between simply entering the scene of the word of God and actually living it. God doesn't ask us to learn His word simply to be more educated, to have that "new background." He asks us to understand His word, incarnate in His Son, so that we can live the life He has for us.

God wants us to have the real experience of life with Him, to love Him and others, to hear His voice, to feel His touch in crisis and in celebration alike. God wants us to be His presence in this harsh world, so that others will seek to have the same peace and compassion and passion for life that we have with Him. God doesn't want us to know *about* Him; He longs for us to *know* Him.

Why look at a picture when you could be at the beach?

Pietà

But we have this treasure in jars of clay to show that this all-surpassing power is from God and not from us. We are hard pressed on every side, but not crushed; perplexed, but not in despair; persecuted, but not abandoned; struck down, but not destroyed. We always carry around in our body the death of Jesus, so that the life of Jesus may also be revealed in our body.

2 CORINTHIANS 4:7-10

Of all the art I saw in Italy, Michelangelo's Pietà in Rome moved me more than any other. I spent 30 minutes just staring at her, wiping tears away, trying to understand how she could be so beautiful, so moving, so sad, so peaceful, all at once.

She is sad because she holds in her arms her murdered Son, bearing the death of a child, the most brutal burden in human experience. And yet she is peaceful because she knows that, as she holds Jesus' body, God the Father holds all of us, and holds for us a promise that our true lives cannot be contained in earthly vessels at all. She didn't understand why it had happened, but only trusted, absolutely, in the will of God.

That body that hangs so limply in her arms is simply a jar of clay, a vessel, like our bodies, made to bear witness to the life God gives us. It's a sobering yet exhilarating thought: that we are made to carry the death of Christ in our bodies, the life of Christ in our hearts. We bear the treasure of God: His only Son.

In our humble jars of clay.

MAY 9

Mother and child reunion

When they . . . repent . . . and say, "We have sinned, we have done wrong . . ." then from heaven, your dwelling place, hear their prayer and their pleas. . . . And forgive your people, who have sinned against you.

2 CHRONICLES 6:36-37

One evening I walked into a hospital room to a scene so divinely moving it could've been a painting: a loving mother holding her young daughter tenderly in her arms. The girl had undergone surgery while her mother had prayed for her child to be out of danger.

The two looked content, radiant, peaceful. What more could a parent ask than to hold her child safely in her arms?

For the rest of my life, I will picture that scene whenever I wonder how God can forgive me one more time, whenever I wonder why He would let me keep coming back, after all the mistakes I've made.

I am His child, and He wants me with Him. He knows for certain that His arms are strong enough to protect me, that His hands are gentle enough to wipe away tears that won't seem to stop, that His heart is deep enough to forgive again. And again. And again. God, my Father, simply aches to bring me from danger to safety.

It doesn't matter where I go. It doesn't matter why. It doesn't matter how long I've been gone. All that really matters is that my loving parent, once more, holds me tenderly, closely enough that I cannot distinguish my heartbeat from His.

What more could a parent ask? Or a child?

What more?

MAY 10

I once was lost

The Mighty One, God, the Lord, speaks and summons the earth from the rising of the sun to the place where it sets. From Zion, perfect in beauty, God shines forth....

PSALM 50:1-2

When I visited the island of Patmos, I learned that the sanctuary of every Greek Orthodox church faces east because Christ is symbolized in the Bible by the sun. The east is the sun's "place of birth," so the sacristy faces toward Christ's "birthplace" in the sun. Our guide told us that if we ever got lost in Greece, we could regain a sense of direction by finding a church and using it as a "compass."

I have been to some ugly and frightening places in my life, places I'm not proud of. How did I get back from that place of unforgiveness, or of pride, or of resentment, or of despair? How did I get back? By turning toward God.

Over and over and over again, I have witnessed as His healing touch restored wholeness and balance and tenderness to a world otherwise gone maniacal and hard. Amid the grit and grimness, "perfect in beauty, God shines forth."

It never fails. I get myself lost out in the big bad world, and finally I remember to turn toward the one constant, toward that Man in the east, stretching out His arms to welcome me back home. God the Father "speaks and summons the earth from the rising of the sun." I've been summoned by the rising of the Son, so I needn't be lost again.

Except in Him.

HOLY ORDINARY 147

MAY 11

All or nothing

Also a dispute arose among [the disciples] as to which of them was considered to be greatest.

LUKE 22:24

I've never been comfortable with finite answers; I always preferred essay questions to those requiring a short, precise, right answer. I especially hate multiple choice tests which combine answers, giving options like "none of the above," or "all of the above."

I suspect God doesn't care for short, limiting answers, either. When he asks a soul to be dedicated to Him, I doubt that He likes to hear, "Would you like me to do this for You, or that, Lord?" Instead, I think He wants to hear an open-ended question, one which will allow Him to be God. I'm trying to learn to ask such questions: not "Which of these would you like?" but "What would you have me do?"

Christ's disciples became so impressed with themselves and the importance of their calling that they forgot who was God and began to argue over which of them was greatest. Instead of focusing on Him, on what He would want, they thought of themselves, their worldly standing, their status.

But the tasks, the calls, the jobs we do for God are not our priority: God Himself is. God doesn't simply want my work, my time, my energy. He wants my soul. He wants me. And He wants me to think only of Him.

So among these things I do on this earth that I think are so important, which of them is greatest? The answer is "none."

And the Above.

MAY 12

Seek ye first

... we have the word of the prophets made more certain, and you will do well to pay attention to it, as to a light shining in a dark place, until the day dawns and the morning star rises in your hearts.

2 PETER 1:19

The day I learned that my sister had died, I was 650 miles away, and had to arrange a flight home at six the next morning. That night I worried so much I didn't sleep. What if I overslept? How would I get there? And so I faced the most difficult day of my life with no rest.

When I first started seeking God, I became so entangled and distracted by religion that I couldn't get to Him. Creationism. Evolution. Inerrancy of the Bible. Souls lost who never heard of Jesus Christ. What if I couldn't figure these things out? How would I get there?

I thought I had to resolve the issues of religion before I could go to God, that the "morning star" would not rise in my heart until I knew the answers. So I stayed in my dark place of despair too long. All that time lost, all that potential joy missed while I agonized over the form my faith would take.

I still don't know the answers. I know only that God longs to hold me close, to light my darkness, to love me as His precious child. Among all the details of religion and its politics, one priority rises above all else: to know God, and by knowing Him, to find His peace and light in the darkest of places.

The devil is in the details.

MAY 13

Let the river run

These are the words of him who is holy and true, who holds the key of David. What he opens no one can shut, and what he shuts no one can open. I know your deeds. See, I have placed before you an open door that no one can shut.

REVELATION 3:7-8

In college, a bunch of us girls decided to go "body-surfing" on a swift little river near campus. We pointed our feet downriver and let the current float us to a safe stopping place, then walked upriver and did it all again.

Though water scares me, I was fine until the current carried me farther downstream than I intended. I panicked when I saw I couldn't swim upstream to my safe place. Finally I let the current carry me on down to where the water calmed and I could reach shore safely.

God sometimes sweeps me away because He needs me to grow. I get complacent with my spiritual life, thinking with great satisfaction of all the things I do "for God." If I had my choice, I would stay in familiar territory, but then I wouldn't become the person He wants me to be. So He moves me along, away from my "safe place," until I trust Him and remember that He is my safe place.

If I stay in my comfort zone, I'll see only one piece of the river, and God has so much more for me than I envision for myself. And as much as that next piece of water scares me, I want to be where God wants me, not where I'm the most comfortable.

So now the river doesn't seem to stop here anymore.

Deep water

. . . during the night an angel of the Lord opened the doors of the jail and brought them out. "Go, stand in the temple courts," he said, "and tell the people the full message of this new life."

ACTS 5:19-20

The water around Santorini, a Greek island formed almost entirely of volcanic lava, is the deepest darkest blue I have ever seen, right up to the shoreline. Because the sea around it is over 1000 feet deep, ships cannot drop anchor there, as anchors cannot go deep enough to find land to grasp.

Choosing to go with God unnerved me initially, because I knew I was entering waters deep and magnificently beautiful beyond my comprehension. I knew I wasn't happy the way my life was, but I was, at least, comfortably and predictably unhappy. Who knew what was waiting in that deep water?

I knew that if I truly invited God into my life, I would have to cast away from secure shallow water, away from anchors that kept me stable in the past. When I launched out, the anchors of human relationships, material things, and status could no longer go deep enough to hold me stable. I would have to trust God completely.

The ability to anchor to familiar ground is a comfortable, stable feeling, but it lacks "the full message of this new life." Anchors don't allow us to drift, or to see the world in all its fullness and depth. Certainly, anchors are stable.

But only because they are dead weight.

MAY 15

Soul support

Ephron the Hittite . . . replied to Abraham . . . "No, my lord," he said. "Listen to me; I give you the field, and I give you the cave that is in it. I give it to you in the presence of my people. Bury your dead."

GENESIS 23:10-11

Nearly four years into my Christian life, I prayed for something I had never prayed for in my life. In a very tumultuous, growth-filled, painful time, I prayed to God not for strength—but for weakness.

For years I had swept grief aside; but in my misguided attempt to be strong, I held God at arm's length. So I was never really at home with Him—not completely. And, like Abraham, away from home, I had no idea how to bury those I had loved and lost.

Finally, one day, I let myself be weak and go to God. Two people came to my aid as surely as Abraham found help when he lost his beloved Sarah. With their lives, they helped me see the beauty of being weak, the beauty of letting God be our soul support. The three of us, together, put my heart in God's hands and gave me a place, finally, to bury my dead. They helped shoulder the burden of my crippling sadness and carry it to God.

After spending years in a distant and uncomfortable land, I believe I have finally found my way home to the strength of God's arms. With the help of God and His people, I can now let the people I love go, because I know they didn't leave me. They simply went to Him. So none of us is alone.

And I can live with that.

MAY 16

By reason of insanity

Let this be written for a future generation.... "The Lord looked down from his sanctuary on high ... to hear the groans of the prisoners and release those condemned to death."

PSALM 102:18-20

In 2003 a federal court ruled that Arkansas officials could force a death-row inmate to take antipsychotic medication to make him "sane enough to execute." A judge felt that medication followed by execution was a better choice than psychosis and continued imprisonment. *A better choice.*

As Christians, we know that a full pardon, a chance to live freely and fully for God, is always available to us. But many "prisoners" do not understand that they can come to God, despite past wrongs, and be forgiven. Many remain on death row, unaware that pardon is theirs for the asking.

If a person is made by God, and made to be with God, but chooses otherwise, can that person be in his "right mind"? Does God sentence us to death for not choosing Him when we're not capable of making a reasonable choice? Doesn't He "hear the groans of the prisoners and release those condemned to death"?

I am free, and I have freely gone to God. But what about the prisoners who don't yet know about Him? Will they be deprived of life, not knowing a better choice exists? I constantly try to understand how a loving and powerful God would want His child—any child—to have a death sentence.

Even a self-inflicted one.

HOLY ORDINARY 153

MAY 17

Undone

Then he said to them, "The Sabbath was made for man, not man for the Sabbath. So the Son of Man is Lord even of the Sabbath."
MARK 2:27-28

Rubik's cube is a puzzle cube with nine squares per face. At first, all squares on one face are one color. But they're all moveable, so the object is to move them around, then restore the colors to the original positions. Afraid I would never solve it, I clung to one hope: theoretically, I needed only to back up and undo each step I had taken. Theoretically.

Since arriving on this earth, man's "progress" has brought many things I wish we could back up and undo, or at least control. Nuclear weapons. The internet. Credit cards. All came into being to serve man, but all could work to undo us. Nuclear weapons in the hands of unstable regimes hang over our heads like a thundercloud. The Internet invades lives and facilitates porn and anonymity. The convenience of credit cards turns into competitive consumption and suffocating debt.

Christ insisted, when pressed about his disciples' "work" on the Sabbath, that the day's holiness was meant as a gift to man, not a burden. The Sabbath is not an end in itself, but a way to draw close to God and listen.

When we venerate the Sabbath itself above serving God, the gift becomes a threat. As with all things, manmade and God-made, we have to concentrate on the one priority that drives us: that God's will be done.

Else man will be undone.

Core Christianity

. . . let us . . . worship God acceptably with reverence and awe, for our God is a consuming fire.

HEBREWS 12:28-29

Earth's inner core reaches over 7000 degrees Fahrenheit; its heat causes materials in other layers of the earth to circulate in currents, which some believe cause our planet's magnetic field.

Looking back, I now wonder what I used to perceive as my "core." I sought for years to be a writer, and now I realize that the missing ingredient was not subject matter or time but passion. I didn't care deeply enough about anything to feel the burning desire to write about it.

Now my innermost core burns with energy that staggers me. No longer fighting anxiety and disquiet, I am finding the most profound peace of my life, and people seem strangely drawn to me.

Passion for God does it, stirring currents around you, creating a spiritually magnetic field. Others move closer, sensing peace and longing to share in it.

At first I thought that people simply preferred my more uplifting attitude, but now I think the reason is something much deeper, much more essential. When you obviously carry within you God's presence and the fire for him, others draw close to see if they can carry it, too. Unsure of what attracts them, they just want whatever it is that you have.

Fervent Christianity stirs the surrounding currents, and inevitably builds the magnetism that lures others inexorably towards God.

And the temperature at the core continues to rise.

MAY 19

Holy Moses

So Moses cried out to the Lord, "O God, please heal her!"
NUMBERS 12:13

The word "heal" comes from the Old English root "hal," which means "whole." Oddly, the word "holy" comes from the same root. So although Miriam had hurt Moses, he asked God to heal her, to stop her pain, to make her whole. Which, in turn, made him holy.

I find it almost impossible to pray for someone who is out to hurt me. Yet it seems that a person begins to approach "holy" when he can pray for the wholeness of others, even those considered hostile to his own interests. Moses prayed for Miriam, who wanted to bring him down. Jesus would later pray, literally as He died, for those who killed Him. They wanted even their enemies to be healed and whole. And so they were holy.

But how can someone like me become "holy" in the face of my humanness and selfishness and frailty? First, I have to stop thinking about how much I hurt and start thinking about what God would have me do. When I can become wholly focused on Him, wholly devoted to Him, wholly committed to His will, I'll begin to see glimmers of the holy in my own life.

I can't do it well now, but someday I will look at a person who hurts me and pray for their healing, and their wholeness. Then I'll be doing what God asks me to do. It is the ideal portrait of Christian faith, when one human prays for another to be healed. One may be called holy.

But both can become whole.

MAY 20

Here and now

They were looking intently up into the sky as he was going, when suddenly two men dressed in white stood beside them. "Men of Galilee," they said, "why do you stand here looking into the sky?"

Acts 1:10-11

After the initial conflict in Iraq, the U.S. military there asked private citizens to voluntarily surrender personal weapons. But many Iraqis hesitated to disarm, because they knew that disarming would make them very vulnerable to their enemies.

Our world holds us in a cycle of fear. We remain armed, not to hurt anyone, but to keep ourselves and those we love from being hurt. Yet knowing that we live in a dangerous and hurtful world, God still asks us to lay down our weapons so that we can pick up His peace and carry it to this world.

When Jesus ascended to heaven, and His followers looked longingly after Him, God's messengers asked "Why do you stand here looking into the sky?" Human lives had been changed for a reason far beyond the peace of their own souls. They would be asked to bring an understanding of God to this world. *This one.*

If we are to bring Christ's peace to this world, though, there are weapons to be surrendered here and now, not when all other weapons and threats are gone. Hearts need healing, hands need holding, hurtful words must go unsaid, here and now. Christ's work waits to be done, here and now. Heaven is already filled with the peace of God; it's our world that desperately needs Him.

Why do we stand here looking into the sky?

HOLY ORDINARY

MAY 21

Lost and found

Anyone who loves his father and mother more than me is not worthy of me ... and anyone who does not take up his cross and follow me is not worthy of me. Whoever finds his life will lose it, and whoever loses his life for my sake will find it.

MATTHEW 10:37-39

The extraordinary combination of events that brought me to God reminds of the old maxim, "For want of a nail . . ." In the progression, a horseshoe nail is lost, which results in the loss of the shoe, the horse, the rider, the battle, and ultimately the kingdom itself. "All for the want of a horseshoe nail."

In 1998, I felt as if nails were being driven into me. I lost much of my family. I lost my job. I lost my home. And ultimately, I lost myself.

But Sufi wisdom says, "When the heart weeps for what it has lost, the spirit laughs for what it has found." My heart wept continually and inconsolably in 1998 for all I felt I had lost, and now my spirit truly soars for what I have found.

While I felt at the time that three nails had destroyed me, now I'm reminded of three other nails that saved me—that saved us all. In retrospect, I can see now that, with the loss of family, a church community was found. With the loss of a job, a calling was found. With loss of myself, my God was found. And at the end of this story, a kingdom is found.

All for the sake of a few little nails.

MAY 22

Need

"Does it make you a king to have more and more cedar? Did not your father have food and drink? He did what was right and just, so all went well with him. He defended the cause of the poor and needy, and so all went well. Is that not what it means to know me?" declares the Lord.

JEREMIAH 22:15-16

When my father was a teenager in the 1920s, his parents could not afford to keep him at home. He and his sister went to live with an aunt and uncle, hundreds of miles away, until the economy improved and they could go home again.

I would do well to remember such economic times every time I use the words, "I need," words cheapened by my materialism. I often say something as thoughtlessly superficial as "I need new golf clubs," or "I need to buy that book." I can easily convince myself that I need material things—"more and more cedar." But possessions are not needs at all; they are simply an empty attempt to validate my worth in the eyes of the world.

My parents were not overly religious, but I cannot think of a time when they made a decision or acted in a way that hurt other people. They "did what was right and just" with all people. They carefully and lovingly tended the three of us, giving us safe shelter, nourishment of every kind, and the constant and abiding knowledge that we were loved. Is that not what it means to know God?

And knowing God—is that not all we need?

Off the charts

Abram fell facedown, and God said to him, ". . . The whole land of Canaan, where you are now an alien, I will give as an everlasting possession to you and your descendants after you; and I will be their God."

Genesis 17:1-12a, 15-16

The Lewis and Clark expedition searched uncharted territory for a route to the Pacific Ocean. As the explorers reached the Continental Divide, they expected to see an easy trek to the Columbia River—their way to the ocean—but instead saw seemingly endless mountain ranges.

Like Lewis and Clark, we have no idea what awaits over the next ridge in this life with God. We hold in our hands no map to brace us, no idea of how much more we must endure. God asks us to walk away in faith, beyond the familiar boundaries of this world in which we are aliens. He asks us to step off the map of the known.

If my life hadn't been changed dramatically by loss, I would never have chosen to deal with the mountains that have been on my path to God. I would have looked for the easy way around, the way without conflict, grief, self-doubt. I wanted someone to tell me what to believe, with no additional challenges to or questions about my beliefs.

Normally, though, easy routes don't get us to the high places. When we reach unfamiliar ground, we have to trust God to guide us from this disquieting, alien world to those high places where we can touch His hand and hear His voice, not through another, but for ourselves.

But it will take some climbing.

MAY 24

Active Voice

When evening came, the boat was in the middle of the lake, and he was alone on land. He saw the disciples straining at the oars, because the wind was against them. . . . They cried out, because they all saw him and were terrified. Immediately he spoke to them and said, "Take courage! It is I. Don't be afraid." Then he climbed into the boat with them, and the wind died down.

MARK 6:47, 49-50

When I studied French in high school, one of the first things we learned was how to talk about the weather. "Il fait beau" in French means that the weather is beautiful, in a sense. But our teacher explained that it literally means, "He makes it beautiful."

As a Christian, the thought that God can be found in everything—even a casual conversation about the weather—sustains me. Before, my worst fear in crisis was that the world was chaotic, the fear that nothing, no one, was in control. Life hurt deeply, and there was no indication it would ever stop hurting. When people assured me that, "Things will get better," it all sounded so passive, so impersonal, so unpredictable.

Being a Christian does not always make tragedies more comprehensible, and it certainly does not make them go away. But now in the midst of fear, I constantly cling to hope, because Jesus Christ came to me in the storm and "climbed into the boat with me."

So I no longer think, in the passive voice, that "Things will get better." Instead, I remember, "Take courage, Jesus is here."

And He makes it beautiful.

HOLY ORDINARY 161

MAY 25

If your horse dies...

... you were dead in your transgressions and sins in which you used to live when you followed the ways of this world. . . . All of us lived among them at one time, gratifying the cravings of our sinful nature and following its desires and thoughts . . . it is by grace that you have been saved, through faith—and this not from yourselves, it is a gift from God. . . .

EPHESIANS 2:1, 3, 8

For years, my spiritual learning curve was absolutely flat; I kept making the same mistakes and wondering why my life never improved. Finally an old adage sank in: "If your horse dies, we suggest you dismount."

Now I see people going that route, and I want to shout at them, "Get off it! Can't you see it's not going anywhere?!" Yet, like me, they think that it'll be better if they choose the right person, or get the right job, or make some other change in their lives. It'll be better "this time."

But a life cannot change until a heart changes, and a heart can only be changed by the grace and might of God. You don't change your heart by saying, "But I'm a good person . . ." You don't change it by saying you know you need God in your life, then leaving Him suspended just outside your door. Even He can't help if you don't let Him in.

You know that change you're making on your own, thinking you'll make it work this time? I'm the voice of experience, and I can tell you it is not enough. It will never be enough. That horse is dead.

It's time to dismount.

MAY 26

A moving experience

To the Lord I cry aloud, and he answers me from his holy hill. I lie down and sleep; I wake again, because the Lord sustains me.

PSALM 3:4-5

Someone left business cards advertising a moving company at the mail drop of my apartment complex; the cards read, "We love to move heavy stuff upstairs."

I've noticed that, since I became a conspicuous Christian, acquaintances come to me for help with the heavy lifting, asking me for prayer. In their moments of most abject fear, people know that nothing on this earth will save or sustain them, and that their only hope is God. Even nonbelievers know that the things that weigh the heaviest in this life have to be taken upstairs.

I used to feel frustrated and helpless when friends were hurting, because I am not capable of dealing with loss, financial crisis, painful relationships, or any of the other roadblocks that make us stumble through this life. Then I realized that perhaps I wasn't being asked to fix the problem, but to pass it along to a higher authority. Friends and strangers who know that I am a strong Christian were asking me simply to ask my God to help.

So when loss or pain or fear or doubt comes, in any form, there is something very useful and loving I can do to help. I can go to the holy hill and ask God to hold us all in His tender embrace. After all, I am a Christian.

I love to move heavy stuff upstairs.

MAY 27

Life sentences

Set me free from my prison, that I may praise your name. Then the righteous will gather about me because of your goodness to me.

PSALM 142:7

In *The Shawshank Redemption,* a prisoner who repeatedly tells the parole board what he thinks they want to hear is repeatedly refused for parole. Finally, when he tells the uncomfortable truth about his "rehabilitation," he is released from prison.

Like that man, for decades I told everyone—including God—what I thought they wanted to hear. I followed rules. I played nice. And I felt so trapped I could barely breathe.

Eventually I heard the voice screaming in my soul. Stop telling God what you think He wants to hear! Stop being pious. Stop fumbling for "suitable" language. Stop lying! Show God your pain. Tell Him the truth.

At last I did tell Him the truth. That I'm not very "holy." That I am angry. That my heart is broken, and that I think He broke it. That—although I didn't understand why—I loved Him still.

He knew, of course. But I needed to say it all out loud. I needed to know it's okay to go to God with my anger, with this sadness that goes on and on. I needed to know that He could heal me, that He could make me whole again. That He can set me free.

So now we both know the painful and terrifying truth: that I have been angry at my God. And He loves me still. I'll never understand why.

But He loves me still.

MAY 28

Son room

For every house is built by someone, but God is the builder of everything. . . . Christ is faithful as a son over God's house. And we are his house, if we hold to our courage and the hope of which we boast.

HEBREWS 3:4, 6

My apartment looks like thousands of other apartments. So I often dream about a house custom-built for me, with a large exercise room, lots of light, open spaces, and a very small kitchen (maybe with a drive-through window for the pizza man). Bookshelves would line every available wall.

God has worked on me all my life to make me a dream house for His Son. I wonder, when God finishes with me, what kind of place will His Son inhabit?

This house will be built on an unshakable foundation, strong enough to withstand any storm or crisis. It will be filled with Light, joy, and warmth, and will be available to anyone who needs shelter or care. It will be cozy enough to feel personal, yet large enough to accommodate all. Every neighbor will be loved and welcomed. This house will be incredibly quiet, so bathed in peace that the voice of God can whisper and still be heard.

Yet so much work remains. Walls that confine the Spirit of God to small portions of the house must come down. The foundation could use some leveling. Some places are so lacking in light that they are dangerous. Yet, with work, my heart and soul can be that house that God builds.

The place His Son chooses to live.

HOLY ORDINARY

MAY 29

Cry for help

Dear children, keep yourselves from idols.

1 JOHN 5:21

In 2002, a 19-year-old German boy gunned down 17 people, then killed himself, in an effort to make headlines. Earlier, as he held 180 students and teachers hostage in the school, they hand-lettered *Helfe,* or "help" on a sign and pasted it in a window.

A few moments of fame were bought and paid for by the slaughter of 17 innocents and a lifetime of pain for the survivors. The shooter desperately wanted attention—wanted to "be somebody." He probably didn't actually know what he wanted, but knew only that he felt desperately empty.

Somewhere inside every person, I believe, is a hunger for God. When that hunger goes unrecognized, the soul searches for meaning in many forms: in alternative spirituality, in the need for social approval or attention, in unhealthy relationships, in inexplicable appetites for money and things, in unbalanced emphasis on work, in idol worship of all types. I know, because I have searched in all of those places.

Disconnected from God, I tried to keep busy so I didn't have time to stop and think about the lack of substance in my life. That inordinately busy, crazed schedule was my sign in the window, my way of begging for help.

Now that I know God is the only force that can fill the emptiness, I look for other signs in other windows, the signs that say, "Need help."

The signs that mean, "Bring God."

MAY 30

The most basic language

For this reason anyone who speaks in a tongue should pray that he may interpret what he says. For if I pray in a tongue, my spirit prays, but my mind is unfruitful. So what shall I do? I will pray with my spirit, but I will also pray with my mind; I will sing with my spirit, but I will also sing with my mind. If you are praising God with your spirit, how can one who finds himself among those who do not understand say "Amen" to your thanksgiving, since he does not know what you are saying?

1 CORINTHIANS 14 :13,16

The worst example of target marketing I've ever seen was a Yellow Pages ad that said, "Learn to read!" It seems unlikely that a person unable to read would look in the printed Yellow Pages for help; I suppose the ad is really directed at people who know someone else who needs help with reading.

Writers and advertisers have to consider their audiences as they create, and we should do the same as we try to evangelize. Quoting Scripture may be very effective for those already conversant in Christianity, but Bible references can truly sound like a foreign language—like 'tongues'—to inexperienced seekers of God. Christians who spout Scripture can scare off those who are seeking God but don't yet "speak the language." The listener shies away, intimidated and insecure about his own ignorance of Scripture.

Christianity has to be translated into language everyone can understand. Listen to troubles. Shoulder burdens. Hold hands. Lift hearts. Accept love. Return it.

Speak the language of God.

HOLY ORDINARY

MAY 31

Owed to a Grecian urn

I know your deeds, your hard work and your perseverance.... Yet I hold this against you: You have forsaken your first love.

REVELATION 2:2, 4

As Athens, Greece began its rise to greatness, one of the first art forms to develop there was pottery. Athenian potters began diverging from traditional styles, and were amazed when the art developed so highly that a pot would be worth more than the grain or oil it held.

It's a revelation we owe to the ancient Greeks: the danger of valuing the pottery of religious expression more than the essence of God it is designed to hold. Millennia ago, the prophets shouted to remind the religious that to love God is to love His people—not to love ritual. Today's churches squabble over the stance or form or theology that is "most right" and will find them the most favor with God. Meanwhile, we have "forsaken our first love"—the love of God—and allow His people to starve in the streets.

But each of us fell in love with the most high God because He stooped to love us in and through our weakness, our fear, our selfishness. We fell in love with God because we knew His tender touch in a frightening moment. We fell in love with God because He loves us even when we cannot find a single reason to love ourselves.

The vessel we use is unimportant. All that matters is the essence of God, contained and expressed clumsily in the work of our hands.

Nothing else compares to that first love.

June

JUNE 1

A great place to live

Do not think that I have come to abolish the Law or the Prophets; I have not come to abolish them but to fulfill them.

MATTHEW 5:17

I grew up in a four-bedroom house situated with a barn on seven acres of land. For me, a little tomboy who loved getting dirty, riding horses, catching bugs, and hitting golf balls, the place was perfect.

That basement held hidden treasure; the barn in winter overflowed with sweet-smelling hay. We had wide open spaces to play baseball, great trees for climbing, a creekful of impromptu science projects, and two quarter horses. (Does that make half a horse . . . ?)

But a physical description of the house couldn't tell how warm I felt every morning I came into the kitchen to find my dad having his coffee and toast. Words wouldn't capture the turmoil I caused when I conspired with my sister to paint my bedroom red. The house was simply a framework for the exuberant, funny, tender life my family built there.

I used to confuse God's law with God, and a life with that law didn't look especially joyful. Knowing what God wants—all the "thou shalt not's"—does give me a starting point. But even if I'd never broken God's laws, I wouldn't necessarily be living a life pleasing to Him. I still have to allow God to fill the house with His love, His strength, His joy. Laws only built this house I live in.

Once I moved in, it was up to me to build a life.

JUNE 2

Same old story

... the Israelites did evil in the eyes of the Lord... They forsook the Lord.... They followed and worshiped various gods of the peoples around them.... Then the Lord raised up judges, who saved them out of the hands of these raiders.

JUDGES 2:11-12, 16

Our group in college used to keep a box full of romance novels to dip into for escape. The plots followed a very predictable formula. Boy meets girl, they fall in love, then have a conflict and break up. But they always end up together, because love conquers all.

The book of Judges, too, follows a formula. Over and over again, we find the words, "The Israelites did evil in the eyes of the Lord...." The people turned from the Lord, to other "gods," then He raised up a leader to bring them back home. A few paragraphs later are found the same words: "The Israelites did evil in the eyes of the Lord." They disappoint God; He welcomes them home again. Same old story.

But this formula doesn't just tell the story of a people long ago. The name of any true follower of God will work in the sentence: David, Solomon, Paul, Peter, or your-name-here did evil in the eyes of the Lord. We turn away from God. Unbelievably, He takes us back every time.

My story is the life story of every Christian. I do what is evil in the eyes of the Lord. He sends someone to bring me back, and we enjoy a very happy ending. Same old story.

Love conquers all.

HOLY ORDINARY

JUNE 3

Coming home

...the Lord your God is gracious and compassionate. He will not turn his face from you if you return to him.

2 CHRONICLES 30:9

After college, I lost touch with my two best friends. We hadn't had any disagreements; I had just been lazy about maintaining contact. And with each passing year, it became increasingly difficult for me to call and rekindle our friendship.

Then came one of the most fearful times in my life. I needed those two people; no one else would do. They instantly came to my rescue without questioning my failure to contact them in better days, without making me promise I would do better in the future. They simply loved me. They held me up. They healed me.

Life can suddenly turn frightening, unsure. Only one certainty remains: that it is time to go to God with whatever fears and worries we have, in whatever condition we find ourselves. He will not remind us of all the years we failed Him, or grill us on whether we can do better "this time." He will not play a divine game of "I told you so." He loves us. He wants to hold us up. He longs to heal us.

In today's climate of fear and unrest, our instinct—the most basic instinct of all—is to run to our compassionate God for His strength, His peace. Anyone who recognizes that the void inside can only be filled by God needs to stop agonizing over past failures and go to Him, now. We all need to go to Him, now.

No one else will do.

His imminence

Let no one on the roof of his house go down to take anything out of the house. Let no one in the field go back to get his cloak....

MATTHEW 24:17 -18

Warning sirens blare the first day of every month, at noon. Car alarms routinely go off in the parking lot, and they are routinely ignored. When I hear an ambulance behind me, sometimes it even takes a few moments to realize I need to pull over to let it pass. I have grown almost deaf to sirens, immune to any sense of urgency.

I'm afraid we've done the same with Scripture passages which tell of the coming of Christ, because the passing of time has made us immune to urgency. But His coming really is imminent; He is poised to appear, if not to the entire world, to one person in our world. It doesn't sound urgent—it's one of those warnings that we tend to ignore, thinking we have plenty of time.

Yet it is urgent. People are hurting, seeking help, dying while we ignore the signs of Christ's coming. For my part, I worry about intimidating them, or embarrassing myself, or saying something stupid, or being challenged and proven ignorant. Meanwhile, people are dying.

I have seen the signs. Christ is not just on the way; He is here, in my life, my heart, my soul. He is here. And today He will appear to someone else, to bring another life to the Father. I need to get myself out of the way. People are dying.

And failing to live.

JUNE 5

The sound of cannon shots

Love . . . always protects, always trusts, always hopes, always perseveres.

1 CORINTHIANS 13:7

In the depths of the Depression, my grandparents couldn't afford to feed both my dad and his sister, so they sent my dad to live with cousins in Clinton, Iowa, on the Mississippi River.

Dad loved living near the Mississippi. The river froze over in winter; when warm spring weather came, the thick ice would begin to thaw and move. My father told me the breakup of the ice sounded like cannons going off nearby.

The temperature didn't suddenly reach a magical level that thawed the ice. It was a maddeningly slow process—no light or warmth evident on the surface, but hidden currents wearing away the ice below. Finally, pressure and heat formed fissures in the thick ice; as it shifted, midwestern spring days resonated with the sound of cannon shots.

I clearly remember the day I found God, but have no idea what started my painfully slow journey. He persevered, though, and wore away my resistance, showing me how Christians live and love. Eventually I figured out that I wanted to live and love the same way.

My life used to be so cold, so quiet. When I finally realized that God wants me now, the ice split and thundered, a sound as awesome and deafening as cannons rumbling right outside my window. It's a sound my dad loved from his childhood.

I pray he's able to hear it again.

JUNE 6

A perfect stranger

... if you suffer for doing good and you endure it, this is commendable before God. To this you were called, because Christ suffered for you, leaving you an example, that you should follow in his steps.

1 PETER 2:20-21

On D-Day, over 5,000 ships and 250,000 people helped give the Allies a foothold to begin driving back Hitler's regime, a fact I understand objectively and painlessly. But the movie *Saving Private Ryan* gave me a sense of D-Day's personal and human cost; it finally hit me that each young man I saw maimed or killed was someone's son, or brother, or father. He was some*one*.

I grew up Catholic, familiar with the Stations of the Cross depicting the events of Christ's crucifixion. It used to be just ritual, but now each icon on the church wall breaks my heart, because I see a scene of pure physical anguish and humiliation. I see the most abject human pain and misery—emotional, physical, spiritual. I see one person's dying on behalf of someone He has never even met. How many of us would choose to endure such agony?

Wondrous gifts of freedom to love and to live are mine because someone's son was brutalized and killed in a distant place I'll probably never even see. I'd like to think that I truly appreciate the sacrifices others have made for me. But this man who gave it all up for me was a perfect stranger.

And He was someone's Son.

The junk truck

This is what the Lord says: Be careful not to carry a load on the Sabbath day or bring it through the gates of Jerusalem.

JEREMIAH 17:21

One day I drove home following something that looked like a junk truck; in the pickup's bed were broken furniture, tools, an old lawnmower, bicycle parts, paint cans, sports equipment—all with jagged corners, dangling parts, pieces missing. I quickly passed the truck because I didn't want any of that stuff flying into my windshield.

Sometimes my heart feels like the back of that truck; for a relatively normal, well-adjusted person, I carry an enormous amount of baggage around. The hurt I cause others weighs heavily on me, and I insist on hanging onto it.

A book called *The Four Agreements* makes the interesting observation that humans are the only animals to pay for a mistake more than once. When I have wronged someone, my mind will not be still and I cannot be at peace. I know that I'm supposed to be in God's image and yet I consistently fail Him—and my other loved ones—miserably. I pay for the mistake again and again and again.

But when I'm with God—truly with God—there is no room for the junk, because He fills my life. He asks me not to just put down that load on the Sabbath, but to constantly purge the garbage so that I am free to love Him and His children. If I insist on carrying it around in the back of the truck, something could fly out.

And someone could get hurt.

JUNE 8

Incomplete

... "He has risen." ... Trembling and bewildered, the women went out and fled from the tomb. They said nothing to anyone, because they were afraid.

MARK 16:6,8

Michelangelo's sculptures in the "Gallery of the Slaves" are controversial: some experts call them unfinished, but others aren't so sure. The figures remain rough, somewhat unarticulated, humans struggling to be free of marble, seemingly in transition, inchoate.

Mark's Gospel wears that same sense of incompleteness; it has no tidy ending, where the women tell everyone what they had seen, where everyone believes and seeks the life of Christ. Although they were the first to know about the greatest event in human history, they told no one.

Fear, like the marble around the "slaves," imprisoned their hearts, so the Word did not immediately spread. Each of us has known that fear, leaving our part of God's work momentarily unfinished. What will my friends say if I tell them Jesus died for me, and rose from the grave? How will it look? Will they think I have lost my mind?

I know the answers in my heart. I hear the words in my head. God has come alive, showing me how to walk away from the tomb. He has given life to my soul. He has entered my world, changing it powerfully, irrevocably.

I should stop every person on the street to tell them that my God lives. And yet, I am afraid.

So the work remains incomplete.

HOLY ORDINARY

JUNE 9

The God who sees me

She gave this name to the Lord who spoke to her: "You are the God who sees me," for she said, "I have now seen the One who sees me."

GENESIS 16:13

I Know What You Did Last Summer is a scary movie that tells the story of teenagers who accidentally kill a man and try to cover it up. They are later tormented by someone who threatens to expose their secret.

But the threat of "I know what you did" holds terror for many people. Few of us hold such a frightening secret, but most people have something in their past that they fear will come out. Of course you love me, we say to the people in our lives. Silently, we add, But if you only knew. . . .

My spiritual outlook changed dramatically when I realized that the God who loves me is also the God who sees me, the God who has always seen me. He knows not only the transgressions I have committed, but He knows how shallow my motives can be even when I do the right thing.

How exhilarating to know that the God who loves me really does see me, not just the spiffed-up public image I present to the world. He loves me even though He knows what I did last summer, and all the seasons of all the years of my life.

I am just now beginning to see Him and appreciate His unconditional care. I see that this depth of love is unknowable to my little human mind. I am beginning to understand that I will never understand. But at least now I see Him, the God who sees me.

The God who loves me, nonetheless.

The rest of the world

The body is a unit, though it is made up of many parts. . . . If one part suffers, every part suffers with it; if one part is honored, every part rejoices with it.

1 CORINTHIANS 12:12, 26

I read a piece on prayer which pointed out that the fervor or the passion of prayer has much more to do with our relationship with the object of the prayer than it does with our relationship with God. As we pray for something very close to our own interests, our prayer is deep and passionate. But when we pray for someone unknown to us, the intensity of our prayer diminishes.

But every time I pray for another person, I really pray for myself, because every person on earth, like me, is part of Christ's body. To pray without passion for certain people would be like saying I want my right arm to stop hurting, but it's fine if my left one aches.

The body of Christ aches today, with loss of loved ones or of security. It aches with anger and resentment that "they have something I can't get." It aches with fear that the terror this time will have my name and address written on it.

Every prayer in me is really for myself, for the health of the body I belong to, so every prayer should be passionate and intense. Bringing peace into one heart today would help bring peace to my heart, to His body.

And so I pray, fervently, for the peace, and the rest, of the world.

JUNE 11

High time

When he arrived . . . two demon-possessed men coming from the tombs met him. They were so violent that no one could pass that way. . . .
MATTHEW 8:28

When I was little my older brother built a treehouse in an oak tree. I never got into it because it required shimmying ten feet or so across a limb thirty feet off the ground; every time I looked down, fear of falling froze me. To placate me, my brother nailed an old door to the lowest branch of the tree to give me my own safe place.

I have always settled for the low branches. When I tried to climb higher, I saw two demons coming from the tombs, so violent that I could not "pass that way."

My unresolved questions of the heart and soul have kept me from getting close to God. I haven't even asked for some answers because I'm afraid of what I might hear. Where did they go? Why didn't I love them better? Where does God want me to go? What would He do with my life if I told Him I was ready to go higher?

This time, another person will be there, holding my hand and allowing me to leave the low branches behind. Just don't look down, He'll tell me. Don't let your fears keep you from going where you know you need to go. I'll lead you across the narrow places, the dizzying heights, past the paralyzing demons of fear.

Take my hand. Look in my eyes. Trust me, alone. Trust me when I tell you that you will not fall.

Except, perhaps, in love.

JUNE 12

The ultimate vaccine

The body that is sown is perishable, it is raised imperishable; it is sown in dishonor, it is raised in glory; it is sown in weakness, it is raised in power . . .

1 CORINTHIANS 15:42-43

I got really frightened when I first read about vaccinations in a biography of Louis Pasteur. In order to keep people from dying of anthrax, he gave them a watered-down case of the disease. I knew at school we received inoculations, which meant that someone was deliberately giving me a dread disease. My fourth grade imagination just went wild with the thought of contracting diseases on purpose.

If we allow him into our lives, God introduces a kind of vaccine against death. We contract a mild form of the disease when we die to ourselves, when we hand our lives entirely over into his keeping rather than insisting that we are in control. When I relinquished my imagined control over my life, I died a little; I wasn't sure I could go on knowing I wasn't directing my own life.

But the body I gave up is so insignificant, so perishable, and the Body I joined is eternal, limitless. What I lost grew from weakness and dishonor. What I gained is filled, and fills me, with the love and life of God, the love and lives of God's people.

For so long, I wanted to shrink God down so that He could be part of me. I finally understand it's much better for me to reach up, to be part of Him.

To be raised in power.

JUNE 13

Plans

This is why Moses was warned when he was about to build the tabernacle: "See to it that you make everything according to the pattern shown you on the mountain."

HEBREWS 8:5

Several years ago, a friend who teaches grade school built in her classroom a "reading loft" to encourage students to read. I can't even assemble pre-fab bookshelves; I make parallelograms. But when I expressed amazement that she could do such a thing, she said matter-of-factly, "It wasn't hard to do. I had *plans*."

With the right plans, truly anything can happen. One human being who will listen to God can teach another to live—and to love—without fear. One human being can turn another toward God. One human being can use old scars to heal someone else's fresh wounds. With the right plans.

My instinct is always to yank everything from the box and hammer away on my own, not a prescription for success. Without exception, God's plans succeed on an unimaginable scale, while mine won't hold up under their own weight.

If I would only listen, if I would only "follow the pattern I was shown on the mountain," I could be built into a dwelling suitable for the spirit of the living God. In fact, I know just the carpenter who could build such a place.

And He has *plans*.

JUNE 14

Rest in God alone

Whatever your hand finds to do, do it with all your might, for in the grave, where you are going, there is neither working nor planning nor knowledge nor wisdom.

ECCLESIASTES 9:10

Jesus called his disciples to him and said, "I have compassion for these people; they have already been with me three days and have nothing to eat. I do not want to send them away hungry, or they may collapse on the way."

MATTHEW 15:32

Whenever I go to the cemetery to visit the graves of family members, I often see a woman who lost her son over twenty years ago to cancer. To this day, she remains crippled by grief, asking everyone who comes by, "Did you know my son?"

I can't imagine losing a loved one and not having the comfort of knowing God. Thinking that all of life simply ends up in the grave, where "there is neither working nor planning nor knowledge nor wisdom" must feel desperate. Who could find rest in the thought that it all ends here, on this earth?

But as Christians, we know about that Light beyond the grave. Jesus came here to get us from life through death to life again, nourishing us so that we do not "collapse on the way." Remaining with Christ, in Christ, draws us near to God the Father, the only place where we can find true rest.

As for me, my heart is filled with hope, all because I finally listened to the question God the Father kept whispering in my ear.

"Do you know my Son?"

JUNE 15

Man and machine

Then they secretly persuaded some men to say, "We have heard Stephen speak words of blasphemy against Moses and against God. . . . we have heard him say that this Jesus of Nazareth will destroy this place and change the customs Moses handed down to us."

ACTS 6:11, 14

Researchers are trying to create robots which can handle tasks more complex than welding or vacuuming. The change will require not just more computing capability, but better interaction between robots and people. The ultimate goal is to make robots much more like their creators.

Sometimes the religious structure looms so large in our lives that it obscures the face of God. The robot of the system performs tasks, checks off lists, seeks and follows the law. "Right thinking" trumps the right to be loved.

The men of the Sanhedrin arrested Stephen and wanted him killed because they felt threatened by the diminishing importance of religious law. They knew that if the law became less important, they would become less important, because their hearts were filled with love for themselves rather than love for God. They even seemed to equate blasphemy of Moses—of the religious system—with blasphemy of God.

So when Stephen put love ahead of the law, when loving became more important than computing, he paid with his life, just as the One before him had done.

And so the creation became more like the Creator, after all.

JUNE 16

I'm telling . . .

Be imitators of God, therefore, as dearly loved children and live a life of love. . . . For you were once darkness, but now you are light in the Lord. Live as children of light. . . .

EPHESIANS 5:1-14

In the movie *The Big Chill,* one man who sees his life as an endless treadmill, a joyless quest to make ends meet, laments, "But nobody said it was going to be fun. At least nobody said it to me." All of us harbor perceptions, often misguided, about what life is going to be like, of what life promises.

Before I became a Christian, I mistakenly perceived a life lived for God as joyless, filled with anxiety over measuring up to rules. I pictured a dull but righteous life of duty, a life of giving up things and people I wanted desperately to hold onto.

I never imagined the joy of being a Christian. I never knew that experiencing God's forgiveness would allow me to forgive others more easily, to let go of resentment and simply love people, including myself. I never dreamed that anxiety would diminish rather than building because I would see that life works better when placed in God's merciful and tender embrace.

I always thought I should become a Christian because it was the right and obligatory and dutiful thing to do. Nobody said that coming out of the darkness and living as a child of the Light would be moving, breathtaking, rich, filled with joy.

At least nobody said it to me.

JUNE 17

A nice little fixer-upper

The law was added so that the trespass might increase. But where sin increased, grace increased all the more, so that, just as sin reigned in death, so also grace might reign through righteousness to bring eternal life through Jesus Christ our Lord.

ROMANS 5:20-21

A few days into the Iraqi war, I saw images of civilians huddled in a cave away from bombs and bullets, and of soldiers a world away from home. The image made me wonder if it's worse to be homeless, or to have a home you cannot inhabit.

As God's child, I can be His home—His dwelling place. But until I looked at "the law" of Christian principles years ago and saw my "trespass," I would never have thought to change. Because of the law, I began to see flaws in my life, and I longed to be a better person. Because of the law, I began to see why my schedule was so full and my heart so empty. Self-examination led me to try church, and a church community led me to God. There I heard Him say, as he says to every seeker, "I want you to be my home on earth."

God lives in each human heart that seeks Him and welcomes Him. But many hearts, like mine, only found God because "the law" got our attention. And although I know this place is small and still needs a great deal of fixing up, I also know that God and I both find joy when I welcome Him home.

It must be painful to have a home you cannot inhabit.

JUNE 18

Door to heaven

After this I looked, and there before me was a door standing open in heaven.

REVELATION 4:1

I am thankful that I went to Greece and Turkey before 2001's terrorist attacks. If the attacks had happened before my trip, I'm not sure I could have gotten past my fear enough to see what the rest of the world held.

God has often shown me enough of the beauty of His world to get me through the difficult and fearful times and places. Every time I experience unconditional love, even for a moment, I glimpse that door to heaven standing open. He has shown me how moving the love of family and friends can be, and that knowledge gives me strength when loss and separation come. He shows me, when I share His presence with others, that this world can be a holy and breathtakingly beautiful place.

Today, this week, this year, this lifetime, I will have to see too many examples of the worst of man's world. But today, this week, this year, this lifetime, I will also see glimpses of what God promises me inside that door to heaven. I can almost hear His words of comfort and encouragement.

Hold on through the pain, the loss, the fear. Hold on, and look through that door, child of mine, to see what an eternity with your God will bring. When times get tough, remember those priceless moments spent with loved ones. You weren't just having a "good day" here on earth.

You were looking through the door to heaven.

JUNE 19

Grace

. . . leaving her water jar, the woman went back to the town and said to the people, "Come, see a man who told me everything I ever did. Could this be the Christ?"

JOHN 4:28-29

Once I adopted a little stray cat, at a time when I, too, felt lonely and lost and picked on. Because he arrived just when I needed him, I named him Grace. I sent a photo of him to a friend, and she wrote back, "Grace is precious."

Probably because he once had to live on his own, alone, afraid, hungry, Grace stands partially in his food bowl when he eats, fearing that he will lose this precious gift to someone else.

In the churches, and in our hearts, we sometimes carry that same attitude. We have found something so life-giving, so priceless, so incredible, that we often believe someone will try to take it from us. We find a God who sees everything we ever did, and loves us still. What if someone tries to take Him away?

But no one can steal grace from me. God will not withdraw His love when He finds out what I'm really like. He will not abandon me, even when I abandon Him. The presence of God need not be hoarded or protected, and it cannot be earned. It must simply be accepted, as the woman at the well accepted it.

My God, in His infinite grace, will continue to hold me, to love me, to caress me, no matter what I have done, no matter what I will do. My friend had it right all along: Grace is precious.

Grace is precious, indeed.

In Father's Arms

You know my folly, O God; my guilt is not hidden from you. . . .
Answer me, O Lord, out of the goodness of your love; in your great
mercy turn to me.

PSALM 69:5, 16

When I was little, I used to lie on the floor to watch television, and most nights would fall asleep there. My Dad would pick me up, take me to my bed, and tuck me in. I loved that tender experience so much that I would pretend to be asleep even when I wasn't. I thought I was really getting away with something.

The more I think back on that time, though, the more I think he knew that I wasn't always asleep. My Dad was always loving, but sometimes had trouble showing it, and now I wonder if he longed for those times as much as I did—having the chance to be close to me, to show tenderness when no one else was looking.

Occasionally I get into a little emotional trough, and I think in a sense I'm pretending to be asleep so that my Father will pick me up, caress me, and take me to my rest with Him. I have realized only recently that this "emptiness" inside me is not pain, is not loneliness, but is simply longing to be close to God. All of those experiences that I have gone through were calls for Him to pick me up and hold me.

And like my earthly Father, I'm beginning to see that God longs for our closeness and intimacy as much as I do. So I pretend to be asleep, and my Father holds me in His infinite tenderness.

And all along, I thought it was my idea. . . .

JUNE 21

Morning

Now if we died with Christ, we believe that we will also live with him. For we know that since Christ was raised from the dead, he cannot die again; death no longer has mastery over him.

ROMANS 6:8-9

Next December, when the days are short and the light seems depressingly nonexistent, I hope to remember this gorgeous Mississippi day of blooming fuchsia azaleas and delicate white dogwoods. I hope to remember.

Many things that bring fear or gloom into my outlook do so because I have no idea when—or if—they will end. I feared the dark, as a small child, because I hadn't amassed enough experience to know that the sun always rises. I used to dread the winter, until years of experience taught me that the spring always appears, with its warm embrace and brilliant color and greening and growth.

In spiritual matters, I struggle with similar fears. Over and over, I have seen God rise before me, comforting me, lifting me above worry, fear, grief, hurt. Yet over and over, when the night stretches long, I slip into wondering, like a fearful child, "But what if the darkness stays this time?"

I know the Light will return. I know that death and the pettiness and dimness of human existence hold no mastery over Christ. And so they hold no mastery over me. I'm struggling to remember the truth. It has been dark before.

But the Son always, always, always rises.

JUNE 22

Acts

He said to them: ". . . you will receive power when the Holy Spirit comes on you; and you will be my witnesses . . . to the ends of the earth."

ACTS 1:8

The cliché tells us that "Actions speak louder than words," a sentiment echoed by the book of Acts in the New Testament. Acts follows the Gospel of John, which ends with these words. "Jesus did many other things as well. If every one of them were written down, I suppose that even the whole world would not have room for the books that would be written."

Human words alone cannot convey the power of God, says John. Enter the Acts of the Apostles. People learn a new skill much more quickly by seeing a demonstration rather than by reading a set of instructions. Nonbelievers will learn what the presence of God means through our actions, and they will recognize the genuineness of our faith when we act with compassion, with mercy, with love.

I believe that the ravenous spiritual seekers in our world are begging us, "Don't tell me what God looks like. *Show* me." Each time we act as Jesus would have acted, we draw near—and draw others near—to our merciful and powerful God. We interest others in a life with Him not by preaching—by words—but by practice, by our acts. Feeding. Healing. Supporting. Loving. The reality is that words can scarcely be heard across a crowded room.

But actions can be heard "to the ends of the earth."

HOLY ORDINARY 191

JUNE 23

Building the kingdom

For the kingdom of God is . . . of righteousness, peace, and joy in the Holy Spirit, because anyone who serves Christ in this way is pleasing to God and approved by men.

ROMANS 14:13

Albert Speer, Hitler's architect, spent 20 years in Spandau prison for his role in the Nazi war machine. While there, Speer used to walk the small prison courtyard, pretending that each mile he traveled was taking him across Europe. Speer studied the sites he would visit, and he pictured those places in his mind's eye to pass the miles and days and years.

Our everyday Christian walk, sometimes a narrow, uninteresting view, holds clues to what God promises us. If on our courtyard rounds we visualize a greater world beyond, we glimpse the kingdom of God every day.

When a friend accepts me and loves me unconditionally, I see several acres of the kingdom of heaven. When my family's deep losses bound us powerfully together, another large expanse of the kingdom came into view. When I sense love or commitment, healing or growth taking place, I get a good look at the kingdom of God.

When he says the kingdom is "at hand," I take him literally and believe that we forge a small portion of it every day, and begin to see God's kingdom long before our lives on this earth end.

I'm still inside the prison walls right now. When I'm free, I know I'll navigate the full kingdom with a tiny sense of déjà vu, because on good days, I see glimpses of it here on earth.

On great days, I get to help build it.

JUNE 24

Compassion

. . . we see Jesus . . . now crowned with glory and honor because he suffered death, so that by the grace of God he might taste death for everyone. In bringing many sons to glory, it was fitting that God, for whom and through whom everything exists, should make the author of their salvation perfect through suffering.

HEBREWS 2:9-10

A friend of mine drove 650 miles one night to attend the funeral of a woman she barely knew, the mother of a friend. She wanted to be there simply to give support, to help shoulder the grief of someone she loves.

The root of the word "passion" means "suffering," so "compassion" is "suffering with." I think compassion, the willingness to "suffer with" another person, is the most grace-filled and Godlike expression within human power. We tell those we love, "I stand with you, my beloved, so close that our tears, our grief, our pain, even our laughter and rejoicing, are one. I'm not just here *for* you; I'm here *with* you."

One Man chose to suffer not only with me, but for me, the living, breathing definition of compassion. When I grieve, or ache, or despair, that Man slips His wounded, yet perfect, hand into mine, to tell me that He is grieving, aching, despairing for me.

I am there with you, my beloved, the Author of my salvation whispers. I will go any distance to be with you, in your pain or in your rejoicing. I love you.

With a Passion.

HOLY ORDINARY

JUNE 25

Haul away

When an evil spirit comes out of a man, it goes through arid places seeking rest and does not find it. Then it says, "I will return to the house I left." . . . it goes and takes with it seven other spirits more wicked than itself. . . .

MATTHEW 12:43-45

After September 11, 2001, it took many months to clean up the debris at "Ground Zero" in New York. Why not plant explosives to bring down the towers' remnants, bulldoze the site, and start over? Why sift through tons of dust and debris, inch by excruciating inch?

But workers at the site found clues in the debris about the attack. They identified weaknesses in the building's structure that could be corrected in the future. They found human remains which allowed families to finally, finally make peace with death, with loss.

Lessons wait among the ruins. Certainly it's easier to cover or ignore pain than to bring it to light and learn from it. But buried resentment or grief really can create "seven other spirits more wicked." Past hurts, left unexamined, can leave the fragile human heart empty or wounded or even incapable of deep trust and love. Wholeness can only come to hearts fully repaired and filled with God's spirit.

So we have to look at the past with His eyes. We have to let His hands carry away the shards of anger, of sadness, of resentment buried within us. He can give us the strength to clear away the debris.

And love—deep, abiding, healing—waits among the ruins.

JUNE 26

The memory of trees

Belteshazzar answered, "My lord, if only the dream applied to your enemies and its meaning to your adversaries! The tree you saw, which grew large and strong, with its top touching the sky, visible to the whole earth, with beautiful leaves and abundant fruit, providing food for all, giving shelter to the beasts of the field, and having nesting places in its branches for the birds of the air—you, O king, are that tree!

DANIEL 4:19-22

I often see crude wooden signs reading, "REPENT!" nailed to trees along the highway. I'll bet a lot of people react to those signs the same way the king in the book of Daniel reacted to his dream. "It can't be about me," we think. "That sign is for someone else."

I've already told God about my checkered past, and I know He has forgiven me. So why would I need to repent? Well, there were those times recently when I hurt others to salvage my fragile self-image. And yes, I do acknowledge that my ego swelled to the size of Rhode Island when someone complimented a Sunday school class I led. Okay, I had almost forgotten about those times when I ignored my friend's needs because I missed spending time with her.

Not only is the sign that reads "REPENT" appropriate to me, there's probably another one right down the road. And by the time I travel those few miles, I'll need another reminder. So, as it turns out, that message nailed to a tree?

It was for me.

HOLY ORDINARY

JUNE 27

Bread and stone

"Which of you, if his son asks for bread, will give him a stone? . . . If you, then, though you are evil, know how to give good gifts to your children, how much more will your Father in heaven give good gifts to those who ask him! . . ."

MATTHEW 7:9, 11

I used to think it was a curse to love deeply. When I lost people I loved so much, I couldn't even think of them without feeling as if I had a jagged piece of metal inside me. Every time I moved, or was moved, it hurt wrenchingly. Why did God give those people to me, only to cause me such pain by taking them away? Had He given me bread, or had He given me a stone?

Then in my pain I reached out to God, and He showed me the heart of Jesus. I saw a man who knows how much it hurts to love, and yet chose the pain in exchange for the love. When I saw the choice He had made to love me, the shards of metal in my own heart melted into flesh and blood, part of me. I am where I am, and who I am, because I have loved.

And finally, He showed me that I have not lost those people at all, that loving is always gain, and never loss. The jagged metal has become precious mettle, the essence of a person who—finally, finally—sees that to love deeply, with all of your heart, is the greatest blessing of all. So God has given me bread after all.

The bread of life—that healed a heart of stone.

JUNE 28

We have met the enemy

... I have no praise for you, for your meetings do more harm than good. In the first place, I hear that when you come together as a church, there are divisions among you. ...

1 CORINTHIANS 11:17-18

If terrorists never perpetrated another act of violence on American soil, they will have achieved a key objective: to make us afraid of our own system.

The prospect of terrorism scares us because our own system of government and commerce were turned against us. Terrorists were able to bring down the World Trade Center by melting into our society, with its freedom to take flying lessons, rent cars, start bank accounts, buy box cutters. Freedom we fought so hard for in revolution, in civil war, in world war now has become a weapon in the enemy's hands.

It's a lesson I need to remember in church, when the tasks I work so hard at step between me and my God. I'm in church to know my God, to learn to love as He loves. Church, above all other places, is where we should remember to love unconditionally. When church activities make me resentful or judgmental, the very system I engage to worship my God will separate me from Him.

True freedom isn't a blank slate, but requires responsibility, vigilance, temperance, wisdom. True freedom—in God and in country—requires us to keep our eyes on why we're here in the first place. Otherwise, we are in danger, because the enemy is here, within our borders.

The enemy is here.

HOLY ORDINARY

JUNE 29

Enough

The Philistines asked, "What guilt offering should we send to him?" [The priests] replied, "Five gold tumors and five gold rats, according to the number of the Philistine rulers, because the same plague has struck both you and your rulers."

1 SAMUEL 6:4

In 2003, the Supreme Court ruled that the University of Michigan could use race as a factor to promote racial diversity in admissions, but that it must stop using a system which awarded applicants a specific number of points based on race. Promoting diversity is laudable, but the system had to go.

Now that we've admitted a centuries-old wrong, we want to implement a neat little system to right it. Reducing the issue to a formula implies that it is under our control. Give me penance, or make me tithe—any number that will let me know I have done enough. The Philistines tried it: having wrongly taken the ark of the Lord, they asked the priests for some hard-and-fast formula to soften God's anger.

God's approach, however, is not so tidy. God says to love Him first, and not to place our little kingdoms above His. God asks us to love each other in the first place, so there will be no discrimination to redress. God asks us to do as He does: to love completely, to never say, "Okay, I'm done; now I have loved enough."

The only number that will redress our past wrongs is one. Worship *one* true God, make Him our number *one* priority.

Love one another.

JUNE 30

Day dreaming

To these four young men God gave knowledge and understanding of all kinds of literature and learning. And Daniel could understand visions and dreams of all kinds . . . In every matter of wisdom and understanding [the king] found them ten times better than all the magicians and enchanters in his whole kingdom.

DANIEL 1:17, 20

The science show *Nova* once ran a story about an epileptic man who thought that, during seizures, he saw God, communicated directly with God, and even became God. He acutely felt the pain of humanity—of atrocities and disasters—during and after seizures. In fact, the man considered refusing medication, because ending the seizures meant ending his visions of God.

Unlike Daniel, we're willing to do the dramatic to be with God, but not the ordinary work of sustaining a deep, abiding, trusting relationship with Him. We want to hear the voice of God in a safe nighttime dream, but don't care to hear Him in the harsh light of everyday life.

Come speak to us, we demand of God. But don't ask us to feel someone else's pain. Give us grand visions of what the world means, but don't ask us to dream dreams frighteningly beyond our small human means to control. Speak to us of the staggering cross your Son bore, but don't ask us to pick up that small cross of loving an unlovable human being. Speak, God, we demand. Speak, and perhaps we'll listen someday.

Perhaps.

July

JULY 1

Christmas in July

Love must be sincere.... Be joyful in hope, patient in affliction, faithful in prayer. Share with God's people who are in need. Practice hospitality.

ROMANS 12:9, 12-13

My office building holds a "Christmas in July" food drive each year to feed people in a downtown homeless shelter. Apparently the sponsors hope to capture the spirit of generosity that donors are more likely to exhibit during the holidays.

It's a lesson that hits close to home. I can be very pious with a Bible or prayer book open in front of me, but I'm less likely to think of God, and of how to treat His people, in traffic or at the office, in the grocery store line or the bank.

But for the sincere and loving Christian, every day is Christmas. Every day of my life I receive gifts from God, and every day I know that I will live forever because Christ came into my world and into my heart. He's not just a holiday God; He's an everyday God, and His Spirit should live clearly in everything I do.

God's people are hungry and hurting every day of the year. God's people need shelter and comfort every day of the year. God's people long for Christ to come into their lives every day of the year, not just on holidays or Sundays.

Today, in the "everydayness" of my life, I can share with God's people who are in need, in Christ's name, to thank Him for the gift of my life.

It'll be like Christmas in July.

JULY 2

Functions

... we see Jesus, who was made a little lower than the angels, now crowned with glory and honor because he suffered death, so that by the grace of God he might taste death for everyone ... he says, "Here am I, and the children God has given me."

HEBREWS 2:9, 13

A mathematical function is a correspondence or relationship between elements, involving the words "if" and "then." One event affects the other; one is a function of the other. But the word function can also be defined as "the action for which a person or thing exists."

Maybe that's where we humans, in our penchant for logic and formulas, fail to understand what God means by the word "love." We think it is a mathematical function, with if and then, when it is actually our function in God's plan, "the action for which we exist," the action for which Christ died. If we can trap love into a formula, then we feel we might somehow control it. If you do what I want you to do, then I will love you. If you measure up, then I will love you. If I can control you, then I can love you.

But loving is not a function of mathematics; it is our function as the living image of a loving God, as children given by the Father to His Son. The love of God cannot be reduced to a formula and predicted and explained and controlled. The love of God is not something I can capture and possess, but something I must allow to possess me. It is my function. Not mathematical.

Divine.

JULY 3

But now I see

For John came neither eating nor drinking, and they say, "He has a demon." The Son of Man came eating and drinking, and they say, "Here is a glutton and a drunkard, a friend of tax collectors and 'sinners.'" But wisdom is proved right by her actions.

MATTHEW 11:18-19

Discover magazine once ran a story about a man, blind from the age of 3, who underwent surgery and regained his eyesight at 46. Yet the man was still unable to use his sight, and even continued to walk with a cane, because his brain had never been programmed to process visual information. He could see, but he didn't know what he was seeing.

The people who saw John the Baptist, and even Jesus Himself, had no idea what they were seeing, because they were still programmed to see on a mean human level. These images of God did not suit their needs, and so they did not see Him at all.

In today's world, we closely examine religion and forget to look at, or even for, God. We see "coincidences," and fail to see His hand at work. We receive gifts, and congratulate ourselves for "earning" them. We see, but we don't know what we're seeing.

It becomes a matter of learning, and then of teaching others, what God looks like in our world. God looks like a friend who brings great joy, a stranger who comforts, an incredible coincidence. God looks like a Man who always, always loves, and He is here in every moment.

If we could only see . . .

JULY 4

I tell you the Truth

"I tell you the truth, this generation will certainly not pass away until all these things have happened. Heaven and earth will pass away, but my words will never pass away."

LUKE 21:32-33

A copy of the Declaration of Independence, one signed on July 4, 1776, came to my hometown in a traveling exhibit. I regret that I didn't get there to see it, to read for myself those words that still ring so clearly centuries later: "We hold these truths to be self-evident, that all men are created equal. . . ."

Cultures change, but at the core of human life is the undeniable truth that we are created in God's image and that we are all created equal. In the New Testament, Jesus uses the words "I tell you the truth" over 70 times. But even if He hadn't spoken those words aloud, truth was "self-evident" in His life and in His love. When asked which law was most important, He went straight to the truth: Love God, love your neighbor, no matter what it costs.

So today, when I love, I speak His truth; His words have not passed away. On the day I recognized God's presence and began to hear the truth of Jesus Christ in my heart, I made my "declaration of dependence." That day I acknowledged that I cannot—and do not want to—make it alone, that true freedom only comes with utter dependence on God.

Christ told us that truth. He lived that truth, and asks the same of us. To live His truth.

In deed.

HOLY ORDINARY 205

JULY 5

The way my Father loves me

Praise be to the God and Father of our Lord Jesus Christ, the Father of compassion and the God of all comfort, who comforts us in all our troubles, so that we can comfort those in any trouble with the comfort we ourselves received from God.

2 CORINTHIANS 1:3-5

A friend once told me a wonderful story of how she, as a little girl, used to go fishing with her father. As she sat in front of him on the riverbank, he would nuzzle and smell her hair. She just realized that she does the same with her grandson, a loving legacy handed down, unspoken, from her father. She is saying, implicitly, "I love you the way my father loved me."

I hope to do the same in a Christian sense. I see now how liberating and comforting it is to feel God's arms around me constantly. So why wouldn't I want others to understand what I understand, to feel what I feel in His care?

At first I thought I was too human to be able to love others the way God loves me. But a man named Jesus Christ, a human, loved us just as His father loved Him. So the real issue when it comes to loving others is not whether I'm able to do it. The issue is whether I'm willing.

Jesus has been here, living in our world, and He's here now, living in our hearts. He taught us the lesson of the strength we give—and find—by loving one another. I can almost hear His voice right now.

"Draw close now. I'm going to love you the way my Father loves me."

JULY 6

The prisoner is you

For if you forgive others their trespasses, your heavenly Father will also forgive you, but if you do not forgive others, neither will your Father forgive your trespasses.

MATTHEW 6:14-15

For nearly two years I dragged around a grudge against a former boss; it weighed me down like a ball and chain. But grudges are not only useless, they're debilitating. The resentment, hostility, and anger I harbored for her didn't cost her one moment's sleep. Yet I constantly fretted, avoided her, and generally allowed my malice to lessen the quality of my life significantly.

Powerfully negative attitudes can become perversely precious to us, like familiar old friends. We say that we have forgiven, then insist on showing evidence to justify our anger. But when we finally burn the evidence—when it's no longer important who was right and who was wrong—we have truly forgiven enough to move on. I clung to my anger, but my spiritual and emotional well-being demanded that I get rid of it. As one quote says, "To forgive is to set a prisoner free and discover the prisoner was you."

Forgiving someone who hurt me so much and regretted it so little represented an imposing obstacle in my path to true Christian living. "She deserved my anger," I wanted to say. "She doesn't deserve my forgiveness."

Thank you, God, for not saying the same thing about me.

JULY 7

Today

"And on the seventh day God rested from all his work." . . . Therefore God again set a certain day, calling it Today, when a long time later he spoke through David, as was said before: "Today, if you hear his voice, do not harden your hearts."

HEBREWS 4:4, 7

I've seen a T-shirt which says, "Golf is life. The rest is just details." Similar shirts about priorities are marketed for all sorts of hobbies and interests.

But to God, "the rest" is not just a detail, but a gift, an integral part of life with Him. We humans have begun to think of rest as laziness; we operate as if staying busy all the time is a virtue. We are even unable to rest, sometimes, for thinking of all the activities we know we will cram into tomorrow. Or rest will not come because we spend all of our energy worrying about what we did wrong yesterday.

But every time I worry about tomorrow, I squander this beautiful gift God calls "Today." And every time I agonize over yesterday's bad decisions or circumstances, I squander the gift of His unconditional love and forgiveness.

I know that the only true rest in this world comes from trusting God, letting all of the details of yesterday and tomorrow dissolve into Him. After all, God gave me this rich gift, a day when I will be able to hear His voice, a day when His tenderness and care will soften my heart. Just for me, "God set a certain day, calling it Today."

Not "to-do."

JULY 8

Belonging

When our fathers were in Egypt, they gave no thought to your miracles; they did not remember your many kindnesses, and they rebelled by the sea, the Red Sea. . . . Save us, O Lord our God, and gather us from the nations, that we may give thanks to your holy name and glory in your praise.

PSALM 106:7, 47

A Greek sculptor and architect named Phidias designed the entrance to the Acropolis, the Parthenon, and a massive statue of Zeus. Where the remains of that statue were discovered, archaeologists also found a small mug, inscribed on the bottom, "I belong to Phidias." A man who designed places that endured the millennia wanted to make sure his cup returned to him.

My Creator has built such wonders as the plant and animal worlds, human life, and the solar system, but He also claims me as His own vessel, His own tool. Incredibly, He seems to value me as much as He values the vast and intricate workings of the universe.

And just as that little cup "wanted to be" with its creator, I want to be with mine, in body, mind, and spirit. I constantly struggle with forgiveness, resentment, defensiveness and all manner of un-Godly things. But I "give thanks in God's holy name" that He still uses me as a vessel to carry His love to others. In my gratitude, I need to make it clear that I know Who created me, and Who holds me tenderly in His hands. You see, I don't simply "belong to God."

I long to be with God.

JULY 9

Breathing lessons

We do not know what we ought to pray for, but the Spirit himself intercedes for us with groans that words cannot express. And he who searches our hearts knows the mind of the Spirit, because the Spirit intercedes for the saints, in accordance with God's will.

ROMANS 8:26-27

Even after taking yoga for a couple of years, I had trouble because I couldn't seem to relax. I especially fought tightness in my left shoulder and in my neck.

Whenever we stretched in yoga practice, the instructor would tell us, "If you have an area that's painful or tight, breathe into it, and then let it go." Breathing deeply and intentionally relieved the tension and allowed me to stretch more.

I decided to take the same approach in my spiritual life based on the quote, "Prayer is exhaling the spirit of man and inhaling the spirit of God." I worry too much and pray too little about what God wants me to do next, personally and professionally, for Him. I'm anxious to "make up for" decades of indifference towards God. I worry too much. I pray too little.

But worry uses time and energy that would be better channeled into spiritual growth. So instead, I will take my concerns to God and trust Him to relieve them. I will spend more time inhaling the spirit of God, through prayer, into that area of my life that causes anxiety. I will breathe into it.

Then I will let it go.

JULY 10

The Bitter River

Devote yourselves to prayer, being watchful and thankful. And pray for us, too, that God may open a door for our message, so that we may proclaim the mystery of Christ. . . .

COLOSSIANS 4:2-3

One of the oldest known maps of the world, a clay tablet from about 700 BC, depicts Babylon at the center of the world, the whole "world" encircled by "the Bitter River." The ancients thought the salt sea—or Bitter River—must be the edge of the world.

How many people today live at the center of such a small universe, trapped by a bitter river of self-absorption? They treasure the role of victim, continually pointing out how they have no control, no way to a better life because the bitter river has hemmed them in.

Other people, in hard times, allow the door to be opened to God's message by "devoting themselves to prayer, being watchful and thankful." They believe that God can redeem even the worst times with a word of truth, a breath of peace. They ride the ocean of tears to a larger place.

I have lived inside the confines of the Bitter River, trapped by a sea of my own tears, by the circularity of the "poor me" syndrome. I escaped when I glimpsed the real person of the risen Christ, when I saw that He, too, was a human who suffered and wept and wondered about His Father's will. Once I recognized Him, I began to explore the larger world, the one on the other side of the Bitter River.

But only because Christ got me a cross.

HOLY ORDINARY

JULY 11

Pulp nonfiction

In bringing many sons to glory, it was fitting that God, for whom and through whom everything exists, should make the author of their salvation perfect through suffering. Both the one who makes men holy and those who are made holy are of the same family.

HEBREWS 2:10-11

My father was in the printing business, so I grew up hearing about all it takes to turn out a printed page. It still fascinates me that paper comes from trees, that wood can be pulverized and so finely suspended in water that it can dry into something we write on.

God, I think, works in the paper-making process when He makes our salvation, through Christ, "perfect through suffering." Our pain, self-inflicted or otherwise, grows like a tree in the forest, so hard and formidable that we cannot imagine it's becoming paper and taking on the aura of holiness in God's hands. Jesus—the Word of God—puts into tangible, legible form the love, forgiveness, and promise God holds for us. And we become the paper, ground-up suffering, mistakes, and worldliness mixed with the water of baptism, something on which God can write His Word.

Jesus is the Word of God, and we are the paper God uses to continually express that Word, a blank sheet on which He writes the promise of being one with Him. And I believe that, despite all evidence He should do otherwise, God believes in me as an expression of His holiness.

My Father is in the printing business.

JULY 12

Someone

But we see Jesus, who was made a little lower than the angels, now crowned with glory and honor because he suffered death. . . .

HEBREWS 2:9

One Saturday, as I traveled to visit a dear friend, I happened across some strangers in need, and my fearful human instinct told me to stay detached. The man and his wife said that if they could get to one of the local churches, maybe someone could help. I wished them well, but it wasn't enough. They had hoped to see the mortality of man conquered and crowned by the glory of God. They had hoped to see Jesus. And so the words echoed in my heart. "Maybe someone can help."

As nice and tidy and Christian as it sounds to wish another person well, it does no good when the gas tank is empty, when hunger pangs come, when rain invades through a hole in the roof. Simply wishing him well is fear conquering love. If I get involved I might get hurt. I might have less for myself. I might see more of another man's need than I care to see.

But people don't long for churches: they long for the presence of God. When they hurt, they don't need good wishes, but human confirmation that someone larger, more loving, more powerful, exists beyond the pain of this world. In their need, it doesn't help to see well-wishers. They want to see Jesus.

"Maybe someone will help us," the man said. I was standing right there, remembering that I love God, and He loves me, that I'm blessed enough to see Jesus in my own life.

That makes me "someone."

JULY 13

Broken wing

Remember how the Lord your God led you all the way in the desert these forty years, to humble you and to test you in order to know what was in your heart. . . . He humbled you, causing you to hunger and then feeding you with manna . . . to teach you that man does not live on bread alone but on every word that comes from the mouth of the Lord.

DEUTERONOMY 8:2-3

In the Kindertransport program during World War II, British families took in German Jewish children to save them from the Holocaust. One adoptee compared the children to birds with broken wings. While it should be beautiful and touching to rescue an injured creature, the bird continually fights against the hands that would save it. Rescue can be painful and frightening.

Don't we often have the same penchant to fight against the only One who could save our lives? It should be a beautiful tableau, the picture of God's hands reaching down to protect me, to bring me to Him, to make me strong. Yet, for years, I fought against Him, trying to escape, anxious to prove that I could "do it on my own" when I was too weak, too broken to even get off the ground.

I knew—as most people do, I think—in the deepest corners of my soul, that only God could save me. So I eventually stopped fighting long enough for Him to hold me, to help me, to give me His strength. But then, in His tender way, He did so much more than rescue me.

He allowed me to fly.

JULY 14

Two simple words

Like a slave longing for the evening shadows, or a hired man waiting eagerly for his wages, so I have been allotted months of futility, and nights of misery have been assigned to me.

JOB 7:2-3

As a result of DNA evidence, a man named Eddie Lloyd was freed from prison after serving 17 years for a rape and murder he did not commit. In an era when everyone seems to point fingers and assign blame, his initial response was to say simply, "Thank you." His first reaction was simply to acknowledge the blessing, to see the beauty in his newfound freedom, in his ability to step beyond the walls.

Like many others who suddenly recognize and welcome the presence of God, I understand the man's gratitude at being freed. My instinct, though, was to question, to ask why I had to waste so much time in prison.

But God opens the doors of the prison only when He knows that we are ready to step out, when we can focus on Him enough to avoid the dangers of self-absorption, vanity, defensiveness, malice. In my case, I needed the boundaries to protect me from myself. Today, God asks me to let go of the years of waste, and to appreciate the chance to live free. He asks me not to mourn the time I have lost, but to celebrate the eternity I have gained.

And perhaps He hopes that I will remember the One who gave me my freedom, and that I will utter two simple words—the words of a human suddenly set free to be with a God.

"Thank you."

JULY 15

Mars Hill

Some of the Pharisees in the crowd said to Jesus, "Teacher, rebuke your disciples!" "I tell you," he replied, "if they keep quiet, the stones will cry out."

LUKE 19:39-40

One unbelievable day I stood on a rock overlooking Mars Hill in Athens, in the place where Paul stood when he talked to the Athenians about their "unknown god." From the account of that event in Acts, it seems that his message was mostly met with indifference or derision, although some became believers.

God didn't ask Paul to preach only to those who seemed fertile ground for the message of Jesus Christ. Paul had no way of knowing if the words he spoke reached one soul. He knew simply that he was to proclaim the message, that God would determine who heard it.

I stood there that day, where Paul stood, where he must have wondered if anyone was listening. Often I stand in a similar place, where I hesitate to speak of Christ. I worry that someone isn't ready to hear it, or that I have no business talking about Christ as if I'm an authority.

But I am an authority on one topic—on how the power of God can enter a life, and change it, and energize it. That's the place I'm standing on right now, and that's the message I'm equipped to pass along.

Someone, somewhere, on this day, is destined to hear this message, powerful enough to make the stones cry out. I wonder who is listening today?

I wonder . . .

JULY 16

Carry on

And the Lord said, "Yes, he has hidden himself among the baggage."
1 SAMUEL 10:22

Just a few years ago, I thought my life was almost perfect, and then one day I turned around to find it shattered. I got that dreaded phone call, the one about a "family emergency." My older sister had died of a heart attack suddenly. Four months later, my father died, his heart irreparably broken by the loss of his child. Six weeks later I lost a job and had to move.

Suddenly everything that had given shape to my life evaporated, and I was left holding incredibly heavy baggage of grief, of loss, of regret. My spirit felt absolutely dead.

But now I understand that my spiritual life took its shape in that time. I stopped relying on people and jobs for my sense of worth. I stopped making decisions based on an ever-changing standard of what would impress people the most. I looked to God and begged Him to forgive me for all the anger I had expressed, for all the love I hadn't. I asked only for the pain to stop, but God gave me instead wholeness, and energy, and strength to help others put down their heavy burdens.

I pray every day that others can use my experiences to understand that God is there, not only in soaring heights, but in the most profound depths. He is there. At least, that's where I found Him.

Right there. In my baggage.

JULY 17

Holy ordinary

My heart is not proud, O Lord, my eyes are not haughty; I do not concern myself with great matters or things too wonderful for me. But I have stilled and quieted my soul . . .

PSALM 131

All my life I've wanted to be famous; I crave attention. I wouldn't want to be famous as the first female serial killer or the person whose cow kicked over the lantern, but otherwise I wouldn't be picky about the source of fame. I always look for the home run over the base hit, the dramatic over the mundane.

Once I began to find God, I kept thinking I would do something "big" like having an incredible revelation or striking it rich so that I can change millions of lives.

Instead, I just do this daily thing that God brings me—not very exciting, not very visible. Yet it brings me great joy. I often hear from people who tell me that a piece God let me write brought light into a dark corner or comforted them. One friend wrote that my words "make the ordinary holy." Others say my morning meditations put God in their minds ahead of the day's memos and purchase orders.

What better work is there, really, than the ordinary things we do to remind people that God is here, that God is everywhere? It's not a winning Powerball ticket, a dramatic vision, a million seller. But it's what God asks me to do every day. And He knows my name.

That's enough for me.

Plumb line

This is what he showed me: The Lord was standing by a wall that had been built true to plumb, with a plumb line in his hand.

AMOS 7:7-8

Several years ago, I went on a Caribbean cruise. When I returned to dry land, I felt unsteady on my feet for a couple of days. Apparently my equilibrium had adjusted too much; the moving ship felt stable, while the solid ground felt shaky.

It's easy for humans to think they know what is solid ground and what is moving, but only God can really make those calls. Amos saw in his God-given vision a stone wall, measured and found to be true by a plumb line, a tool used to determine absolute straightness and remove the distortion of the human eye.

Every gift, talent, relationship, circumstance of the human life can be a stone on which the kingdom is built. But we could save ourselves a lot of repair work and rebuilding in our lives if we would only use God as the true plumb line before building. Rather than going to Him when the wall falls down, we go to Him in advance to find out which walls He would have us build, which stones He would have us use, where we should place those stones.

Prayer is the plumb line, the true straight path between God and His kingdom builders. Today, instead of asking Him to fix my work, I will ask Him to design and guide it. Is this my work, God? Which stones should I pick up? Which stones belong to others? Where do my gifts belong?

How would you have me build your kingdom?

JULY 19

Seeing is believing

Some of the Pharisees said, "This man is not from God, for he does not keep the Sabbath." But others asked, "How can a sinner do such miraculous signs?" So they were divided. Finally they turned again to the blind man, "What have you to say about him? It was your eyes he opened." The man replied, "He is a prophet."

JOHN 9:16-17

Interested in taking a drawing class, I picked up a brochure about a class. It didn't promise to teach students new ways to position or use their hands to draw. Instead, the flyer described how the class would change the way students see.

Some people who long for God, for a strong and comforting spiritual presence, think they need training in spiritual "techniques" when they really need to change the way that they see. Lives change not through learning to "summon" God with a perfect worship service, the ideal music, or all the right religious words. Lives change when God is seen, when we begin to recognize His presence moving in our days.

The best we can offer spiritual seekers is a change in vision, a pointing out of God's working in our own daily lives. We can insist, as the newly sighted man did, on giving God the credit when we are blessed. We can refuse to credit the doctors, coincidence, luck, the market, or our own acumen, and insist on giving the glory to God. We can help draw others into a relationship with God by teaching them, finally, to see Him. In our lives, in theirs.

In everything.

Safe place

Hasten, O God, to save me; O Lord, come quickly to help me.... I am poor and needy; come quickly to me, O God. You are my help and my deliverer; O Lord, do not delay.

PSALM 70:1, 5

When I called a roadside assistance program for the first time, I was miles from anyone or anyplace I knew. What impressed me most about the service was the responder's first question: Are you in a safe place?

In my few years as a committed Christian, I have felt comfortable in answering that yes, I am in a safe place. Plenty of problems have arisen: crises, minor and major tragedies, conflict, resentment, doubt. But through it all, I see clearly the bottom line, that God is here, for me. God is here with me.

My instinct is to keep my little needs to myself rather than bothering God. I once went to a healing service because I was depressed and grieving, and at first thought I shouldn't be there. The others seeking healing were fighting degenerative diseases, and tremendous fear and loss. My need seemed so small in comparison to theirs. But it felt overwhelming to me, so I asked God to "hasten to save me."

God knows I am poor and needy; I know He is my help and my deliverer. It soothes and holds me up to know that I constantly have the option of connecting to the most powerful and loving force in the universe. And so yes, no matter what happens, I am in a safe place.

I'm in our Father's arms.

JULY 21

The never-ending story

How beautiful on the mountains are the feet of those who bring good news, who proclaim peace, who bring good tidings, who proclaim salvation, who say to Zion, "Your God reigns!" . . . When the Lord returns to Zion, they will see it with their own eyes.

ISAIAH 52:7-8

It has always bothered me that the fantasy movie *The Never-Ending Story* has a sequel called *The Never-Ending Story II—The Next Chapter*. It just doesn't sound right—that a story that never ends could have a sequel.

But maybe this passage from Isaiah tells of the "next chapter" of a never-ending story, too. As Christians recognizing and glorifying God now, we are "those who bring good news, who proclaim peace . . ."

We are the people gifted with the message of God, that all can come and worship and find peace with this newborn King. We are the people who already know that God loves us and holds us up, whether we are coming down the mountain, fresh from having seen His power, or whether we are climbing a mountain of fear in our lives.

We are the ones blessed enough to know—now—the richness of life with God, the comfort of His caress. We are the ones who know that He is here, now, that He has been here forever, that He will be there with open arms for any soul who chooses to turn toward Him.

God is here. God has always been here. God will be here. It's a never-ending story.

I can't wait to read the next chapter.

JULY 22

Press on!

Who is this coming from Edom, from Bozrah, with his garments stained crimson?... Why are your garments red, like those of one treading the winepress? "I have trodden the winepress alone; from the nations no one was with me."

ISAIAH 63:1-5

The Spartans of ancient Greece based their entire society on war. In it, only warriors who died in battle and women who died in childbirth were buried with honor. Spartan warriors even wore crimson garments to hide the stains of blood, their own and their victims'.

But a garment stained red can also symbolize the greatest peace. Isaiah's vision is of Christ, stained in crimson because He has "trodden the winepress alone."

When I feel alone, when I fear I cannot survive one more ounce of pain, Christ approaches and reminds me that he has already trodden the winepress. He opens His arms to me and wraps my suffering in His own.

I want to wear my suffering conspicuously so others will tend me more carefully and see the depth of my sorrow. But God asks me to mingle my small wounds with the incalculable suffering of His Son. In the mingling, all things are consecrated, and even pain becomes holy.

That figure walking toward me, garments stained with His blood and my own, is the God of peace asking me to surrender my pain. And when I allow Him to embrace me in sorrow as well as in joy, I walk away with the most precious gift of all. The peace of God.

Wrapped in the cloak of Christ.

JULY 23

Spiritually fit

... train yourself to be godly. For physical training is of some value, but godliness has value for all things, holding promise for both the present life and the life to come.

1 TIMOTHY 4:7-8

A few years ago I bought a treadmill and started training for an upcoming 5K run. A friend who routinely runs three to four miles a day agreed to enter the race with me; we agreed that my only goal was to finish the race running rather than walking.

I built stamina and could soon run three miles on the treadmill. Then my buddy told me it was time to run outside, with no air conditioning and no TV. She said the treadmill could help me train, but running outside in the world requires more focus. Hills appear. Other runners upset your rhythm. Big scary dogs get interested.

Happily, though, running outside also holds advantages over a treadmill workout: you breathe fresh air, with changing scenery that isn't electronically generated. From other runners' techniques and strides and struggles, you learn how to run your own race a little better.

We Christians sometimes limit ourselves to training on treadmills: attending church and Sunday school, maybe some Bible study, to train our spirits for the real race. But it's not enough. The religious treadmill is a great tool to get you in shape and keep you spiritually fit. But they don't hold races on treadmills.

Eventually you have to take your act outside.

JULY 24

First person singular

. . . to prepare God's people for the works of service, so that the body of Christ may be built up until we all reach unity in the faith and in the knowledge of the Son of God and become mature, attaining to the whole measure of the fullness of Christ.

EPHESIANS 4:12-13

My dad used to say of people who were too self-centered, "That man is Big I and little u." But our language sets us up to think of ourselves as the "big I." The word "I" is the only pronoun capitalized in all uses, and when we conjugate verbs, we learn that the "first person" is "I." We start by learning to say I make, or I love or I know, and then we worry about what u do. No wonder it's so hard to learn to put the desires of our God and our neighbor ahead of our own.

For over four decades, I didn't care in a deep and tender way about other people. Then I started hanging around "God's people" and found the paradoxical magnificence of Christian love: the more I think about other people, the happier I become. When I insisted on putting myself in the position of "first person," I was miserable. The smaller i become, the happier I am.

Finally I see that, in this life, God is the original "first person singular." The gifts He gives me are not to entertain or glorify me, but to build up and extend the body of Christ. My life became rich and deep when I realized that it's not about me at all. It's about Him.

And it's about time.

HOLY ORDINARY

JULY 25

Safely home

... when time had fully come, God sent his Son ... to redeem those under the law, that we might receive the full rights of sons. Because you are sons, God sent the Spirit of his son into our hearts, the Spirit who calls out, "Abba, Father." ...

GALATIANS 4:6

"Be sure to start home when the streetlights come on." I can almost hear the first time my dad said those words, because to me they meant responsibility, autonomy. Dad let me stay later at a friend's house, knowing that if I followed his instructions, I wouldn't be trying to get home after dark.

That was how I learned responsibility—in small steps. Initially, my parents "laid down the law." Then, I learned from my brother's example; four years older than I—a hero and a role model. As I matured, my parents let me go more and more, hoping they had equipped me with the discipline, morality, and compassion to make good decisions.

God knows that, as baby Christians, we're not always capable of discerning His will, so He sets down rules to guide us. As our faith matures, we look at the model of Christ—the ultimate "older brother"—to see how to live. Finally, through His Law and then His Son, God trusts that He has put a light in our hearts to show us the way.

I no longer fear the dark, because the Light travels with me. The Spirit of the Law, dwelling in me, can be trusted to guide me.

I know now I'll get safely home.

JULY 26

Something to carry

"The arrows of the Almighty are in me, my spirit drinks in their poison; God's terrors are marshaled against me. . . . What strength do I have, that I should still hope? What prospects, that I should be patient?"

JOB 6:4, 11

I once read a story in which a youth asked a lonely old man, "What is life's heaviest burden?" and the old man replied, "To have nothing to carry."

Certain days, certain anniversaries, I remember only the burdens I carry—losses of my life, loved ones gone or indifferent, opportunities missed, doors unopened. Yet I must thank God that I'm not like that old man—sad, broken down, alone—someone with nothing to bear.

Human love, I know, cannot compare to God's love in depth or breadth, but the loss of love, or of a loved one, makes me feel that "the arrows of the Almighty are in me." God is in control; why couldn't He let them stay with me longer?

But then I realize that they have. In my heart I carry the memory of my parents' gentle humor, my sister's incredible generosity. All are gifts they have given me, pieces of them that remain with me today. So love borne for others is not lost at all, but simply changes form.

And partly because of their influence, I understand that I have "something to carry." I carry the love of God, expressed and embodied by the people in my life, by all whom I have loved, by all whom I have lost. I carry the heart of God.

And His burden is Light.

HOLY ORDINARY

JULY 27

Firewood

... God is on my side ... you have rescued my soul from death and my feet from stumbling, that I may walk before God in the land of the living. ...

PSALM 56:9, 13

Firewood waits, stacked up at the place next door. It's the end of July. And it is hot.

I've never been much good at storing up enough money, or time, or firewood in abundant times to prepare for lean or frantic or cold days ahead. So I used to have little to warm my spirit in winter. My enemies in those raw winter days? Grief, regret, self-deprecation, anger at myself, anger even at God.

Until recently, I never allowed God's presence to enter my life consistently, but thought it was something to demand only when needed. Just get me through this day, Lord, I would ask. This moment. This winter.

Every time a storm came in, I had to go out in it to find firewood to stave off the cold and the dark. I stored nothing of God within myself to warm me and to shelter me. So my empty and broken spirit wandered around, seeking strength, yet unequipped to find it.

Then I opened my heart, asking God to pour Himself into all of its tired and aching places, places that echoed in their vastness, their emptiness. With God's spirit constantly flowing into me now, I know I can face change, uncertainty, even loss.

Right now, the weather is fine. But when winter comes this time, I'll still be fine.

Because God comes first.

Pantheon

. . . I urge you, as aliens and strangers in the world, to abstain from sinful desires, which war against your soul. Live such good lives among the pagans that, though they accuse you of doing wrong, they may see your good deeds and glorify God on the day he visits us. . . .
1 PETER 2:11-12

One afternoon in Rome our group went separate ways to explore. When it was time to meet, after asking directions and consulting my map, I finally found my way to the Pantheon. I was really proud of myself until I realized we weren't meeting at the Pantheon. I wasn't lost, but I was certainly in the wrong place.

When it was built in about AD 118, the Pantheon was dedicated to "all the gods." I've been there: honoring multiple gods like the approval of other people, the need for attention, money, job status. I was "living the good life among the pagans," among the others who honored the little gods. I wasn't lost, but I was certainly in the wrong place.

I went so many ways in error; some mistakes were even made in the name of spirituality. Finally I noticed that as I dedicated myself to "all the gods," I found many things that placated, but none that filled. Until I found God, with a capital "G."

In about the 7th century, the Pantheon was consecrated as a Christian church, which allowed it to survive. So the temple once dedicated to all the gods was saved because it finally focused on the one true God.

I know how it feels.

JULY 29

Redeemable

Then he showed me Joshua the high priest . . . and Satan standing at his right side to accuse him. The Lord said to Satan, "The Lord rebuke you, Satan! . . . is not this man a burning stick snatched from the fire?" . . . Then he said, "See, I have taken away your sin, and I will put rich garments on you."

ZECHARIAH 3:1-4

My brother and I used to roam around the woods and hills exploring, and one summer day we came across forty or fifty discarded pop bottles. Glass bottles could be returned for cash back then, so we gathered them up and cashed them in. Spending that money felt delicious, because it seemed as if we had created treasure from nothing.

Much later, in an adulthood without direction, I felt lost, discarded, worthless. Then something miraculous happened; God's people picked me up and carried my spirit to Him for redemption. He took away my darkness, "put rich garments" on me, and sent me in search of others waiting to be claimed. Wouldn't you think He would be satisfied just to bring back those who seemed beyond redemption? Isn't that miracle enough?

Instead, He uses those of us who came closest to destruction to find the next soul. God saves me—like a burning stick from the fire—and I help fuel someone else's passion for Him. And so, the one seemingly beyond redemption becomes not only redeemed, but part of the Redeemer. It feels delicious, creating such treasure.

From nothing.

Life

You killed the author of life, but God raised him from the dead. We are witnesses of this. By faith in the name of Jesus, this man whom you see and know was made strong.

ACTS 3:15-16

Recently a 92-year-old man was released from a California prison, although he had begged authorities to let him live out his days behind bars. Shortly after his release, the man committed suicide, unable to face life on the outside.

Living in freedom can be very frightening. Decisions must be made. Responsibility must be shouldered. So, too often, we choose to live a "religious" life, imprisoned by rules. We're frightened by the prospect of freedom, by the call to find love and compassion for every human being. It's much easier to live in confinement, to look at yardsticks, to say who measures up and who doesn't, than to offer every person love without boundaries. It's much easier, but it makes for a very small world.

But how will I know the way to live if those walls are not there for me? I will know by looking at the Son of God, the author of life, and by letting Him make me strong. If I lean on Him, Christ will hold me and heal me just as He used Peter to heal the lame man.

With God in me, I will find the courage to love others and myself. With God in me, I will find the courage to get up and walk out the door, to leave those comfortable walls behind.

They tell me there's a big, beautiful world out there.

JULY 31

God's green earth

Someone in the crowd said to him, "Teacher, tell my brother to divide the inheritance with me." Jesus replied, "Man, who appointed me a judge or an arbiter between you?" Then he said to them, "Watch out! Be on your guard against all kinds of greed; a man's life does not consist in the abundance of his possessions."

LUKE 12:13-15

One weekend, driving to a conference, I passed road construction where acres of trees had been cut down. The remaining stumps and the fires burning removed stumps made what had once been a forest look like a battlefield. And not only trees were lost: animal habitat, erosion protection, natural beauty, and trees that literally make fresh air were gone because man needed to make his road just there. The whole ecosystem took a hit.

Interdependence is among the toughest lessons, in ecology and in spirituality. We get so wrapped up in the need to build our own road in the world that we forget that we're part of others, part of God. When I hurt someone as I hurry through, or bring someone down to show my superiority, I don't simply damage one person. I make a direct hit on the body of Christ, because, like the components of the ecosystem, we are all members of one God.

We all have to make our own spiritual roads. But as we do, we have to remember that the body of Christ is all one, that we are all part of each other, and part of our God. We need to remember the ecosystem.

And forget the ego-system.

August

AUGUST 1

No currency is necessary

"Sacrifices and offerings . . . you did not desire, nor were you pleased with them. . . ." Then he said, "Here I am, I have come to do your will."
HEBREWS 10:8-9

Money in itself carries no intrinsic value. Your family can't eat it. It won't shelter you from a storm. You can't wear it. While our society has come to worship money, it's just an arbitrary system we humans have developed to assign value to things and trade for what we really need. If each person on this earth possessed all the material things they needed—or wanted—we wouldn't have invented money at all.

And the rules observed by Christians have no intrinsic value. You're not a good Christian just because you go to church or because you know every line of the Bible. You're not even a good Christian if you spend all of your time helping others.

Accumulating "Christian currency" is just one way we determine whether we're living as God would ask us to live. Certainly going to church, reading his word, and helping others can strengthen your relationship with him. But those activities represent only an outward expression—a medium of exchange—in our quest to live in God's will.

Simply seek to live your life God's way; tell him, "Here I am, Lord. I have come to do your will." He'll take care of the details of your Christian service. God will feed you, clothe you, keep you safe.

No currency is necessary.

AUGUST 2

Take courage

When evening came, the boat was in the middle of the lake, and he was alone on land. He saw the disciples straining at the oars, because the wind was against them . . . he spoke to them and said, "Take courage. It is I. Don't be afraid." Then he climbed into the boat with them, and the wind died down. . . .

MARK 6:47-48, 50-51

After my first few days at college, my parents dropped me off for freshman orientation as they were driving out of town. I felt a jumble of emotions: mild fear, excitement, determination, as I knew this was where I would start learning how to live life on my own. I knew, as they drove off, my parents had to trust that my years with them had prepared me for going out on my own.

Christ prepared the disciples, too, for living life without having Him physically present. He left them alone in the boat, knowing it would be a struggle for them, yet also knowing that He could step in to help if they couldn't handle the situation.

It's easy to forget in our anxiety that God is always there—to get so wrapped up in worry that we forget how carefully He protects us. When I deal with a minor crisis, I feel Him near me, offering through the hands and hearts of friends the strength and wisdom I need to go forward. The words my friends speak are things like, "Let me help," "You'll be fine." "You have to take better care of yourself."

But it isn't their voices—or even their words—that I hear. I hear the wind dying down. Then I clearly discern a message I need desperately to hear.

"Take courage. It is I. Don't be afraid."

AUGUST 3

What you don't know . . .

. . . if you spend yourselves in behalf of the hungry and satisfy the needs of the oppressed, then your light will rise in the darkness, and your night will become like the noonday. . . .

ISAIAH 58:10

I need to make a list of everything I don't know so I can learn about it. Of course it sounds dumb, but that's the dilemma I faced when I sensed something was missing in my life. I didn't know what I didn't know.

My days felt empty and dark, but I had no idea that they could be fuller or brighter. In fact, my sight adjusted to the darkness so I thought that dim view was normal. I didn't see much; I simply groped around and survived.

But humans instinctively seek light. In the darkness, we move toward any glow, no matter how faint. If we move closer to it, soon we discern shapes and movement. When other people in our lives flash a small spark of divinity, we begin to sense the brightness waiting just outside the door.

That's the way I began to "know what I didn't know." I saw that the friends who enjoyed peace—who were comfortable with themselves—had some presence in their lives that I didn't have; it brought them completeness and peace, continuity and meaning. Now I've identified that presence as God—living in a human being.

Because I know how frightening the darkness can be, I now look to shine God's light through my life into all the darkest corners, pointing it toward anyone else who may be desperately searching.

I want to help them know what they don't know.

AUGUST 4

Where do you come from?

Then you will say, 'We ate and drank with you, and you taught in our streets.' But he will say, 'I do not know where you come from; go away from me, you evildoers!'

LUKE 13:26-27

Wondering where someone "comes from" means you want to know the underlying motivation behind their actions. If someone makes a request of you and you ask, "Where are you coming from on this?" you seek to identify the reasoning behind the request.

Jesus doesn't care how much time you've "hung out" with Him or how many times you've heard Him teach; He wants to know what force directs your life. Just because you've been there to hear a lesson doesn't mean you've committed to live according to it.

Today, many of us would offer Jesus a resume as proof that we deserve the kingdom of God. "I go to church every Sunday," we might say. "I pray every night." Or maybe, "I'm a leader in my church."

But where do you "come from" in all of those activities? Do you come to church because you love God so much that you simply must worship to express that love? Do you pray because you cherish a personal, interactive relationship with God? Are you a church leader because His love overwhelms you and you want to join in His work? If such questions can be answered affirmatively, then he knows "where you come from."

And rest assured that you can know where you're going.

HOLY ORDINARY

AUGUST 5

Birds on a wire

Do your best to present yourself to God as one approved, a workman who does not need to be ashamed and who correctly handles the word of truth.

2 TIMOTHY 2:15

At dusk one night, I saw a telephone or electrical wire that must have held 20 sparrows, lined up, watching the world.

That wire wasn't designed as a rest stop for sparrows, but to deliver power or communication to thousands of people. But in their little bird brains, those sparrows had no interest in illumination or communication—only in momentary support.

The Bible frequently falls victim to the same fate as that utility wire. Some people have no interest in using it to understand God's will or bring His power into their lives. They cling desperately to some parts of the Bible while ignoring the parts that make them uncomfortable or disprove their cases. Like those sparrows, they're not seeking communication or power, but support—evidence to advance a personal agenda. They're just birds on a wire—unaware that it could put them in touch with a living, loving God, unaware of the power within their grasp.

The Bible is not just a place to lean on to make a case, but a connection designed to bring God's presence directly to a needy and hurting world.

The power is there, waiting for us to tap into it. The Bible is the best news in the world.

Why are we just sitting on it?

Ashes and dust

For I eat ashes as my food and mingle my drink with tears. . . . But you remain the same, and your years will never end. . . .

PSALM 102:9, 27

. . . flee from idolatry. . . . Is not the cup of thanksgiving for which we give thanks a participation in the blood of Christ?

1 CORINTHIANS 10:14, 16

In the year 79 A.D., the volcano Vesuvius erupted and destroyed the city of Pompeii, Italy. Lives disappeared in an instant when poisonous gases arrived. Seeing those ruins even today can send a message of fear, of panic, of hopelessness, across centuries and miles directly into our time and place. But the ash that covered Pompeii and the surrounding area ultimately would make the land very fertile, lush and green with vineyards and other vegetation.

I have made huge mistakes in my past, but now I know that God will use them to fortify the soil in my life for His work. My disasters, too, will turn into vineyards, into wine, into hope and strength for those facing that timeless message of fear and emptiness.

The lesson of Pompeii, of unimaginable growth spurred by stark disaster, is one I carry in my heart and soul today. God not only forgives every mistake I have made, but will use those mistakes to speak to those who don't yet know Him.

I remember, clearly, those days of disaster, and I thank God for giving them to me. Because they are no longer just volcanic ash.

They have become the blood of Christ.

AUGUST 7

Masterpiece

Save me, O God, for the waters have come up to my neck. I sink in the miry depths, where there is no foothold. I have come into the deep waters; the floods engulf me. . . . My eyes fail, looking for my God.
PSALM 69:1-3

Not long ago, an Eagle Scout was threatened with expulsion from scouting because he considered himself an atheist. He said that as he learned about science and evolution, he became increasingly uncomfortable with the thought of God. Sunk in the "miry depths" of a debate between science and religion, his "eyes failed."

When I went to Italy and saw the Pietà and the statue of David, I was stunned that stone could capture and communicate humanity with such exquisite beauty. I cannot imagine thinking that those two pieces just happened by accident, but that's the choice this young man feels compelled to make. He's trying to force himself to believe that our magnificent and intricately scientific universe came into being by random circumstance.

Our world is a work of art far beyond anything Michelangelo ever produced. Yet right now, the eyes of an intelligent young man fail, "looking for his God" because he thinks that God and science cannot coexist.

Whatever happens to this particular man, the creation/evolution debate will rage on. But to me, one undeniable, ineffably beautiful fact stands out.

Every masterpiece begins with a Master.

"Life as a house"

Whoever lives in love lives in God, and God in him. . . . There is no fear in love. But perfect love drives out fear, because fear has to do with punishment. The one who fears is not made perfect in love.

1 JOHN 4:16, 18

In the movie *Life as a House,* a terminally ill architect decides to tear down the house his father left him and build another. He says that he hated the old house ever since his father had put it in his name. He laments his "25 years of hating what you live in—hating what you are."

I hated the place I lived in for over 40 years, in a sense, because I lived in a house of fear. It was certainly not physical fear or even emotional fear; I had the most perfect childhood, a wonderful family, beautiful, loving friends. But I was always a little afraid, of what people might think, of what I might become, of what I might not become. I hated what I lived in. I hated what I was.

Then I found God, and I found in Him deep and abiding love which gradually brought down the walls of fear. The more I trust Him, day after day, the more of the debris of the old place is carted away. I worry less about what other people think of me and listen more to what God asks. I love more, and more deeply. I trust more, and more peacefully. I live more, and more joyfully. I fear less.

Finally, I love what I am, because I am in God. Finally I love this place I live in; it's my Father's house.

We finally put the place in His name.

The deep end

Jesus answered them, "Destroy this temple, and I will raise it again in three days." The Jews replied, "It has taken 46 years to build this temple, and you are going to raise it in three days?" But the temple he had spoken of was his body.

JOHN 2:19-21

When I learned to swim, my dad had to work hard to convince me to take my feet off the bottom of the pool and let go of the side. I wanted to stand in the shallow end and move my arms frantically until I took off. But he said, "You have to let go. Trust the water to hold you up."

I still struggle with trust. I get addicted to sameness and predictability, seeking too often to keep my feet on the ground. As a result, I often limit myself to some very shallow places.

The Jews who spoke to Jesus of the temple had no desire to go any deeper into God. When He spoke of rebuilding the temple, they stayed anchored in the safe and shallow world of temporal matters. They thought only of putting stone on stone until an edifice rose again. Yet if they had trusted God, and let the water hold them up, they could have seen not only a building rising up, but a God. And their own eternal life in Him.

Our God goes deeper than we can imagine, and when we go deeper with Him, and in Him, we need not fear getting in over our heads. Think bigger, God asks us. Trust. Let go of earthly supports, worldly images. Leave the shallow places behind. Strike out, in faith, for the deep water.

And I will hold you up.

AUGUST 10

Marketplace

[The people] ran throughout that whole region and carried the sick on mats to wherever they heard [Jesus] was. And wherever he went—-into villages, towns or countryside—-they placed the sick in the marketplaces. They begged him to let them touch even the edge of his cloak, and all who touched him were healed.

MARK 6:55-56

A new restaurant opened near my home in a building where at least four other restaurants had failed recently. Though the spot seems a good location, it is simply not accessible.

Accessibility is critical to good business, and to God business. Our human instinct is to set up—morally, geographically, spiritually, doctrinally—where we want to be, then insist that the people without God come find their own way to Him.

Yet in Jesus' time, many sick people were carried to Him in the marketplace for healing. Their friends did not let them remain off the beaten path, and they didn't try to decide who deserved to be healed. They simply brought those in pain, and let Jesus decide.

We're so anxious to be right, and to make others come to God on our terms rather than on His. We're so anxious to filter the sick, to decide whom God should heal. We're so anxious to name every sin, to identify everything that's offensive to God, and to label it for our own purposes. But identifying sin is not our job; it is God's alone. Our job is much simpler: to carry the wounded to Jesus.

And to let God be God.

AUGUST 11

One car length

When God made his promise to Abraham, since there was no one greater for him to swear by, he swore by himself, saying, "I will surely bless you . . ." And so after waiting patiently, Abraham received what was promised.

HEBREWS 6:13-15

Too often I have railed about cars weaving through traffic, running lights, and going unsafe speeds to get ahead. Then, at the next light, I'm right behind that car, thinking, "You went through all of that to gain one car length?"

Then, again, who am I to talk? God gives me so much—so many gifts, opportunities, friends, ideas—that I get all wound up and run on ahead of Him. Instead of waiting patiently, as Abraham did, I zoom my spiritual life in and out of traffic and run it at breakneck speed. With one hint of direction from God, I assume I know the rest of the story.

But at the stopping places—times when I'm forced into quietude and meditation—I realize that I'm supposed to listen, let Him choose the route and speed, and enjoy the journey. I'm not sure where I think I'm going in such a hurry.

I feel so impassioned for God, and I see so much spiritual hunger in the world, including my own, that I simply cannot wait to see what He has next for me. I cannot wait, and so I go through all kinds of spiritual panic to run ahead.

I will surely bless you, God says, so relax and let me do my job. Slow down; have patience; listen; trust.

I'll meet you at the Light.

AUGUST 12

Lover's quarrel

Looking at his disciples, he said: ". . . Blessed are you who weep now, for you will laugh."

LUKE 6:20, 21

Robert Frost's epitaph reads, "I had a lover's quarrel with the world." Those words struck a deep chord in me, as I seem to be having a "lover's quarrel" with God.

I love God so much He takes—and gives—my breath, but I question Him and quarrel with Him constantly over the pain He allows: over Columbine and 9/11, childhood disease, abuse, the inhumanity of His human creation.

I love you, God, I tell Him, but I don't understand some of the things that you do or allow to happen in your world. I believe that you are all-powerful and all-loving, but why do people who love you have to weep at all when you could let them laugh? Why do prayers work to salve and heal the deep wounds in your world, yet not to prevent them?

But this quarrel is certainly not one-sided. God cannot understand how He can love and love and still see me turn away in fear or selfishness. When my life works so well in His hands, He is incredulous that I would keep trying to seize control of it. He wonders why I say I love Him, yet constantly hurt and disappoint Him. We love each other, no doubt about it. And yet we quarrel.

I don't understand you, will never understand you. I can't believe what you do sometimes, but I love you and want the best for you. And I will do anything to be with you.

Was that His voice I was hearing? Or mine?

AUGUST 13

Praying for peace

... "I am the Lord your God, who teaches you what is best for you, who directs you in the way you should go. If only you had paid attention to my commands, your peace would have been like a river...."
ISAIAH 48:21

The most painful moment in my life is probably also the moment when I came closest to praying as God would want me to pray.

My dad, home from the hospital but very ill, slept on a daybed in the living room while I slept on the couch. Around one a.m., I heard him stir and call to me. He asked me to sit in a chair by him until he fell asleep. In an uncomfortable kitchen chair, I stayed by him, my hand on his arm.

Once in a while, dad took long pauses between breaths; twice I thought he had completely stopped breathing. When I realized the emotion I felt was not panic, but relief, I experienced the most profound pain and sorrow I've ever known. It wasn't because I had just realized that my dad would not live forever. It was because, seeing his pain, I didn't want him to.

Looking back, it surprises me that I didn't ask God to save my dad, because my prayers normally focus on what I want. Instead, I asked simply for him to be at peace, and a few days later, he was gone.

Praying really isn't about us; it's about God—about seeking His will and bringing peace into our hearts. Isn't that what we all want, for ourselves and for those we love—to have peace?

Why would we pray for anything else?

AUGUST 14

Running the blockade

When Jesus had entered Capernaum, a centurion came to him . . . "Lord," he said, "my servant lies at home paralyzed and in terrible suffering." Jesus said to him, "I will go and heal him. . . ."

MATTHEW 8:5-7

The city of Vicksburg nearly drove Ulysses Grant crazy in 1862. With travel on the Mississippi River paralyzed by Confederate fortifications, Grant tried to dig a canal to reroute the river's course so he could bypass enemy batteries. Finally he abandoned the river assault, laid siege to the city by land, and cut supply lines until the southern troops relented.

Decades ago, I made the kind of mistake you have trouble living with no matter how merciful you believe God to be. It hurt other people, and it hurt me. For years, it lay on my heart like a stone; the guilt from it prevented my free passage throughout God's kingdom.

Down deep, I knew God forgave me long ago, yet I couldn't forgive myself. Finally I realized that the issue was no longer the offense I committed; it was my own self-absorption. Who am I to know better than God what can be forgiven and what cannot?

Finally, I surrendered to forgiveness; with that blockade gone, I could come and go on the river with freedom. I began to lean only on God; in return, He sometimes lets me glimpse the kingdom through his merciful and forgiving eyes.

To this day, that view takes my breath away.

AUGUST 15

The secret is out

Listen, O heavens, and I will speak; hear O earth, the words of my mouth . . . I will proclaim the name of the Lord. Oh, praise the greatness of our God! He is the Rock, his works are perfect. . . .

DEUTERONOMY 32:1, 3

I need to tell you about a place I've been.

A few years ago I stood in a cave on the island of Patmos, the cave where John received the vision that became the book of Revelation. I had my own revelation in that place.

I don't do a very good job of telling others about Christianity. I help strengthen the message for those who are already Christians, but I don't do much to start others thinking about their spiritual lives. It's as if I stood in that cave, received a vision of how God's love can change a life, and only told others about it if they happened into the cave.

What would have happened to Christianity if the early followers of Christ had received the Word but had done nothing to pass it along to others? They would be with God, but few others would be able to follow them. I thank God they proclaimed the news about Christ, and I need to do the same for others who haven't yet found this place where I live.

My revelation in that sacred place on Patmos told me to step out of the cave, to find other people who don't know about Christ, to be bolder and more vocal about proclaiming how God entered my life and changed it.

I need to tell you about a place I've been.

AUGUST 16

Bridge to grace

As for the saints who are in the land, they are the glorious ones in whom is all my delight.

PSALM 16:3

U.S. efforts in Afghanistan included "Coalition Humanitarian Liaison Cells," groups which described themselves as "Peace Corps with guns." They ranged around the country building bridges, repairing roads, providing supplies to schools. Though technically part of the "war" effort, they met basic human needs for food, shelter, education, transportation.

Whether they realized it or not, those soldiers were "the saints who are in the land," doing God's work by extending tangible and practical help to people in need. The people they helped were certainly not Christians, and may not even believe in God, but they saw His grace in action.

Those hands at work building bridges were the hands of God. Afghanistan is not the only place in the world that needs bridges, education, roads, food. People we know close to home hunger for God, and we can feed them by offering them generosity of heart, and thus the body of Christ.

People we know can't reach God yet, and we can be the bridge to grace by holding them close on His behalf. People we know need the hands of God, and we can be His hands. Being a Christian means meeting basic human needs in the name of God—not simply being active in church programs. It's not about counting the things we do for God.

It's about doing the things that count.

AUGUST 17

Grand canyon

The men of Ephraim . . . did not keep God's covenant and refused to live by his law. . . . When the Lord heard them, he was very angry . . . for they did not believe in God or trust in his deliverance.

PSALM 78:9-10, 21-22

In the movie *Grand Canyon,* a story of the small choices that determine the meaning in modern life, a woman who loves a married man confides to another person. She laments, "It hurts when you love someone, and they don't choose you."

But the tragic story of unrequited love isn't just a story of man and woman, but of man and God. He creates us, redeems us, sustains us, yet we forget Him. He opens His arms to protect us, yet we turn away to fight our battles alone. And amazingly, He continues to forgive each wrong turn we make, each time we fail to "trust in his deliverance."

My Christian life has not been, as I envisioned, one big choice, one step across a grand canyon between seeking God and turning from Him. Instead, it is a series of smaller chasms where I can choose Him or not choose Him. I can do the right thing, in this moment, this decision, and approach God. Or I can live for myself, take some seemingly harmless road, and widen the gulf between me and Him.

The saddest story of unrequited love is lived out, not just in the lives of nonbelievers, but day to day in the life of every Christian. When we turn away, it has to hurt our tender-hearted God. It has to hurt.

When you love someone, and they don't choose you.

AUGUST 18

Open house

How great is your goodness, which you have stored up for those who fear you, which you bestow in the sight of men on those who take refuge in you. In the shelter of your presence you hide them from the intrigues of men; in your dwelling you keep them safe from accusing tongues.

PSALM 31:19-20

Once when I visited an unfamiliar city, I stayed in the home of people whom I hadn't met before. As they left me alone there for the weekend, they told me to make myself at home.

Why can't more churches feel so welcoming and warm, so spacious and comfortable—so open to those needing love, and help, and God? Why can't we invite people in, telling them, "Make yourself at home. We'll figure the rest out later"?

Shouldn't a spiritual traveler find church a place to take refuge, a "dwelling safe from accusing tongues"? Bringing people to God requires the courage to be genuine, accepting, vulnerable. It asks a willingness to offer a stranger a glimpse of a God who has been, for us, a safe, warm, loving place.

Religion should be less about mistrust, and more a process of opening: accepting and stepping into the channels God sets before us, and opening up a clear channel for others to see the way He works. We can open our church doors all we want. But these places of God will not be filled with the people of God until, on His behalf, we do something much more courageous.

We have to open our hearts.

AUGUST 19

Holy wars

"To what can I compare this generation? They are like children sitting in the marketplaces and calling out to others: 'We played the flute for you, and you did not dance; we sang a dirge, and you did not mourn.' "
MATTHEW 11:16-17

One generation never understands the next; we don't even speak the same language as our parents or our children. For example, my parents pictured war on the beaches at Normandy and Iwo Jima, while I picture it in the jungles of Southeast Asia. Today's kids will think of going to war in office buildings, airports, post offices, laboratories, of battlegrounds in New York and Washington. For them, the battle is here.

The scariest struggles—national, personal, spiritual—are those close to home. War used to mean we steeled ourselves to go "over there" to fight a foreigner. But once we truly turn towards God, from religion to relationship, the battleground gets very close to home. In fact, you *become* the battleground. People and things that look innocent or even holy turn out to be enemies. Complacency and self-righteousness look so peaceful, so orderly. Why worry? We're at home.

It's no longer enough to send armies away to fight the holy battle. Others no longer go off to war for our souls. Sadly, suddenly, the battle is joined.

The war has come to us.

AUGUST 20

God's living canvas

. . . the Lord God formed the man from the dust of the ground and breathed into his nostrils the breath of life, and the man became a living being.

GENESIS 2:7

Vincent van Gogh believed that every object on this earth lives and breathes with life—with an almost palpable physical energy. In his paintings, every table, chair, tree, and field emits a vibrant aura that seems to make the canvas move.

Like van Gogh, I see the world as alive, vibrating with energy and light. Perhaps van Gogh understood God better than most people do; both painted their vitality, their love for the world, onto every canvas that came into their hands.

To understand God—the incredible combination of His power and His tender care—you must see Him in everything—literally every thing. Such vision will make your world come alive; your every action and thought will hum with God's loving energy. Every stone, every leaf, every sunset, every person is God's canvas. You are part of His artwork.

My God is a living God, and His vitality surrounds me. He lives when a butterfly flits past me. He lives when the winter comes. He lives when I realize it is just a season of life. God lives in all persons I love in this world, and He certainly lives on the day when I finally understand that they cannot stay here. He lives and breathes and loves, this magnificent God of mine.

And because He does, so do I.

HOLY ORDINARY

AUGUST 21

Up close and personal

. . . you are to seek the place the Lord your God will choose from among all your tribes to put his Name there for his dwelling. To that place you must go. . . .

DEUTERONOMY 12:5

The hotel I stayed in when I visited Athens, Greece was in the heart of the city, a population of 4.5 million sprawling all around us. From the roof of the hotel, I took pictures of the nearby Parthenon because I couldn't get over being so close to ancient history. The day I saw those pictures, I was stunned to see a foreground dominated by ugliness: twisted metal, broken concrete, people living in squalor.

There's a danger in seeking to be close to God in ways that allow us to forget about the condition of other humans. Whenever a criminal is put to death, millions of people say they are praying for that person. But to simply say "God help Him" is like zooming in on the summit and ignoring all the problems in the foreground. We have to put ourselves in his shoes, to wonder what went wrong, to see how to keep another person from becoming so lost in our world. We have to consciously love him just as God loves him—and us.

I'd prefer to zoom past all the ugliness straight to a view of God. It's great for me to sit here and talk about getting close to God, but to do it I have to care for another human being today. I have to reach out to another human being today. When I acknowledge the world's pain and try to salve it, I will see God up close.

And I will see Him today.

AUGUST 22

Your life line

The next day the great crowd that had come for the Feast heard that Jesus was on his way to Jerusalem. They took palm branches and went out to meet him, shouting, "Hosanna!" "Blessed is he who comes in the name of the Lord!" "Blessed is the King of Israel!"

JOHN 12:12-13

Surfing the internet one day, I found a website which offered, "Amazing free palm readings!" This service is offered over the computer, now, not in person. The user (a.k.a., the victim) is asked to place his palm on the computer monitor and wait for a prediction to appear on the screen. As screwy as it sounds, I fear that some people are so desperate for direction and hope in their lives that they will try it.

The people who shouted for Jesus and waved palm branches sought direction, too, thinking that their lives would hold more meaning when they were freed from oppression. They could not predict that peace would come at the price of the King's life, and of their own. They could not know that true power on earth comes not from politics, money, or status, but from the willingness to leave such things behind.

The real meaning of life is found in a Man whose hands would open to accept not a scepter, but a nail. The real meaning of life is found in a God who would die for us so that our life line could go on forever. The real meaning of our lives, the hope for our futures, can be read right there, in the hands of God.

It's written in His palms.

HOLY ORDINARY

AUGUST 23

Holy smoke

My enemies say of me in malice, "When will he die and his name perish?"

PSALM 41:5

But it is the spirit in a man, the breath of the Almighty, that gives him understanding.

JOB 32:8

My dad was born in Appomatox, Virginia; his given name, much to his later embarrassment, was "Georgie." When the original courthouse there burned, and the official record of his name went up in smoke, he changed his name to George. He saw that fire as his chance to reinvent himself, to cast off the name he hated and take on one he could live with.

Every day that I wake up and acknowledge God at the center of my life, I have the opportunity to reinvent myself in a much deeper way. I "die and my name perishes," but His name—the breath of the Almighty—gives me power, understanding, a fresh start.

I'd like to say that all the major mistakes I have made are in the distant past. But some of the acts I have committed against God came after I "changed my name" to become a Christian.

Yet somehow, inexplicably, God will forgive me again. Somehow, the moment I speak to Him in prayer and repentance, every transgression will go up in smoke. I can change my name, again, and take on His name, because my mistakes will vanish in the wind.

On the breath of the Almighty.

AUGUST 24

City of God

As he approached Jerusalem and saw the city, he wept over it and said, "If you, even you, had only known on this day what would bring you peace—but now it is hidden from your eyes."

LUKE 19:41-42

In May, 2003, an educated, intelligent Palestinian woman blew herself apart near an Israeli mall, killing three people and wounding scores of others. Her mother said of her, "If I had known that you were going to do this, I would have tied you up with a rope."

God must know how the Palestinian mother felt. He raised us up and showered us with gifts, and yet we insist on hurting each other, and Him. We forget about God, and when we do, "what would bring us peace is hidden from our eyes." So as Jesus approached Jerusalem, he wept, not only over what it had become, but over what it could have been.

God's cities and God's people are made in His image, but then they have free will to live in that image or to destroy it. I struggle often with the knowledge that each human being is made first in His image. The Palestinian bomber. Osama bin Laden. Me.

And yet so many choose to use their gifts to destroy cities and people of God when they could have built them up. I wonder, does God look at what we have done, and lament as the suicide bomber's mother did? Does God look at what each of us has built, and weep as Jesus wept over Jerusalem?

If He had known we were going to do this, would He have tied us up with a rope?

HOLY ORDINARY 257

AUGUST 25

Questing and answer

Then they said to him, "Please inquire of God to learn whether our journey will be successful." The priest answered them, "Go in peace. Your journey has the Lord's approval."

JUDGES 18:5-6

My sophomore year in college, my friends and I went on a quest when someone asked a simple but useless question (What do you call the hat that Sherlock Holmes wore?). The question occupied us, gave us something to seek, made us visit reference books and libraries that we never would've seen otherwise. When we found the answer, I felt vaguely disappointed, wondering, "What will I look for now?"

Sometimes we humans enjoy this journey so much that we almost fear reaching the destination. Do we fear actually finding God, and having nothing else to seek? It seems, though, that each answer about the presence and will of God prompts a larger or more difficult question. And every time we have the courage to ask the next question, we draw closer to Him.

The key, as the people in the book of Judges saw, is to listen for God's answers, to let God bless the journey. What lesson lies in this experience? Where should I go next? How should I spend my energy, my time, my money, my passion?

The questions will always be there. But the Good News is that, with prayer, God will always be here, in my heart, to allow me to journey in peace.

He's my final answer.

Walk this Way

For you, O Lord, have delivered my soul from death, my eyes from tears, my feet from stumbling, that I may walk before the Lord in the land of the living.

PSALM 116:8-9

Many years ago, a familiar sight in my neighborhood was a young man who walked all over a three- or four-mile square area. I never saw him sitting in a park, stopped at a store, or talking with anyone. I never saw him do anything but walk.

It seems that anyone who loves to walk and enjoy the outdoors is pursuing a healthy lifestyle, but I always had the sense that the young man was walking away from something troubling rather than just exercising.

I kept walking for the longest time to avoid committing to a relationship with God. I studied and read about Him, and considered the theological, moral, and ethical implications of believing in God. As long as I was studying, I didn't have to take the daunting step of sustaining a strong relationship with Him. It looked like a healthy walk, but I was really walking away from God.

Then I had to stop, wounded so deeply by tragedy and loss that I could not take another step. I stopped, and finally realized that God didn't want me to study Him, but to love Him, that He didn't want me to walk aimlessly, but to approach Him. I opened my life to accept His endless mercy and grace, and He "delivered my eyes from tears, my feet from stumbling."

Now, I continue to walk, but with a difference. Now I walk in the "land of the living."

Because now I walk with God.

AUGUST 27

Learn something every day

> ... I keep asking that the God of our Lord Jesus Christ, the glorious Father, may give you the Spirit of wisdom and revelation, so that you may know him better.
>
> EPHESIANS 1:17

Among the legacies—of wisdom and advice, of humor and tenderness—that my dad left me was the admonition to "Learn something every day." He taught me many things, but the most important was that a person can never know enough.

Knowledge, to me, holds intrinsic value. Some people do not agree; they think everything they study should be of some "practical" value. "Why do you want to know about that?" they ask, when I pick up a book on astronomy or Sufi poetry or weather phenomena. But I want to know everything about the universe; to know God, I have to understand His work.

What kind of God allows humans to develop a language so powerful that words can heal a heart or science so advanced it can replace one? What kind of God arranges immense stars and planets in the nighttime sky, then gives us the imagination to see lions and archers and bears in them? What power sculpts the magnificent Himalayas and then gives us the passion to see their peaks for ourselves? What kind of God is this?

To this day, I love the smell of printer's ink because it reminds me of my dad's workplace. I understood him better, and loved him more, once I had seen his work. The art paints pictures of the artist.

This lesson, my Father has taught me well.

The breath of God

When I am afraid, I will trust in you. In God, whose word I praise, in God I trust; I will not be afraid. What can mortal man do to me?
PSALM 56:3-4

I sat quietly on a porch one summer morning, listening. The air was generally still, but when it did stir, the music of wind chimes floated by. The more agitated and unstable the air felt, the louder the music became.

The life with God is a paradox of calmness and agitation. We try to live for Him, and increasingly find peace. But when peace becomes complacency, the air has to stir, or there's no more growth to Him, and in Him.

Changes sweep across our mortal lives with stunning speed, and we pursue God, at least in part, so that we can say, "When I am afraid, I will trust in you . . . I will not be afraid. What can mortal man do to me?" And sometimes the only transgression mortal man has committed against us is to love us as a mortal, to make us want to stay forever in one place when God needs one of us to move on, and to move closer to Him.

The air continues to stir in my life; the atmosphere feels stormy. Change—to some degree painful change—is on the way; I can feel it in the air. The wind is beginning to pick up. But that wind is the breath of God.

So the music isn't far behind.

AUGUST 29

Freedom

Would not his splendor terrify you? Would not the dread of him fall on you? ... Keep silent and let me speak; then let come to me what may.
JOB 13:11, 13

As the threat of war in Iraq grew, a news story suggested that the leaders of some nations feared deposing Saddam Hussein because they feared what a liberated Iraq could mean to the region's stability. What if their own people wanted more freedom for themselves? How would the Iraqis handle subjection to a marketplace instead of to a dictator?

Since I started connecting to God and beginning to feel truly free of this world, some people around me seem unsettled and nervous. Longtime friends who "don't get" God begin to suspect that their fast-paced, hollow lives really hold no meaning, that all they have invested in their lifestyles evaporates in eternity. Even some practicing Christians look suspiciously on a new believer's passion and energy and joy. Some would rather bind themselves dispassionately to religious ritual than free themselves through a powerful relationship with God.

Rituals are easy and finite; relationship, like any freedom, requires commitment, constancy, care. But freedom in God, it seems to me, is the only way to live, no matter how nervous it may make those around us, no matter how much "His splendor may terrify them." I've heard it for years, but now I believe it, that "The best things in life are free."

As are the best lives.

AUGUST 30

Verbs

And now, dear lady, I am not writing you a new command but one we have had from the beginning. I ask that we love one another. And this is love: that we walk in obedience to his commands. As you have heard from the beginning, his command is that you walk in love.

2 JOHN 1:5-6

My sister was the queen of malapropism; she frequently scrambled or confused words and clichés. Often, however, her phrases were much better than the originals. For instance, when she had an uneasy feeling about someone, she didn't say they gave off bad vibes, but "bad verbs."

She was probably closer to the truth than the rest of us. Usually when someone makes me uneasy, it's because they mouth all the right words but don't act in a way consistent with those tidy words. And verbs are action words, so maybe they do give off "bad verbs."

Christianity is not a passive faith, of nouns and adjectives, but a faith of action. Christ commands us to love Him by loving each other, looking out for each other, forgiving each other. He asks us to "walk in love," to go out among His people and actively, openly, and unconditionally love them.

He never commands us to scorn, to judge, to punish, to resent, or to marginalize. He asks us to walk in love, to actively care for His people, and His words of action are very simple. Respect. Forgive. Hold. Heal. Tend. Love.

Good verbs.

AUGUST 31

Glory

At once the Spirit sent him out into the desert, and he was in the desert forty days, being tempted by Satan. He was with the wild animals, and angels attended him.

MARK 1:13

A movie called *Glory* tells the story of the first unit of African-American soldiers to fight in the Civil War. In training, one man is particularly proud of his marksmanship. But when his commander begins to duplicate combat conditions, firing a pistol into the air and shouting, the man gets so flustered he can barely get his weapon reloaded.

When I first became a committed Christian, I considered myself a sharpshooter. This life is easy, I thought. Go to church, study about God, hang around with these warm, compassionate, Godly people, and through it all find, finally, a life that is more substance than flash.

Then the Spirit sent me out into a desert, where I had to reinterpret every aspect of my life. Old environments and friends no longer fit. Other Christians insisted on telling me their truths about God and His nature.

But there's glory in the field, amid the noise and the clutter, the busyness and the pace. There's glory in walking out of that church building on Sunday morning and holding God in my heart when a work deadline, or an angry motorist, or a diagnosis looms on the horizon. The real glory is in constantly, consistently, remembering that I live in God's hands, that I live in God's grace.

Especially under fire.

September

SEPTEMBER 1

Sanctuary

"This is what the Sovereign Lord says: Although I sent them far away among the nations and scattered them among the countries, yet for a little while I have been a sanctuary for them in the countries where they have gone...."

EZEKIEL 11:16

One course where I play golf is bordered by protected areas. Golf balls hit into those areas must be abandoned, to preserve the habitat of the wildlife and plants growing there. Some forms of life are so precious, yet so delicate, that they need help surviving in the modern world.

Christianity sometimes seems to be such a vulnerable life form, unable to make it in the real world without help. But God didn't say that He would build His people a sanctuary, or give them a safe place to live, but that He would *be* their sanctuary. The true people of God can't cower in a protected area; we have to enter the chaotic, noisy, frightful world and carry His presence to it.

God's people today find sanctuary in the knowledge that Christ lived in this world, yet still lived only for God. We find sanctuary in a life that says, "This is what God looks like. He's not a God who can only survive in a church or tabernacle, but one who lives and works in this world. He is a God of blue collars and white collars as well as clerical collars. This is a God who is real."

The living God is our sanctuary. Living in Him, for Him, protects us from everything in this world.

Including ourselves.

SEPTEMBER 2

Profit and loss

But whatever was to my profit I now consider loss for the sake of Christ.... What is more, I consider everything ... rubbish, that I may gain Christ and be found in him ...

PHILIPPIANS 3:7-9

On my e-mail one day I received a message entitled, "Check out some attractive Russian brides." Clearly this message was not for me personally; all of my friends know that I'm not into attractive Russian brides. But the spam continues to arrive in someone's effort to get ahead materially.

Our world has become a giant mass marketing campaign to pull humans down to the lowest common denominator, to make us want the next hawker's product. But as a Christian, my priorities don't match those of most of the world: I no longer value myself over God, things over people, status over relationships. And even as a Christian, an insidious change of priorities can happen. If I'm not vigilant, I can begin to value my church or my religion over my God.

Now, as a Christian, losses become gains. Every time I incur a loss—material, physical, emotional—my spirit grows stronger, and I gain in my relationship with Christ and with other people in need. When I suffer a loss, I "gain Christ and am found in Him."

So please remove my name from your marketing list. Don't tell me about attractive Russian brides, enhancing body parts I don't even have, or having my palm read over the Internet. I'm not into those things. I am a Christian.

I'm into Jesus.

SEPTEMBER 3

Here I am

... as for you, I will take you, and you will rule over all that your heart desires. If you do whatever I command you and walk in my ways and do what is right in my eyes ... I will be with you.

1 KINGS 11:37-38

I love to tell people that I once had a "furniture sale" marriage: 12 months, no interest. A man vowed to remain with me "until death do us part," but as it turned out he only stayed long enough to confirm that I wasn't his mother.

Vows are taken and given so casually nowadays that we scarcely think about making—or breaking them. I get all pious and pretend I would do anything God asks, but I usually back down. "I will gladly give you anything," I tell Him, but too often I add, "except that."

God teaches us love by showing us love, love so deep that you're willing to give up your life—your life—to save someone else. He doesn't want one-seventh of my week or one-tenth of my income—He wants my life. He wants me to do what His Son did— to open my hands to Him and say, here I am, do with me what You will. What *You* will.

God asks me to entrust myself into His keeping, for His work, no matter how frightening or painful that work may be. He vows that, if I put my life in His hands, He will make me new. He will make me whole. He will give me everything my heart desires. Everything.

Accept that.

SEPTEMBER 4

I believe, I can fly

Then Jesus said to the centurion, "Go! It will be done just as you believed it would."

MATTHEW 8:13

A favorite pop song that appeared a few years ago included the words, "I believe I can fly; I believe I can touch the sky." I loved the suggestion that even a mortal human being like me can rise to extraordinary heights—intellectually, spiritually, emotionally.

I used to think of the words as, "I believe *that* I can fly; I believe *that* I can touch the sky." But my newfound Christian perspective changes the meaning entirely. Now I rely on God's power instead of my own pitiful little reserves, and I say, "I believe, *so* I can fly; I believe, *so* I can touch the sky." I literally feel now that everything is possible.

Since I put my life in God's hands, I find myself accomplishing feats that I never even considered possible in the past. I always wanted to write, but encountered mental and emotional obstacles at every turn. I always wanted to touch other people's lives, but I feared rejection and unpopularity. I always wanted to like myself, but I found it impossible in light of my past mistakes.

But now I believe, and so I can write. Now I believe, and so I touch people. Now I believe, and so I like myself because I know I am made in the image of a forgiving and awesome God. I believe that God makes all things possible.

I believe. I can fly. I can touch the sky.

HOLY ORDINARY

SEPTEMBER 5

A safe place to rest

God will speak to his people, to whom he said, "This is the resting place, let the weary rest," and "This is the place of repose,"—but they would not listen. So then, the word of the Lord to them will become do and do, do and do, rule on rule, rule on rule . . .

ISAIAH 28:12-13

In 1998, I had to drive the 630 miles from Mississippi to Illinois to visit my dad in the hospital and attend a class reunion. I was supposed to leave at noon, but didn't get on the road until after 8 p.m. because of a long, difficult meeting with my boss. I kept falling asleep at the wheel and pulling over, but didn't stop for a prolonged nap because I knew of no safe place to rest.

My spiritual life was in the same condition. I had been involved in religious activities, had read all the right books, and yet God wasn't in my life. I still had nowhere to go with my anxiety and frustration, no one to hear my cries or shoulder my burdens. Living in fear meant that I had no safe place to rest.

I was so frightened—a long, difficult road ahead, and no safe haven where I could regain my strength. I felt that if I kept going, kept doing, I would eventually find a relationship with God. Instead, I found out that more activity wasn't the answer. I needed to learn to rest in God, to trust in His protection. Ultimately, though, God didn't just find me a safe place to rest.

God is my safe place. He is my rest.

SEPTEMBER 6

God on the dock

When God saw what they did and how they turned from their evil ways, he had compassion and did not bring upon them the destruction he had threatened. But Jonah was greatly displeased and became angry. . . . He prayed to the Lord, ". . . Now, O Lord, take away my life, for it is better for me to die than to live." But the Lord replied, "Have you any right to be angry?"

JONAH 3:10, 4:1-4

West Coast dockworkers chose to strike in 2002, and they were willing to allow tons of produce and meat to rot on the docks to force contract negotiations to go their way. Meanwhile, innocent people went without food or paid higher prices because of the loss.

I have, in the past, been a world-class holder of grudges. Very recently, though, I realized that the animosity I harbor accomplishes nothing positive and in the bargain closes out the spirit of God. Like the produce on the West Coast docks, spiritual energy was wasted, and people were going hungry.

Jonah had finally done as God had asked, and then God changed His mind and chose not to destroy the Ninevites, who repented. Jonah saw God as *too* loving, *too* forgiving, and felt so betrayed by the incredible mercy of God that he preferred death to life.

Who in the world would choose death over life because of a grudge? I did it, for many years. The body of Christ, which could feed the world, waited on the dock because of my anger, my failure to forgive. Meanwhile, people were starving.

Including me.

HOLY ORDINARY

SEPTEMBER 7

Listening to the profits

A silversmith named Demetrius, who made silver shrines of Artemis, brought in no little business for the craftsmen. He ... said: "Men, you know we receive a good income from this business. And you see and hear how this fellow Paul has convinced and led astray large numbers of people here in Ephesus and in practically the whole province of Asia. He says that man-made gods are no gods at all."

ACTS 19:24-26

Jurassic Park is a movie in which scientists re-create dinosaurs for use in a theme park. The creators plan to control the dinosaurs with massive electrical fences, but when the power goes out, the dinosaurs begin to take over.

Today we have incredible technology to transplant human organs, communicate with others around the world in seconds, and even clone animals. Man's technology is so powerful that we begin to think we can create anything, or anyone. Including God.

But if I try to create God and use Him for my own profit, as the silversmiths at Ephesus used Artemis, then I have lost sight of Him. God is not something to be put on a resumé, and the seeking of God is not a virtue I should use to make others admire me. God is life, and love, and limitless.

God cannot be created, or even defined, by me. It works the other way around. Paul had it right, that "manmade gods are no gods at all." Manmade gods ultimately can accomplish nothing of importance.

But God-made men? Now that's a different story.

Before God

In the morning, O Lord, you hear my voice; in the morning I lay my requests before you and wait in expectation.

PSALM 5:3

When I first got my driver's license, a friend taught me how to drive a car with a manual transmission. Initially, I killed the engine every time I turned a corner, because I forgot to downshift. I had to keep popping the clutch to get the engine going again.

Unfortunately, I still use that technique too often when rounding corners in my spiritual life. I hurry through changes and decisions, running ahead of God rather than "waiting in expectation" for His will. For years, every time I went around a corner, the engine stalled because I hadn't downshifted long enough to understand what He wanted me to do.

A dear friend and spiritual guide is helping me learn to turn corners more effectively, to pray not reactively, but proactively. Instead of "Please God, get me out of this," I'm learning to pray, "Please God, tell me what I should do next." Instead of just praying for circumstances, I pray before them: before trouble comes, before decisions are made, before someone gets hurt, before I go the wrong way. Before I turn the corner.

The most devoted Christian life is filled with turns: decisions, calls, relationships that require God's guidance. Slowing down long enough to ask God's way, to "lay my requests before God and wait in expectation," will keep that life running more slowly. So this morning, as my day begins, only one thing goes before God.

My prayer.

SEPTEMBER 9

Tornado warnings

. . . he speaks falsely, while his heart gathers slander; then he goes out and spreads it abroad. All my enemies whisper together against me. . . . But you, O Lord, have mercy on me. . . . I know that you are pleased with me, for my enemy does not triumph over me.

PSALM 41:6-7, 11

Once, as I watched a movie on TV, a message on the screen said a tornado had been spotted nearby. I looked outside and saw only clear blue sky. Another warning flashed, and the sky remained bright. Finally I realized I was watching a movie I had taped three weeks earlier, when tornadoes were in the area. The seemingly "urgent" warning was three weeks old.

Since I've become a strong Christian, I still agonize around old friends who don't understand why I or how I changed my life. I find myself wanting to appease them—maybe being more covert about my faith so I won't make them uncomfortable. What if they think I'm not the same old friend they've always known?

But the truth is that I'm not the same person; I'm a new person in God. My old friends—and even my old self—become enemies who threaten to "triumph" if I don't remain true to Him. Those earthly evaluations applied, like that videotaped tornado warning, to another time, another person.

Now I try to let only God—not man—measure my life, a yardstick that always finds me wanting.

Wanting less of me. And more of Him.

SEPTEMBER 10

The gate of heaven

In their fright the women bowed down with their faces to the ground, but the men said, "Why do you look for the living among the dead? He is not here; he has risen!"

LUKE 24:5-6

The entrance to the holy cave on Patmos bears the inscription, "As dreadful as this place is it is nevertheless the house of God and this the Gate of Heaven." When I read those words, I knew that I had been to that place before.

Places I saw a few years ago terrified me; I had reached the end of my self, the brink of my world. I suspect the women who went looking for Jesus' body felt the same way. He had been right there with them, and now He had been murdered. As they considered what had come to pass, the darkness must have felt overpowering.

A technique frequently used on my neurotic, worrying self is the question, "What's the worst thing that could happen?" The assumption is that your fear is worse than the actual outcomes. In my case, I felt that the worst that could happen *did* happen: I lost everything that was important to me, and I was driven to my knees.

But then the light started creeping in, one night when another Christian gave me strength to get through my grief. An awful moment became awe-full; when I looked up, I couldn't believe what I was seeing. I still can't believe it.

I was kneeling at the gate of heaven, so close I could almost touch it.

From that dreadful place.

SEPTEMBER 11

Jacob's ladder

. . . my eyes are dim with grief. I call to you, O Lord, every day; I spread my hands out to you. . . . You have taken my companions and loved ones from me; the darkness is my closest friend.

PSALM 88:9, 18

On September 11, 2001, firefighters from Engine Co. 6 helped an elderly woman out of one of the Trade Towers. When the woman made the group stop on the fourth floor so she could rest, the tower collapsed around them. After waiting hours in the stairwell for rescue, they finally looked up to see light above. They climbed up and out, to salvation.

Sometimes my life crashes down around me, jobs and people and comfortable places lost in a vortex of destruction. When it happens, only the love of God remains standing, the love of the One who gives me those gifts in the first place. Perhaps the collapse tells me to depend on Him only, to understand that even the most important parts of my human life are just temporary companions. Perhaps the loss reminds me to seek only the Light above, that the way to salvation is up.

My parents and my sister taught me how to love and how to be loved; they helped get me into that stairwell, to the one place where I could survive. When they were gone, when the walls of loss and loneliness crashed down around me, that ability to love, turned towards God, was the only thing left standing. And, against all earthly odds, it is enough.

Thank you, God. It is enough.

The twelfth of September

Jesus said to her, "I am the resurrection and the life. He who believes in me will live, even though he dies; and whoever lives and believes in me will never die.... Do you believe this?"

JOHN 11:25-26

All the world recognizes yesterday's date—September 11th—as a terrible day, a heart-wrenching anniversary. But for someone, every date marks the passing of a loved one or a way of life. Someone out there cringes and cries and mourns on September 12th, too, and on every day of the year.

Our world overflows with loss. Loved ones die empty, and fail to live, every day, because they haven't yet seen God. As Christians, we can only answer those echoes of loss and emptiness with the voice and the presence of our God. He alone can fill that unnamed longing for something more meaningful in this world, something lasting. Some*one* lasting.

We can tell each aching soul that any anniversary they face—no matter how much it hurts—can be handled by God's tender touch. We can pray constantly that those who don't know Him will meet Him and feel Him in their lives. We can pray that, a year from now, someone will celebrate September 12th as the day that they encountered God and first felt His arms around them.

Yesterday, indeed, was a dreadfully tragic anniversary, a day when we prayed for all of those who were lost.

Perhaps today we should pray for those who still are.

SEPTEMBER 13

Limitless

We proclaim him . . . so that we may present everyone perfect in Christ.
COLOSSIANS 1:28

The first time I came to Mississippi in 1973, floodwaters also came to the state. When we crossed the Mississippi River at Memphis, it looked to be miles wide. It was impossible to tell where the riverbanks had been; they became irrelevant.

A few years into my Christian life, I had a powerful experience that made me think of those lost boundaries. For a moment, I closed my eyes and felt as if my body disappeared; only my soul remained, connected directly, totally with God. I felt peaceful, yet powerful. Strong, yet humbled. Not near God, but *in* Him.

To be "perfect in Christ," means all boundaries disappear. The line between me and Him. Between me and you. Between life and death. And life again.

I used to worry about what would happen if I lost my sense of self. After that experience of being in God, though, I realized that the only things lost are my limitations, which were self-imposed in the first place. In the moment that He enveloped me, what surprised me most was the sound.

It wasn't noisy or violent or frightening, like the crash of walls falling or fences swept away by force. It didn't feel like a lost battle or a takeover bid. It was peaceful—the sound of snow falling into a river. In that hushed and holy moment, the snow and the river became one. All boundaries were gone.

And only God remained.

SEPTEMBER 14

Small sacrifices

... Andrew, Simon Peter's brother, spoke up, "Here is a boy with five small barley loaves and two small fish, but how far will they go among so many?"

JOHN 6:8-9

Thousands of men from Arab countries volunteered during the Iraqi conflict for suicide bombings to kill American soldiers. The most sophisticated military in the world, it seemed, could be set back by one man willing to sacrifice his life.

That's the bad news. The Good News is that incredible positive change can also be wrought in this world by one person's offering himself to God. One small boy's lunch, in the hands of God, feeds five thousand. One Man's life, placed tenderly in the hands of God, continues to feed the world over 2000 years later.

I'm not sure what I would do if God asked me to sacrifice my life as Christ did, as so many martyrs have. And probably it won't be asked of me, at least not in one dramatic moment. But He does ask me, every day, to sacrifice a little piece of myself—my ego, my time, my agenda—so that someone else may be fed.

It's easy to say, "I'm only one person," or "I have only this small gift," and to question, "How far will it go among so many?" But in the hands of God, one small sacrifice—even the offering of your life a few minutes at a time—can feed someone who hungers.

How much can be accomplished by one child of God offering one small gift? How far will one sacrifice go among so many?

Far enough to feed the world.

HOLY ORDINARY

SEPTEMBER 15

Some restrictions may apply

. . . love your enemies, do good to them, and lend to them without expecting to get anything back. Then your reward will be great, and you will be sons of the Most High . . .

LUKE 6:35

To my amazement, a toy I bought for my cat bore on its package disclaimers, I suppose to protect the manufacturer from cats with lawyers. The disclaimer said cats should be supervised while playing with the toy, in case any small parts came off and put the cat in danger of choking.

It seems sometimes that everything in our society today carries a disclaimer. No one wants to make a plain, matter-of-fact statement; everything is footnoted or asterisked or otherwise disclaimed.

When God gave us commandments, He didn't operate that way. For example, I carefully examined this passage of the Bible, as well as those about loving my neighbor, and for the life of me I can't find the word "except" in them. I keep hoping God will say, "Love your enemies, except You-Know-Who." But He never puts a footnote at the bottom of the page reading, "This commandment does not apply in case of extreme annoyance, dislike, hormonal imbalance, obnoxious behavior, pain, or anger."

God speaks a simple, forthright language. He asks me to love Him, to love my neighbor, to love myself. And very plainly, He asks me to love my enemy.

Excepting none. Accepting all.

Two things have I heard

One thing God has spoken, two things have I heard: that you, O God, are strong, and that you, O Lord, are loving.

PSALM 62:11-12

My freshman year in college found me 600 miles away from home, and I was one homesick puppy. Knowing how much I missed home, my mom wrote me a letter every day the first semester. Her letters gave all kinds of little details about my family and hometown, some serious, some funny. (My favorite was one that ended, "P.S. I was going to send you $5, but I had already sealed the envelope.")

Anyway, it almost didn't matter what news my mom chose to relate—I got her message just by seeing that letter in the mailbox. Whatever her incredibly neat, tiny little handwriting actually said, she communicated three sentiments to me every time she mailed a letter. I knew without question that she missed me, that she loved me, that she was proud of me.

Sometimes, especially when I fight difficult anniversaries, friends hold me up until I can regain my equilibrium. The words are usually something like, "Let me help you" and "I'm praying for you," but the message—from God Himself—tells me that I am cared for, that I will always have His strength when mine is gone.

Like those letters from home, the form and content may vary, but two constant things I have heard.

I love you. I long to be with you.

SEPTEMBER 17

Lots to forgive

... the master of the banquet tasted the water that had been turned into wine. He did not realize where it had come from, though the servants who had drawn the water knew.

JOHN 2:9

I used to kid a realtor friend, telling her I could only remember two of the three most important factors in real estate value. They are, "location, location, and . . ." What's the third one? Oh, yeah—"location."

Some ideas are so critical that we could hear them over and over and still not quite grasp their importance. For instance, the three keys to my spiritual growth are forgiveness, forgiveness, and forgiveness. In a few cases, I have not forgiven; in fact, I still want to hurt someone else back. And yet deep down, I want to forgive, even when I am in the right.

I feel that desire to forgive only because Christ is here, in my life. And since He created that desire to forgive, He will perform whatever miracle is necessary to allow me to forgive.

I wonder if Jesus' friends ran short of wine because He was there. Perhaps many people went to the wedding only to glimpse Him. And since Christ's very presence may have created the need for more wine, He miraculously provided more wine. Where God points out a need, He supplies the means to fill it.

He constantly reminds me of the three keys to loving and getting past the hurt. "Let it go. Let it go." What was the third one, Lord?

Oh, yeah. "Let it go."

SEPTEMBER 18

The Son and the moon

Do not gloat over me, my enemy! Though I have fallen, I will rise. Though I sit in darkness, the Lord will be my light.

MICAH 7:8-9

When the earth's single moon rises into the nighttime sky, it prompts poetry and art, music and romance. Moonlight holds a curious, mystical power over us humans.

But the moon, itself no more than a large rock suspended in space, possesses neither light nor warmth. In fact, we would not even see the moon in the night sky if not for the sun, because the moon is capable only of reflecting light, not of generating it.

For decades, I thought I was the sun and that everything in the world revolved around me. But inside, spiritually, I was dark and lifeless, my spirit eclipsed by its own self-centeredness. Once I admitted that I was only a reflector, and not a source, of light, my life began to revolve around its true source of energy, the Son of God. It was then that others began to see light in me, as I began reflecting God's image.

Without God's light, I am invisible. Without God's light, I am nothing; I hang cold and lifeless, wondering why no one notices me. But "though I have fallen, I shall rise; though I sit in darkness, the Lord will be my light."

Alone, I am nothing, but I can be God's moon, suspended beautifully in the night sky, revolving around Him.

Reflecting the power and light of the Son.

SEPTEMBER 19

A child's wish

The first thing Andrew did was to find his brother Simon and tell him, "We have found the Messiah" . . .

JOHN 1:41

At my favorite lunch place is a large fountain which fascinates the children. I often see a parent near it, digging in purse or pocket for coins; the child waits, palm open, anxious for a penny or two to throw in and "make a wish."

When Andrew says, "We have found the Messiah," I picture that hopeful child waiting on the parent's gift that might change the future. I see the whole world, holding its breath for eons: a child, palm open, seeking the Messiah to redeem the world. And suddenly, in an ordinary moment, Jesus is here.

God's coming into a life can be just so breathtakingly ordinary. He comes when we worry about work, or health, when we rejoice, or grieve. He walks up one day, and we realize "We have found the Messiah," the only One capable of taking away our sin. And in seemingly that most ordinary of moments, He cleanses our whole grubby past in the fountain of forgiveness.

I love those magnificent, mundane moments when Christ comes to me. I clutch my little worldly treasure—my gifts, my relationships, my worship—in my hand, and I cannot wait to throw them into the fountain of redemption so they can be immersed, baptized, washed clean. I suspect today will offer many ordinary moments when I can throw my treasure in with God.

And all our wishes—His and mine—will come true.

SEPTEMBER 20

Wisdom

"But where can wisdom be found? Where does understanding dwell? Man does not comprehend its worth; it cannot be found in the land of the living. . . . It cannot be bought with the finest gold, nor can its price be weighed in silver. . . ."Where then does wisdom come from? Where does understanding dwell?. . . God understands the way to it and he alone knows where it dwells. . . ."

JOB 28:12-13, 15, 20, 23

The U.S. Board on Geographic Names says "Fairview" is the most common name for populated places in the United States, followed by "Midway." My favorite place names, though, are less common, places like "Normal, Illinois" and "Hard Times, Louisiana."

Job asks "Where wisdom can be found," and in my life, I've found it much more often in Hard Times than in Fairview, or Midway, or even Normal. I think we find wisdom not on a smooth road, but on a dangerous, frightening, often treacherous one. We find it when we have the willingness to revisit those painful places to help others, to say lovingly, "I know it hurts. I have been there."

Wisdom is not a common place, not a middle-of-the-road place, but one where you are willing to be vulnerable and open, to God and to others. Wisdom is a place that only God can take us. It's a place I have glimpsed, with Him, and in Him.

I found it just the other side of Hard Times.

SEPTEMBER 21

Global warming

"I revealed myself to those who did not ask for me; I was found by those who did not seek me."

ISAIAH 65:1

I once heard an interview with an expert on investing in gold. He said that world geopolitical factors could mean significant changes in gold prices, that, for example, prices could vary significantly if "World peace broke out."

I love the thought that peace could "break out" just as war and violence do. What if acts of peace could happen as spontaneously as acts of war? What if humanitarianism and tolerance could break out, sneaking up on us, changing the whole world? What if . . .?

But there is little peace among nations today because there is little peace in individual human hearts. We acquire and consume material things to make us feel more important, and continue feeling empty. Other nations see our profligacy and strike back in resentment. We fear each other, so we plan for war instead of planning for peace.

I have wished for many things in my life, but never had the sense to ask for, or plan for, peace. The peace of God only began coming into my heart when I hadn't the strength to keep the walls of fear intact. God "revealed Himself to me when I did not ask for Him."

Just a few years ago, my heart was utterly broken, and I wasn't even looking for God. Now I know that He used that awful time, that crack in my heart, for the best possible good.

That's when peace broke in.

SEPTEMBER 22

Rewards

"You alone are the Lord. You made the heavens, even the highest heavens, and all their starry host, the earth and all that is on it, the seas and all that is in them. You give life to everything, and the multitudes of heaven worship you...."

NEHEMIAH 9:6

In February of 2001, a Cleveland man returned to authorities $640,000 that had fallen from an armored car. The serial numbers were recorded, so he knew he couldn't spend it anyway. Yet the company considered giving him a reward for returning the money. *Their* money.

God routinely leaves me gifts, dropping talents or friends or circumstances out of the back of the truck, even letting me think I found them through my own skill. When I picked up that priceless gift He left for me—His breathtaking gift of grace—He not only let me keep it, but continues to reward me for picking it up.

Sometimes, not often enough, I stop and realize where those gifts originate, and I try to return them to God. It is so easy for me to think that I deserve a reward for giving this life of mine back to its Creator, its rightful owner. And when I make the slightest move to give something back to God, He gives me the really good news—that those His gifts are multiplied into a life deeper, richer, and more beautiful than any I could imagine.

Keep the treasure you "found," He tells me.

And here's a little something extra for remembering that it was never really yours.

HOLY ORDINARY 287

Water into wine

Dear friends, we are now children of God, and what we will be has not yet been made known. But we know that when he appears, we shall be like him, for we shall see him as he is. Everyone who has this hope in him purifies himself, just as he is pure.

1 JOHN 3:2-3

A few years ago at a meeting, I heard a speech by a person who had hurt me mortally a few years earlier. As she ended her remarks, she began to lose her voice; I knew I should get her a drink of water to help out, but I didn't do it.

Most people there knew of our past conflict, and some know that I have now turned my life over to God. So helping her would've sent a compelling, real-life message about the power of faith to change lives. It might have even changed hers. Yet my motivation would have been primarily selfish: I wanted to be seen as the better person, the one to first extend a hand of reconciliation.

But that's such a small, human goal; why should I seek to be simply better than the next person when I'm a child of God? In fact, when I forgive and heal and love, I become part of Him. It would have felt like a miracle, to care for someone whose presence once filled me with loathing. Christ loved others no matter what offense they had committed, so He would have made it happen.

A simple glass of water—a symbol of my selfish humanity—could have become the wine of divinity, in the right hands. In God's hands.

But not yet in mine.

SEPTEMBER 24

Know question

Knowledge puffs up, but love builds up. The man who thinks he knows something does not yet know as he ought to know. But the man who loves God is known by God.

1 CORINTHIANS 8:1-3

Once, when faced with a difficult but critical golf shot, I said aloud, "I don't think I can do this." My golf partner chastised me to "think positive," so I told her, "Okay, I'm *positive* I can't do it."

I have never had confidence in my own abilities, and have never been good about stretching into new territory. When I face an opportunity that isn't within shouting distance of my comfort zone, I think and pray about it, my mind filled with noise and doubts. All of the doubts have to do with my limitations: human limitations.

Yet there's no doubt that, when God asks us to do His work, He fills the toolbox with all we need to do it. I keep wanting to ask how I can do such a thing, who will help, when it will have an effect, what I need to know.

But the only question that really falls in my realm is, "Does God want me to do this?" The question is not how or where or when or why. The question is *if*. When I know He wants me to do it, I can be confident that He will handle the rest. Still, this job frightens me here, in my complacent little world, so I asked Him one more time. "God, do I know enough to do such work?" He answered my question with one of His own.

Do you know Me?

HOLY ORDINARY

SEPTEMBER 25

God changed His mind

[The king] issued a proclamation in Nineveh: ". . . Let everyone call urgently on God. Let them give up their evil ways and their violence. Who knows? God may yet relent and with compassion turn from his fierce anger so that we will not perish."

JONAH 3:7, 9

I have always wanted to try woodcarving. One book I read about it suggested starting out with a more "forgiving" substance, such as soap. As it said, with soap, "Even failures don't go to waste; they can always be used for washing."

God operates in an equally forgiving mode, and too rarely, we remember this world's impermanence and God's steadfast forgiveness. We fail to remember that all of this world will pass away. Including our mistakes.

In the story of Jonah, the Ninevites had lived a life distant from God. Yet when they repented and "gave up their evil ways and their violence," God decided not to destroy them. And because they had failed, they learned firsthand about the forgiveness and compassion of God. For when they truly repented, God changed His mind.

All in this world is transient; all accomplishments and all failings will pass away, and only God, in His infinite forgiveness, will remain. We have to remember that we are dust, and to dust we shall return. But God whispers something else.

"Even failures can be used for cleansing."

SEPTEMBER 26

Constant

Blessed is the man who does not condemn himself by what he approves. . . . May the God who gives endurance and encouragement give you a spirit of unity among yourselves as you follow Christ Jesus. . . .
ROMANS 14:22B, 15:5

Physicists have long considered a few measures, especially the speed of light and the charge of the electron, to be "constants." But today, scientists are beginning to suspect that these "constants" are not constant at all, but are changing almost imperceptibly.

Nothing remains constant in the world of man. A job I thought I would keep until retirement lasted seven months. Financial security seems an oxymoron in today's business climate. The most "constant" and abiding love, in the hands and hearts of man, becomes inconsistent. Even a person with the best possible intention to love goes away—through life changes, illness, death, emotional distance.

When we seek only earthly things, we "condemn ourselves by what we approve," because what we seek is transient. So what can we hold constant in this life, if not the love of those we trust the most? Ultimately, all we can hold onto is the One who gave those marvelous gifts of love to us in the first place.

Our world is filled with "inconstant constants." Money evaporates. Jobs change. People go away. Even the speed of light is changing.

But its Source never does.

HOLY ORDINARY

SEPTEMBER 27

The crux of Christianity

Into your hands I commit my spirit; redeem me, O Lord, the God of truth. . . . My times are in your hands. . . .

PSALM 31:5, 15

The movie *Stigmata* follows a young woman who begins to suffer the wounds of Christ. Confused, she tells a priest, "I feel like my heart is breaking. Why am I so sad?"

She is inexpressibly sad because she has glimpsed the place where Jesus lived, where He was mortal enough to feel human pain, but divine enough to take it on for others who would not even acknowledge the sacrifice. To stand in such a place, it must feel as if your heart is breaking.

The word "crux," which means the main feature or the heart of a matter, comes from the Latin word for "cross." The crux of the Christian experience is the Cross, that intersection of man and God. One man chose to live at that intersection of the human and the divine, committing His Spirit, His every breath, to His Father's will.

To communicate the love of God, we will have to suffer, in small ways and utterly unimaginable ones. The crux of our faith—the Cross—reminds us that Christ gave His life to bring us to that place where we are willing to die to ourselves so that another will live. We see His example, and, at least in a moment here and there, we commit our spirit, our breath to God.

"Our times are in His hands." We sacrifice our will, to do His.

And that's the heart of the matter.

SEPTEMBER 28

Everything your little heart desires

Jesus then took the loaves, gave thanks, and distributed to those who were seated as much as they wanted.

JOHN 6:11

... Simon ... offered them money and said, "Give me also this ability so that everyone on whom I lay my hands may receive the Holy Spirit." Peter answered: "May your money perish with you, because you thought you could buy the gift of God with money!"

ACTS 8:18-20

I once looked at people whom I considered spiritual, and wondered how they could "do without" some of the activities that seemed central to my life. Now that I seek God earnestly, I see that He doesn't give us everything we desire; He changes our desires.

I used to want money, fame, material goods—and once even prayed, in my superficial way, to have more of those things. Now I find richness in those moments when I know God and feel Him in my life, in knowing that every moment can be spent with Him.

Until recently, if I had been asked to tell the story of the loaves and fishes—of Jesus feeding the five thousand—I would've said that he took the young boy's gifts and multiplied them. But now I realize that nothing in this passage says that Jesus multiplied the food; it says only that those who were there had as much as they wanted. Today I understand that, in changing a life, God doesn't always bring more food to the table.

Sometimes He just takes away the hunger.

HOLY ORDINARY

SEPTEMBER 29

Some assembly required

But a Samaritan . . . took pity on him. He went to him and bandaged his wounds . . . and took care of him. . . ." Which of these three do you think was a neighbor to the man who fell into the hands of robbers?" The expert in the law replied, "The one who had mercy on him." Jesus told him, "Go and do likewise."

LUKE 10:25-37

When a major auto manufacturer opened nearby, a place employing thousands of people assembling cars, I couldn't wait to tour the plant. I couldn't wait to see something that begins as nothing more than a frame to be built, piece by piece, until it can be driven away.

As Christians, we ask God, "Make me holy as your Son is holy." But when it comes down to the nuts and bolts of becoming like Him and building the kingdom, we balk. I want to be with God, not with some beaten and bloodied stranger in a ditch.

But truly being with God requires uncomfortable and often unappealing day-to-day investments of time and care. It requires caring for the wounded man along the way, even if we don't "care for" him. It requires allowing ourselves to be helped out of the ditch. It requires absolute, unconditional, across-the-board loving of other human beings as ourselves, not finding the loopholes to love a little less or prosper a little more.

And if we take on the name of Christ, yet pass by a hurting stranger, that stranger may feel much more than just unloved.

He may be driven away.

SEPTEMBER 30

My most grievous fault

Out of the depths I cry to you, O Lord . . . I wait for the Lord, my soul waits, and in his word I put my hope.

PSALM 130:1,5

Earthquakes rattle our world when tectonic plates deep within the earth change position. The shift produces stress in rock, which is forced into sudden jolts. On the surface, bridges and roadways collapse, buildings crumble, and life becomes chaos, all from shifts in a fault line miles under the surface.

Faith experiences move us when values and perspectives shift deep within us. My "fault line" lay in trying to intellectualize a power that can only be understood with the soul and the heart. Fissures ran deep when I thought I must manage life on my own, only to learn that help is as close as a whispered prayer. The great quake in my soul came when I realized that a relationship with God required only my assent, that He was waiting and ready for me.

A shift of that magnitude had to translate into changes visible on the surface. Many people say that, when their faith in God takes a quantum leap, others note a perceptible, physical change.

Now I frequently hear comments about changes in my appearance. I "have a glow" about me. A checkout clerk called me a "happy soul." A friend whom I hadn't seen lately asked if I had fallen in love.

When my smile seemed to affirm her guess, she said, "Do I know him?"

I hope you do, my friend. I hope you do.

October

OCTOBER 1

Room to forgive

His lightning lights up the world; the earth sees and trembles. The mountains melt like wax before the Lord, before the Lord of all the earth.

PSALM 97:4

I have a friend who is always perfectly groomed, always organized, with a beautiful home, one that welcomes with warmth and style. Then there's that one room . . .

In her home office, it looks like a bomb went off—files, documents, quotes, addresses, phone numbers. She could close the door and not think about it, but that doesn't fix anything. In the back of her mind is the constant thought she must do something about it. So physically, it's stationary, but emotionally it follows her wherever she goes.

I have places in my heart that I'm still afraid to go—fears unexpressed, even to God, or myself. I have shadows of emotions, of relationships, of doubts I'm too frightened to confront. Mistakes remain unforgiven, not by God, but by me.

I close the door and try to think about the other bright and warm rooms of my life, but sometimes all I can think about is what's in that room. I know I need to do something about it, so it invades the rest of my life.

I trust God; I trust His power. I believe that He literally can melt mountains like wax, that He can make the earth tremble. I know that He can make all of my disorder and resentment disappear instantly. Instead, I close the door, because I am so weak.

There are still places in my heart I'm afraid to go.

Love that stoops and rescues

Also a dispute arose among them as to which of them was considered to be greatest. Jesus said to them, "The kings of the Gentiles lord it over them; and those who exercise authority over them call themselves Benefactors. But you are not to be like that. Instead, the greatest among you should be like the youngest, and the one who rules like the one who serves. For who is greater, the one who is at the table or the one who serves? Is it not the one who is at the table? But I am among you as one who serves.

LUKE 22:24-27

My yoga teacher showed me that the practice of yoga requires both flexibility and strength. As does life. Her words brought to mind a hauntingly beautiful quotation that says, "Grace is love that stoops and rescues."

Gods of other religions may be flexible—the spiritual version of "If it feels good, do it." And gods of other religions may be strong, but without the element of humanity, those gods know nothing of hurting, or weeping, of dancing, of desperately wanting solace through a torturous and fear-filled night. And while I hesitate to use the word "flexible" to apply to God, I do picture His bending over to touch us with His Son while other gods hover aloft, out of man's reach.

Our God, the God who sent Jesus Christ to us, understands our humanity, yet has the power to gather us into His arms. And how can a human heart fail to be touched and empowered by a God who, out of pure and unconditional love, sacrifices His immortality to feel, and then to heal, our pain?

In His grace, He stoops. By His strength, He rescues.

OCTOBER 3

Liberation

"Never again will they hunger; never again will they thirst. . . . For the Lamb at the center of the throne will be their shepherd; he will lead them to springs of living water. . . ."

REVELATION 7:16-17

In an interview, Holocaust survivor Elie Wiesel once spoke of his father's death in the concentration camp, saying, "Since my father died, I was not there." Wiesel also described the American soldiers who liberated the camp as, "the first free persons to look into hell," seeing the tragic hollowness of humans deprived of food, water, dignity.

We think of such imprisonment as distant in either time or place, but people today often become captives in other ways. They become tied to stressful but empty jobs, unmanageable credit loads, family crises, addictions, with no outlet to satisfy the hunger and thirst for the presence of God.

We Christians are the free persons who "look into hell," as we watch friends and family pursue material success and human relationships that can never truly fill them. Every Christian carries in his heart the power to liberate the prisoners, to lead them to "springs of living water."

By clearly making the presence of God the focus of our lives, we open the gate and show those prisoners what the free world looks like. We feed them with the love of our God, who gave us His Son as our gate to eternal life.

The Father who says, "Since my Son died, I am there."

OCTOBER 4

Devaluation

*... The earth is filled with your love, O Lord; teach me your decrees
... The law from your mouth is more precious to me than thousands of
pieces of silver and gold. ...*

PSALM 119:54, 72

When I visited Turkey, I received a small coin which equaled 100,000 Turkish lira but was worth less than 25 American cents. The economy had been even worse earlier, when one American dollar equaled 950,000 lira. Technically, I had enough in my pocket to be a Turkish millionaire. Practically speaking I couldn't buy much.

Many people spiritually have pockets full of devalued currency, but empty lives from chasing all the wrong things. We Christians have to show them how they can be rich beyond measure by opening their hands to accept the unconditional love of God. We have to show those who don't yet understand how powerfully God works in and changes our lives.

A line in the musical *Les Misérables* says, "To love another human is to see the face of God." As we Christians show glimpses of our precious God to others, to love another human is also to *be* the face of God. The kindness and help we show someone today may be the only glimpse of God they've had in a long time.

So why cling to those other worthless coins when I could look at another human and see the face of God, or love another human and be the face of God? We can't just love people who are rich, like us.

We have to help the poor.

OCTOBER 5

Definition of terms

... Suppose a brother or sister is without clothes and daily food. If one of you says to him, "Go, I wish you well; keep warm and well fed," but does nothing about his physical needs, what good is it? In the same way, faith by itself, if it is not accompanied by action, is dead. ...

JAMES 2:15-17

When I was in eighth grade, a teacher asked our class to define the word "fatal," and one of my friends said it meant "serious." When the teacher said, "Actually, it describes something that kills you," my buddy said, "Well, that's pretty serious."

As Christians we throw around buzzwords and expect people to understand what we know in our hearts. We talk about faith, Good News, salvation, but it can sound so fluffy and meaningless, so impractical. We talk about "Good News," for example, and then judge people in the name of religion, which sounds distinctly like bad news to me. We talk about being saved, then forget about all the other lives out there that still need saving.

So what does the "Good News" mean when you're hurt or hungry or cold or grieving? It means that I, in God's name, will reach out to heal, feed, warm, soothe you. It means that you are never alone; I am here with you, and God is here with both of us. It means that you need no longer fear death, because we become part of God and go on living forever.

We live forever, my friend, my loved one. Forever.

And that's pretty serious.

World peace

Jesus called out with a loud voice, "Father, into your hands I commit my spirit." When he had said this, he breathed his last.

LUKE 23:46

Movies and sitcoms which spoof beauty pageants frequently show contestants being asked in interviews what they hope for most. Each woman answers sweetly, "world peace."

Unfortunately, many people wishing for world peace don't even believe that peace can come to their own hearts for one day. Yet in one of the most moving passages in the Gospels, Jesus breathes His last words, "Father into your hands, I commit my spirit." And even though we're reading those words thousands of years later, we can almost hear the stillness, the peace, of that moment.

God asks us, in much smaller ways, to breathe those words each day of our lives. If I could say every day, with conviction, "Father, into your hands I commit my spirit," then peace would come to this heart, this day. I would know that every difficult choice was made with my spirit in God's hands. If, during one day, I made each decision in prayer, thinking of God first instead of myself, then peace would come, at least to this one person.

Perhaps the road to world peace is one taken in the smallest of steps, for each person to invite, and to obey, God's will for one day. In other words, the elusive "world peace" may have to be built one human heart at a time.

So today, Father, into your hands I commit my spirit.

OCTOBER 7

The Promised Land

When the Lord your God brings you into the land he swore to your fathers, to Abraham, Isaac and Jacob . . . a land with . . . wells you did not dig, and vineyards . . . you did not plant—then when you eat and are satisfied, be careful that you do not forget the Lord, who brought you out of Egypt, out of the land of slavery.

DEUTERONOMY 6:10-12

Each time I drive home to visit family, I love to see the sign that reads, "The people of Illinois welcome you." It's a reminder that the warmth and comfort and joy found in any state come not from geography, but from personal relationship.

And the beauty of the Promised Land, offered to Abraham, Isaac, Jacob—and to me—is not a matter of more territory, more water, more food, but of more constant communication with God. It's not a place I may "someday" reach, but a state I can choose to inhabit now.

I reach the Promised Land each time I choose to stand on God's side of the line rather than on my own side, or on this world's side. I fulfill His Promise each time I put God ahead of worldly worry, material gain, even this human life. I live His Promise every time I love when I could hurt back, when I forgive and move on, when I heal a wounded heart instead of adding to the pain.

Such gifts come from God, with the territory of the Promised Land, if only I will accept and use them. You see, ultimately, it's not really the Promised Land I'm interested in seeing, anyway.

But the One who gave the Promise.

OCTOBER 8

Let the river run

These are the words of him who is holy and true, who holds the key of David. What he opens no one can shut, and what he shuts no one can open. I know your deeds. See, I have placed before you an open door that no one can shut. . . .

REVELATION 3:7-8

In college, a bunch of us girls decided to go "body-surfing" on a swift little river near campus. We pointed our feet downriver and let the current float us to a safe stopping place, then walked upriver and did it all again.

Though water scares me, I was fine until the current carried me farther downstream than I intended. I panicked when I saw I couldn't swim upstream to my safe place. Finally I let the current carry me on down to where the water calmed and I could reach shore safely.

God sometimes sweeps me away because He needs me to grow. I get complacent with my spiritual life, thinking with great satisfaction of all the things I do "for God." If I had my choice, I would stay in familiar territory, but then I wouldn't become the person He wants me to be. So He moves me along, away from my "safe place," until I trust Him and remember that He is my safe place.

If I stay in my comfort zone, I'll see only one piece of the river, and God has so much more for me than I envision for myself. And as much as that next piece of water scares me, I want to be where God wants me, not where I'm the most comfortable.

So now the river doesn't seem to stop here anymore.

HOLY ORDINARY 305

OCTOBER 9

Precious mettle

Since an overseer is entrusted with God's work, he must be . . . one who loves what is good, who is self-controlled, upright, holy and disciplined.

TITUS 1:7-8

In Paulo Coelho's allegory *The Alchemist*, a young boy learns of the sorcerer's stone, said to turn any substance into gold. He is told by his teacher, though, that instead of seeking only gold, it is better to ask everything and everyone to evolve into a higher form, because the world needs more than gold. The man encourages him to seek to evolve as highly as he can, because others around him will then be drawn to improve themselves.

Our society seems stuck in a rut of searching for a sorcerer's stone, a way to turn everything into worldly success. We want the magic substance that allows us to turn everything into "gold." But is gold really what we want? In many of life's moments and tasks, gold is absolutely useless. Gold does not make a good nail or hammer. Gold is not edible. Gold is ineffectual in drying a tear. Embracing gold is a cold way to get through a dark night.

God needs all types of metal—and mettle—to accomplish His purposes. When we seek Him first, we immediately help draw others nearer to Him through our self-control, our uprightness, our holiness. Then, perhaps, all around us will begin to evolve toward Him, to seek something higher. But our first job is to "love what is good."

Not what is gold.

OCTOBER 10

The Son also raises

" 'This is what the Sovereign Lord says: . . . you, my people, will know that I am the Lord, when I open your graves and bring you up from them. I will put my Spirit in you and you will live. . .' "

EZEKIEL 37:12-14

One of my high school English teachers, Mrs. Westray, used to tell us impatiently, "Crops are raised; children are reared." She would hate knowing that nowadays it's considered acceptable usage to talk of raising crops *and* children.

One type of raising—raising from the dead—seems to be the major focus of many Christians trying to bring others to faith. Some emphasize almost exclusively the infinite consequences of failing to turn to God.

But God promised me not only that He would bring me up from the grave, but that He will "put His Spirit in me and I will live." Being with God isn't just a matter of changing the fact of death, but of raising the quality of life. Through my relationship with Him, God brings more equilibrium to my everyday human existence. His strength becomes my strength when crisis enters my life. His love becomes my love when it enters someone else's.

Certainly children of God can be, and are raised, every day. We're raised, not only from the grave, but up toward God even in the most ungodly circumstances. I know, because I'm part of a recent crop.

So my apologies to Mrs. Westray. But as a child of God and a follower of His Son, I have been raised.

And will be again.

HOLY ORDINARY

OCTOBER 11

Bread or burden

" 'Woe! Woe, O great city, where all who had ships on the sea became rich through her wealth! In one hour she has been brought to ruin! . . . The music of harpists and musicians, flute players and trumpeters, will never be heard in you again. No workman of any trade will ever be found in you again. The sound of a millstone will never be heard in you again. . . ."

REVELATION 18:19, 22

The so-called "Danforth lady" was a woman whose remains went unidentified for 40 years until a forensic artist reconstructed what the woman probably looked like. In the intervening time, no one had even known that there had been a victim.

Our world can be so anonymous. With our elaborate legal system and acute sense of self-interest, we can rationalize almost anything as acceptable, easily forgetting those who pay the price for our wealth, wealth which can be emotional as well as material. When I work hard to make myself look important, usually someone gets hurt, and often those victims go unnamed.

Intelligence, talent, and other resources can be used to tend or to destroy. A millstone grinds the grain or hangs around the neck. And God lets me choose whether I will use my millstone to help feed the hungry, or will simply lay it on an unnamed victim as dead weight. The victims, or those who benefit, may go unidentified. But I know exactly the identity of the one who decides how my millstone will be used.

That would be me.

OCTOBER 12

Who would know?

Tax collectors also came to be baptized. "Teacher," they asked, "what should we do?" "Don't collect any more than you are required to," he told them. Then some soldiers asked him, "And what should we do?" He replied, "Don't extort money and don't accuse people falsely—be content with your pay."

LUKE 3:12-14

With the fall of Baghdad in 2003, liberated citizens went looting, and coalition soldiers were accused of stealing money found in the vacated buildings. But the property belonged to murderers, and was almost certainly collected by illegal and immoral means. So what would it hurt to take a few hundred thousand dollars, or the belongings of those enforcing a despotic regime?

But even world-class rationalization crumbles before the merciful yet unflinchingly righteous presence of God. Followers of John the Baptist asked how they, ordinary folk, should act after their baptism, and he told them simply to do their jobs with the presence of God in their hearts.

Good and evil aren't measured by the probability of being caught, or by the moral fiber of the victim. Sin is never solely perpetrated on the victim; it is an assault on God.

When a person chooses to do something good, God celebrates at the being He made in His image. When a person chooses to do evil, God mourns the being He made in His image.

Who would know if I did this one dishonest thing? Who would know?

God knows. And God weeps.

HOLY ORDINARY

OCTOBER 13

Take a deep breath

This is what the Lord says: Be careful not to carry a load on the Sabbath day or bring it through the gates of Jerusalem . . . but keep the Sabbath day holy. . . .

JEREMIAH 17:21-22

In chronic obstructive pulmonary disease, or COPD, air cannot flow out of the lungs effectively, so "used" air takes up space and prevents oxygen-rich air from entering. The disease, a leading cause of death in the U.S., often goes undiagnosed; as one doctor said, "One gets a sense that people are too accepting of their disease."

The human mind, body, and soul can be frighteningly adaptive. We learn to limp instead of getting well. We sit in church, thinking it's enough just to go through the motions, when God longs to revive us with His own rich and life-giving breath. We hold toxic resentment, anger, self-righteousness in our hearts, leaving no room for Him. We become accepting of our disease.

When God asks us not to "carry a load" on the Sabbath, He isn't only asking us to forgo work one day a week. He asks us to leave animosity at the gate, to expel all "loads" that separate us from others, and from Him. He asks us to find holiness in all circumstances, in all persons, to purge the stale air from our souls. To have room for Him.

I refuse to adapt to the superficiality of this world, to simply "get by." I refuse to become accepting of my disease. I want it all: to live holy, and wholly, in Him.

I want to take a deep breath again.

Deep voice

For since the creation of the world God's invisible qualities—his eternal power and divine nature—have been clearly seen, being understood from what has been made. . . .

ROMANS 1:20

In the Baroque music of the 1600s, a practice called "basso continuo" developed, in which all parts of a piece were built on the bass line, the lowest musical part. After composition of the bass line—the "rock" on which the piece was based—the other parts were improvised around it.

While I acknowledge man's sinful nature—especially my own—I firmly believe that our lives as Christians are composed as "basso continuo," that our essence is that of the deepest voice. Before we were sinful, before we wandered, we were made in the image of God.

The profound ache for something more, the innermost peace after a difficult decision, the tears that come when another feels loved—all are the deepest echoes of God's presence. Taken alone, life's circumstances make little sense. But with God at the base, pain and joy, exuberance and disappointment, love and fear, all express and ring out with God's voice in this troubled world.

Before all else, I am of God—of His essence, His creation, His expression, His love. I am made to resonate with His beautifully moving and life-changing music. I am here to listen for, and to harmonize with, the deepest voice, the highest call.

I am made to be like Him.

OCTOBER 15

A measure of hope

For no one can lay any foundation other than the one already laid, which is Jesus Christ. If any man builds on this foundation using gold, silver, costly stones, wood, hay, or straw, his work will be shown for what it is, because the Day will bring it to light.

1 CORINTHIANS 3:11-13

A week and a half after the terrorist attacks of September 11, 2001, CNN reported with senseless precision that 59,982 tons of debris had been hauled away from the World Trade Center site.

Humans love numbers that measure activity, even meaningless activity. We counted trucks because we could not get our minds to accept that we were finding no life. No one wanted to hear the number zero, the total number of survivors found after the first 48 hours. We just feel more productive when we can measure what has been done, even if we're only measuring degrees of hopelessness.

Inventorying rubble leaving the site of disaster is just the crisis-mode version of what we do every day before God. When we find no sign of life, we're quick to point out all the things we have done. I went to church. I gave my ten percent. I helped build houses for the poor. I served the homeless breakfast on Thanksgiving Day. I never hurt anyone. Doesn't that count for something?

But God, our Father, reminds us that only one measure counts. Do you love—deeply, completely, selflessly—as my Son did? Do you love?

It's the only thing they cannot haul away.

Light

"What do you want me to do for you?" he asked. "Lord," they answered, "we want our sight." Jesus had compassion on them and touched their eyes. Immediately they received their sight and followed him.

MATTHEW 20:32-34

One day in grade school, our teacher explained the difference between "invention" and "discovery." Thomas Edison invented the lightbulb, because it had never existed before. But Ben Franklin discovered electricity when he went out in that storm and flew a kite. Electricity had always existed, but it had remained untapped.

My life changed irrevocably, not because of invention, but because of discovery. I "discovered" God, and accepted His grace, a priceless force that existed before time. I finally tapped into the gift offered to each human being through the life and death of Jesus Christ. And since that discovery of God, my life has been electrified.

I journeyed all those years, thinking I had to invent a spiritual life myself, when God was simply waiting for me to discover the dreams He had for me. Like the blind men who met Jesus, I couldn't see Him, even when He was right in front of me. In His compassion, though, He gave me my sight, and I began to follow Him.

Now, with this newfound vision, I "discover" God everywhere. I discover that His Light and power can enter the bleakest day, the darkest heart, the most frightening place.

All because one Man went out into the storm.

OCTOBER 17

You should meet my Father

I no longer call you servants, because a servant does not know his master's business. . . . I have called you friends, for everything that I learned from my Father I have made known to you.

JOHN 15:15

My college friends have endured throughout my adult life, because we did everything together: meals, double-dates, classes, vacation. But I felt I understood those friends even better when I had been to their hometowns and met their families.

I certainly felt closer to my college roommate after visiting her hometown. She shared with me the places of her life—the house where she grew up, her school, her church. I met people who had helped her through tragic, difficult times. I helped her avoid the guy she had dated in high school. Our friendship grew stronger because I had a precious glimpse of her roots.

And she had a deeper understanding of me after she met my family, especially my dad.

Whenever she groaned at a bad pun or smart-aleck remark, I no longer had to say, "You should meet my father. He's the master." Even now, years after my dad's death, I often find myself wishing more of my friends could have met him.

The "new me," my reinvented Christian self, longs for others to see how deeply God affects me, too. The cross I wear around my neck declares, "I'm a Christian." It defines who I am, and how I try to live my life."

But you really should meet my Father. He's the Master.

A re-formed Christian

. . . says the Lord . . . "See, it is I who created the blacksmith who fans the coals into flame and forges a weapon fit for its work."

ISAIAH 54:16

In the movie *The Patriot,* Benjamin Martin only joins the militia because a coldhearted British officer murders one of his young sons. He later becomes a hero, but arrives there quite reluctantly.

When Martin leaves home to fight, he carries a sackful of his dead son's toy lead soldiers, later melting each one down to make a musket ball for his rifle. Fire reduces the painted toys to basic lead to be re-formed into weapons of war.

I wonder what God will form me into next. I'm certainly not someone who clearly hears God's voice directing my life. In fact, I often worry that I'm drawn to work more by my desires than by His will.

How do I tell the difference? Has he given me talents and passion for jobs because He needs me to do them? Or do I conveniently use that to pursue my will instead of His? What will it take for me to declare one day, with confidence, "I know what God wants me to do"? What will it take?

I think God sticks me in the fire occasionally so that I can be reconstituted into a tool "fit for its work." I suspect my only job is to purify the substance of my life, so that He can put it in the right form. Who could have ever guessed that I'd ever amount to more than just another toy soldier?

I never dreamed I'd fight in the real war.

OCTOBER 19

Going up

Since my people are crushed, I am crushed; I mourn, and horror grips me. Is there no balm in Gilead? Is there no physician there? Why then is there no healing for the wound of my people?

JEREMIAH 8:21-22

Scientists discovered in Italy a set of footprints that they believed to be about 350,000 years old. The tracks were made by three humans descending the treacherous slope of a volcano, probably to flee a volcanic eruption.

That urge to run away from powerful and uncontrollable forces which exist up the mountain is described time and again in the Bible. Jeremiah talks in this passage about how he mourns for his people, who continually run away from the power of God. But it's often very difficult to give crises, fears, or grieving completely over to God.

One of my greatest faith struggles is the question of why, if God is all-powerful and all-loving, He even allows some tragedies to occur. Like Jeremiah, I myself have wondered, "Is there no physician there?"

I know eruptions—crises—are coming for me; I already hear the rumbling. I just pray, that amid the noise and the haste, I don't run down the mountain, lowering myself to the level of frightened and defensive humanity, but up into the presence of God. I hope I can heed His voice instead of all the others.

God, give me your strength to get through this frighteningly human day.

Help me rise above it.

OCTOBER 20

Tools and weapons

But I tell you that men will have to give account on the day of judgment for every careless word they have spoken. For by your words you will be acquitted, and by your words you will be condemned.

MATTHEW 12:36-37

Sometimes it's hard to distinguish between tools and weapons.

You can use a hammer to construct a house, or to deliver the blows that destroy it. A screwdriver, designed to build and repair, becomes a weapon when sharpened and carried into the darkness. In the same way, a word can be soothing enough to heal someone's soul or sharp enough to pierce it fatally.

Many people today find it difficult to say, "I love you" because past experiences have made it unclear whether the expression is a tool or a weapon. Those three words may have been wielded to manipulate them into unhealthy circumstances, or opened them to unnecessary pain. Other people who are casualties of those words have seen too many situations in which the words speak of love but the actions speak of indifference or intolerance or manipulation, or sometimes even of hate.

God has given us marvelous gifts of communication: the abilities to listen and to counsel and to exhort and to cleanse. But those same gifts could also be used to criticize and mock and discourage and shame.

It's my decision. To pick up a weapon—and destroy. Or pick up a tool—and build.

HOLY ORDINARY 317

OCTOBER 21

Jump

As the time approached for him to be taken up to heaven, Jesus resolutely set out for Jerusalem. And he sent messengers on ahead, who went into a Samaritan village . . . but the people there did not welcome him. . . . When the disciples . . . saw this, they asked, "Lord, do you want us to call fire down from heaven to destroy them?" But Jesus turned and rebuked them. . . .

LUKE 9:51-55

The Perfect Storm is a fictionalized account of boats caught at sea when major storm systems collided. In it, as a rescuer was lowered from a helicopter into a sailboat, the pilot tells him, "We can't go any lower. You gotta jump from here!"

I picture just such a gap between the life of faith in oneself and the life of faith in God. We cling to lifelines and comfort zones, but at some point we have to commit to God. Jesus "resolutely set out for Jerusalem," knowing He would soon return to heaven,

His disciples claimed they would follow Him anywhere. But though they said they wanted to go with God, they also wanted to reserve the option of human vengefulness.

Many of us seekers claim to follow God, but sometimes we can't resist the urge to make threats in His name. And we straddle the world of man and the world of God, hoping for a sign, some absolute proof, that our lives should be in His hands alone. But at some point, He can't "go any lower." We have to have faith, to leave our humanness behind.

We have to jump from here.

OCTOBER 22

In the presence of our God

May the Lord make your love increase and overflow for each other and for everyone else, just as ours does for you. May he strengthen your hearts so that you will be blameless and holy in the presence of our God and Father when our Lord Jesus comes with all his holy ones.
1 THESSALONIANS 3:12-13

After the terror attacks of 2001, I heard a great deal about the terrorist alert system, which assigns a level of urgency to the threat of terrorist activity. I still wonder what to do when that status rises. Do I travel less? Avoid crowds? Become more vigilant about strangers?

Then I think about that dreadful fall day when people faced disaster in a much more immediate way. Some of them helped crash an airliner to save other lives. Some sacrificed themselves to get others out before the towers collapsed.

Many of those heroes, looking their own destruction squarely in the eye, made phone calls to parents, spouses, children simply to say three life-giving words: "I love you."

All of us will face an earthly end. But all I can do is live for God. Then, when the "terrorist warning" level rises, I'll do exactly what so many people did September 11, 2001. I will try to save the others. And I will make sure people know how much I love them.

In other words, the two things I should have been doing all along.

OCTOBER 23

At the small table

... we pray this in order that you may live a life worthy of the Lord ... : bearing fruit in every good work, growing in the knowledge of God, being strengthened with all power according to his glorious might so that you may have great endurance and patience, and joyfully giving thanks to the Father. ...

COLOSSIANS 1:10-12

One relaxing Saturday at a bookstore I saw a young father—big, athletic—squeeze into the small chairs at a children's table to read and play with his son and daughter. Perhaps, when those children themselves become parents, they will remember the magic of having dad sit down at their level just to be with them.

God knows that in our deepest, widest, most electrifying dreams we cannot possibly understand His love for us. So through the humanity of Christ, He stoops to sit with us at the tiny children's table, to enter our small earthly lives and give us a glimpse of Him. He gives us strength to get through everyday tough spots. He infuses us with His patience, His endurance, as the unloved and unlovable of this world reach out to us for help.

Someday, as we remember how it felt to see God at our small table, we may pass such tender care on to His other children, and to our own. For today, the deep and profoundly moving things of God are beyond us, so we must be content with living an earthly life worthy of Him.

Tomorrow, perhaps, this table will look small even to us.

OCTOBER 24

Saving the heard

An argument developed between some of John's disciples and a certain Jew over the matter of ceremonial washing. They came to John and said to him, "Rabbi, that man who was with you on the other side of the Jordan—the one you testified about—well, he is baptizing, and everyone is going to him."

JOHN 3:25-26

The CNN web page once ran a teaser on an upcoming story, saying "A terrible disease threatens to destroy one of nature's most beautiful creatures. What can be done to save the heard?" In that typographical error, I saw the story of this Scripture passage. "What can be done to save the heard?"

The tragic irony of religion is that it tries to fit heaven into the confining compartments of earth. People who consider themselves the most religious—the "heard"—are often the ones farthest from understanding what God wants from us. They want to debate ceremonial washing when prophets long to speak of a cleansing that could put us in heaven, here and now.

Does God become frustrated with us when we work so hard to make Him fit our small imaginations, our small dreams, our small hearts? He beckons us to "go to Him," and we agonize over narrow religious rituals: how we will worship, and where, and when. Why spend our time focusing on this world when we could be talking with God, and of Him? Why remain bound to earth when we could be bound for heaven?

What can be done to save the heard?

HOLY ORDINARY 321

OCTOBER 25

Taking away

In that day the Branch of the Lord will be beautiful and glorious, and the fruit of the land will be the pride and glory of the survivors in Israel. Those who are left in Zion, who remain in Jerusalem, will be called holy. . . .

ISAIAH 4:2-3

One of our guides in Italy suggested that sculpture is the only art form created by taking something away rather than adding. In the same way, each of us Christian believers becomes God's work of art through subtraction rather than addition.

But art can only be created by the steady, loving hand of God, not by the hand of man. We cannot be left to our own devices to decide what will be taken away and what will remain in our lives. I would have chosen to take away the pain, to leave my loved ones. I would have taken away the hunger, leaving a deadly complacency. I would have taken away the need for others, which would have disguised my need for God.

Every human life holds pain. But the human life which finds its meaning in God also finds meaning in the pain. When God shapes us through our suffering, dependency on other humans is taken away. Self-reliance is taken away. The instinct to judge is taken away.

Ultimately, under the hand of God, His chosen people survive, and pure holiness remains. And so God, like the sculptor, creates art by taking away.

The chisel is positioned. The hammer falls. The masterpiece emerges.

The form of the risen Christ.

OCTOBER 26

Fusion

As Jesus was on his way, the crowds almost crushed him. And a woman was there who had been subject to bleeding for twelve years. . . . She came up behind him and touched the edge of his cloak, and immediately her bleeding stopped.

LUKE 8:42-44

As the 21st century opened, scientists hoped to achieve thermonuclear fusion, the process that powers the sun, and to harness it as a source of energy. Fusion, the combining of atoms, is much safer than fission, the splitting of atoms, because it does not produce long-lasting, deadly radioactive waste.

The woman who slipped up behind Jesus sought His power, but couldn't deal with more fallout. Cast aside as unclean in her illness for years, she somehow knew that fusing with Jesus, even touching His garment, might bring her healing.

Yet the beauty of the Christian faith is that we needn't be satisfied with the anonymity of a crowd, but have a God who stops, touches, heals. I don't want a God at a distance; I want Jesus, the God sensitive enough to stop for me, to heal me. Don't give me public miracles, but personal wholeness. Don't tell me about a Man who can feed five thousand unless He can stop long enough to feed me.

I want a God who offers, and teaches, compassion, personal touch, tenderness. I want a God who knows, and heals, me. I want my touch, eventually, to be the touch of such a Man, of such a God. I want fusion with Him.

I want the same process that powers the Son.

OCTOBER 27

Holy weak

... Paul answered, "Why are you weeping and breaking my heart? I am ready not only to be bound, but also to die in Jerusalem for the name of the Lord Jesus." When he would not be dissuaded, we gave up and said, "The Lord's will be done."

ACTS 21:13-14

The Greek state of Sparta existed almost solely to fight wars; everything in their society revolved around that goal. Newborn Spartan babies were examined; strong, healthy ones were allowed to live to become warriors, and weak ones were "exposed," left in a mountain chasm to die.

In physical battle, strength certainly is an advantage, but in spiritual battles, weakness can be used equally effectively by God. Paul had been weak, not knowing in his early life about the true God, and even working to persecute Christians. Yet, armed with God's spirit, Paul would become one of His greatest warriors, not just willing, but anxious to give His life to God.

Spiritually, I have found myself in those mountain chasms, too weak to survive this world alone. I have been without hope or strength. I have hurt and have been hurt, and failed to forgive. I have doubted God's will, and I have run from it.

Yet God pulled me to Him so that I could draw His warmth, His Spirit, His strength, and go out to do His battles. From that coldest, darkest, most vulnerable place, I learned that God can't just use me in spite of my weakness.

He can use me *because* of it.

OCTOBER 28

Buy the Way

One day Peter and John were going up to the temple. . . . Now a man crippled from birth . . . saw Peter and John about to enter, [and] he asked them for money. Peter . . . said, "Look at us!" So the man gave them his attention, expecting to get something from them.

ACTS 3:1-5

When I took marketing in college, we learned to sell benefits, not features. Features describe how a product works, but benefits describe the value a product holds for the customer.

People outside the church mostly hear about the features of Christianity, but see no benefits: too little evidence of changed lives, too little focus on God, too little welcoming, too little love. As Christians, if we emphasize the feature of knowing we are forgiven, then we must forgive. If we emphasize the mercy of God's judgment, then we must let Him judge. If we say that God is love, then we must love.

When others look at us and "expect to get something from us," what do they get: a community seeking God, or a community of self-appointed judges and critics? Do they sense the presence of God, or the presence of self-righteousness, judgmentalism, unforgiveness, hypocrisy?

When we say, as Peter did, "Look at us!" we have to let others see peace, forgiveness, strength, love—all the benefits we find in God. When we stop selling the features and start living the benefits, perhaps eventually they'll stop looking at us at all.

And they'll find themselves looking at Him.

HOLY ORDINARY

OCTOBER 29

Blessed peace

Suddenly there was such a violent earthquake that the foundations of the prison were shaken. At once all the prison doors flew open, and everybody's chains came loose.

ACTS 16:26

A journalist described the end to Angola's long-raging civil war as a "negative peace," an absence of conflict, but one without justice or opportunity. Still, though, as an official told the people, "You are no longer refugees. You are Angolans."

Civil war rages in the human soul when priorities cannot be reconciled or roles conflict. For many of us, an earth-shattering change is necessary to make us examine those priorities and roles and to set them straight with God. And when peace does come, it is initially an uneasy, negative peace.

Not that long ago, I settled for that "negative peace;" nothing was visibly shaking, but nothing was on solid ground, either. I was imprisoned by flawed choices, flawed relationships, flawed priorities. When the earth moved, and my world fell apart, the chains came loose, and I found God. Nothing less would have brought me to Him.

God doesn't wish for us to have negative peace—a simple absence of conflict. He wants us to know blessed peace, the unshakable understanding that we are His, and that He holds us and protects us from war, civil and otherwise. The walls have been shaken; we are no longer refugees from our own choices. We are children of God.

And we are free.

OCTOBER 30

Door number One

Love the Lord your God with all your heart and with all your soul and with all your strength. These commandments that I give you today are to be upon your hearts. . . . Write them on the doorframes of your houses and on your gates.

DEUTERONOMY 6:4-9

In college I heard the following riddle. Suppose there are two doors facing you, a man sitting in front of each one. Behind one door is heaven and behind the other is hell. One of the men is good and always tells the truth; the other is evil and always lies. The truth-teller is not necessarily sitting in front of the "good" door, nor is the liar necessarily in front of the evil door. What one question can you ask that will help you identify the good door?

We constantly face such choices, some mundane, some grave, often with no clue which choice brings joy and growth and which one brings desperation and destruction. Something that appears as positive opportunity may tear us down. Circumstances that we think may destroy us work later to lift us closer to God. Which door is which?

In the Jewish faith, these words from Deuteronomy are placed above the doorway of each home as a reminder that God is above us constantly. We Christians, too, are supposed to remember that He is always above us, that He is our first love, our first counselor, our first line of defense.

Heaven is being with God; hell is separation from Him. So remembering Him always writes His name above every door we enter.

And every door becomes a door to heaven.

HOLY ORDINARY 327

OCTOBER 31

The princess and the Power Ranger

"Sacrifice thank offerings to God, fulfill your vows to the Most High, and call upon me in the day of trouble; I will deliver you, and you will honor me."

PSALM 50:14-15

One Halloween, as I worked in my office, a man who works in our building brought his two small children by. They were dressed in their Halloween costumes: a little "princess" of about 5, and a 7-year-old Power Ranger.

The children carried plastic pumpkins with candy in them, and I panicked momentarily when I saw them because I had nothing to give them. But then they said, "Trick or treat" and offered their candy to me. It was one of the most poignant experiences of my life.

That day I had the same sensation that I often have when I think of all that God has done for me. I know that I am supposed to live for Him, to "sacrifice thank offerings" to Him, and usually I don't do a very good job of it. Then, just as I struggle, as I wonder what to offer Him, He gives me even more. He shows me, by His example, that love is not a transaction, but a gift. Love is a *gift*.

God doesn't wonder what He will receive in return when He offers gifts. He does exactly what I should do, in my relationship with Him and in my relationships with other people: He loves without expectation of a return on the investment. He brings gifts to all of us who should be making sacrifices to Him. In other words, He simply loves.

He's the sweetest gift of all.

November

NOVEMBER 1

Just us

...[Barnabas] ... encouraged them all to remain true to the Lord with all their hearts. He was a good man, full of the Holy Spirit and faith, and a great number of people were brought to the Lord.

ACTS 11:23

The History Channel once ran a program about America's founding fathers: Jefferson, Franklin, Washington. Ads for the show said, "They were not just icons; they were men." The implication is that to be an icon is less important and less difficult than to be a human being, especially in a position of power.

Jesus is God, but His humanity more than His divinity, and His goodness more than His greatness, transform my life. If He had been simply an icon, His life would have little bearing on the life of an ordinary human like me. But He was a good man whose love brought Him together with others when greatness could have distanced Him from them.

And later, other good men like Barnabas brought the people to God day in and day out by treating others with justice, mercy, tenderness. Not by being great, but by being good.

"Society," that faceless group, perhaps listens more to great men than to good ones. But human beings who need hope in their lives are much more likely to respond to goodness. And it's not a case of lowered expectations, but of heightened ones. We're called to be more than great, and we're certainly called to be much more than "just human."

We're called to be humans who are just.

NOVEMBER 2

Getting well

Filled with compassion, Jesus reached out his hand and touched the man. "I am willing," he said. "Be clean!"... Jesus could no longer enter a town openly but stayed outside in lonely places. Yet the people still came to him from everywhere.

MARK 1:41, 45

A movie called *Baby Boom* tells of a female account executive who leaves New York City to live on a Vermont farm. The house becomes a money pit; when the water stops working, the woman learns her well has run dry. She tells the plumber, "There's a hose out back. Why can't you just fill it up again?"

For years, I relied on manmade wells, convinced I could make things work. But illness entered my life. And death. Then despair. And when those inevitable visitors arrived, the wells of self-reliance, of legalism, of earthly comfort all ran dry.

Like me, the people who found healing with Jesus had to admit that their reservoir of strength could not handle disease, crisis, death. They had been dipping into the well of legalism, and found it empty when they needed true healing or genuine care. Then they saw the source of all healing, in Person, and they could not stay away.

That source of wholeness is right here, in our world, easily within our reach. He has already said, "I am willing," so it is clear that, in His grace, He wants to heal me. I can no longer walk away. My well has run dry.

Thank God, my well ran dry.

NOVEMBER 3

The light of day

In him was life, and that life was the light of men. The light shines in the darkness, but the darkness has not understood it.

JOHN 1:4-5

For centuries, sailors and explorers navigated by the stars. Today, we steer by the stars in more figurative ways; we're frequently exhorted to focus on a star, to fix our dreams upon it.

But some stars we see in the nighttime sky no longer exist. They have already burned out; they're just so distant that their last, dying rays of light haven't reached earth and our human eyes yet.

I once heard a woman speak about her life before God, an existence in which she alternated between prison time and drug use. Sadly, she said, at the time she never realized her life could be anything else. She thought she was headed toward a bright light, but the light she chose was extinguished, or never existed at all.

I understood exactly what she meant. Once, I thought my life was fine, but it wasn't a life at all. I had just a series of days—some good, some bad, depending on the day's entertainment. The star I followed—immediate gratification and diversion—looked good in the nighttime sky, but in reality it had no substance at all.

We're not steering through darkness; without God we are the darkness. But we need only look up at midday and count the visible stars to understand the power of God's light and God's love in our lives. When we allow his light—his Son—into our lives, our dying stars become irrelevant and we navigate in full daylight.

In that "true light," finally, we will find our way home.

NOVEMBER 4

Part-time Job

In all this, Job did not sin by charging God with wrongdoing.

JOB 1:22

On a road I often travel is a business sign that reads, "Barnett and Barnett." I thought, if two people share the same name—brothers, or father and son—then wouldn't it suffice to put the name on the sign or the business once? Yet we crave proof that we have gotten our share of credit, our share of ownership.

Like the people who want their names on the business sign, I often claim success for my own and only question God when the bad times come. I'm certainly no theologian, so I struggle with this issue. If God causes all the good things to happen, and He is all-powerful, then doesn't He cause the bad things, too?

And yet, I try (usually unsuccessfully) to follow Job's example, to not "charge God with wrongdoing." I don't know all the reasons behind God's work. I will never know why some things happen, good or bad.

But this much I know is true: since I invited God into my life, I have found peace. Since He entered my heart, I have found joy. As my relationship with Him has deepened, all of my human relationships have deepened. My gifts have been multiplied in His hands. My sorrows have been divided, and shared, and turned to good. Wonderful and poignant changes have blessed my life, and I know undeniably who owns that success, who gets the credit. I know whose name goes on that public sign.

God. And Son.

HOLY ORDINARY 333

NOVEMBER 5

No laws have been broken

And what does the Lord require of you? To act justly and to love mercy and to walk humbly with your God.

MICAH 6:8

When I was a teenager, my mom said that I could repaint my powder blue bedroom a more exciting color. But when my older sister and I went shopping, I impulsively decided to get fire-engine red instead of the teal that mom had approved. When mom got home from work, I thought she was going to kill us. We protested, "But you didn't say we couldn't paint it red!"

The adult version of that refrain is, "I haven't done anything illegal." I just found a way around the tax law, or a way to spin the facts to obscure the real truth, or did what everyone else is getting away with. God said "Thou shalt not steal," but He never mentioned pirating music from the Internet, copying software to avoid buying it, or letting the insurance company pay me a bit more than I'm owed.

But the words from Micah cover all of those "thou shalt nots" with a neat, tight little quilt of "thou shalts." The prophet says, "Act justly, show mercy, walk humbly with God." If my life contradicts those admonitions, I am not lucky to have gotten away with it, or incredibly clever, or officially blameless. I am *wrong*.

Sometimes I get tired of rationalizing before God and man that I have broken no law. And it may be true that the law remains unbroken.

But God's heart? That's another story.

NOVEMBER 6

The empty box

"If you are returning to the Lord with all your hearts, then rid yourselves of the foreign god . . . and commit yourselves to the Lord and serve him only, and he will deliver you. . . ."

1 SAMUEL 7:3

On a trip to Greece, one stop we made in the Aegean Sea was Mykonos, a beautiful blue-and-whitewashed place dotted with shops and restaurants. As we sat relaxing in a restaurant, a friend decided to show us a bracelet she had bought. But when she opened the box, she found it empty, and had to return to the shop to recover the jewelry she had paid for.

For years, I went to church, but didn't connect with a soul, including my own. I paid for a box called religion, expecting to find inside it all of the things we seek in God. Love when we feel unlovable. Forgiveness when we feel dirty and shameful. Comfort when the test results aren't so good.

The box I held in my hands was beautifully detailed, ornate with ritual, flowery words, uplifting music. But when I opened it, I found it empty, devoid of love, of commitment, of true joy.

The practice of religion can be one of those "foreign gods" that Samuel cautions us about. We serve our church or our religion with such zeal that God becomes almost a footnote, an afterthought. But I change disappointment into joy when I fill the box called religion until it overflows with God. It's a wonderful present to give someone.

A wonderful presence.

HOLY ORDINARY 335

NOVEMBER 7

Orientation

" 'As for those of you who are left, I will make their hearts so fearful in the lands of their enemies that the sound of a windblown leaf will put them to flight. . . .' "

LEVITICUS 26:36

A map used in the Middle Ages, called a T-O map, placed the east rather than the north at the map's top. In the map, a T lay within a circle, dividing the world into the three known continents. The top of the T was Jerusalem, because the world focused on Jesus Christ, on His world, His direction. The T symbolized Christ, arms outstretched on the cross, the world in His embrace.

We Christians return to that map, seeking to orient our world to Jesus. People who don't hear God's voice move constantly and find nothing, at the mercy of schedules, of material success, of appearances. "The sound of a windblown leaf will put them to flight," because their maps have no consistent orientation, no meaning, no stability. No God.

If I do not point my life towards God, then life becomes only what my tiny human imagination can make it. Orienting a life using God means that the possibilities for that life are endless. My world opens into His arms—into everything He can imagine for me. I leave behind the life of man, small, petty, mean, self-absorbed, and I open up my arms to accept the life of God. I am no longer chasing—or chased by—the wind, because I am pointed, always, toward Jesus.

I live my life in His embrace.

NOVEMBER 8

Unbelief

[Jesus said] "Everything is possible for him who believes." Immediately the boy's father exclaimed, "I do believe; help me overcome my unbelief!"

MARK 9:23-24

One day when my dad was trying to keep me busy, he taught me to peel the ultra-thin layer of foil away from the paper on the wrapper of a stick of chewing gum. He said that, when he was a boy, he would peel and save the pieces of foil until they were the size of a baseball, then sell them to the scrap man for candy money. It was hard for me to imagine that those tiny bits of foil could ultimately add up to be worth something.

Learning to trust God can be a maddeningly slow process. I go through one experience where I don't quite have the faith I know I should have. He helps me through, and I begin to trust the slightest bit more. And I say to God (again), "I believe."

Then, the following day, I complete the verse: "Help me overcome my unbelief!" He helped me and protected me a moment ago, yet in this moment I forget and reenter my customary shell of anxiety. "I believe," my voice insists aloud, for my benefit as well as for others'. Inside, my soul whispers, "Help me overcome my unbelief. . . ."

Today the tiniest scrap of evidence will remind me that God is in control, that He will not hurt me, that He is the only one who can save me. Perhaps someday those tiny fragments, put together, will be a faith that can keep the anxiety away altogether. Someday, it will happen, I believe.

Help my unbelief.

HOLY ORDINARY

NOVEMBER 9

Spear of influence

"The days are coming," declares the Sovereign Lord, "when I will send a famine through the land—not a famine of food or a thirst for water, but a famine of hearing the words of the Lord...."

AMOS 8:11

One of Adolf Hitler's many obsessions was his desire to possess the spear of Longinus, the spear which, according to tradition, pierced Jesus' side as He hung on the cross. Legend suggests that the one who possesses the spear and understands its powers can conquer the world.

Hitler must have felt that devouring the whole world would surely fill the vast emptiness in his soul. In his megalomania, Hitler never understood that he didn't need the spear, but the One whose side it pierced. His need to *see* God somehow became a need to *be* God; in an effort to sate his hunger he consumed millions of lives—entire nations—and topped it all off with a cyanide capsule. Yet for all his consumption, he lived an empty life, and died an empty death.

On smaller scales, though, many of us try in futility to fill an unnamed hunger with possessions or people or relationships. I've certainly tried feeding that hunger with things that cannot nourish a soul. I filled my schedule with busy-ness. I filled my bank account on occasion. I filled my living space with things. I filled my head with facts. But my soul remained empty.

Until I let God consume me.

NOVEMBER 10

Who will be strong for me?

When Mordecai learned of all that had been done, he tore his clothes, put on sackcloth and ashes, and went out into the city, wailing loudly and bitterly. . . . [Esther] . . . sent clothes for him to put on instead of his sackcloth, but he would not accept them.

Esther 4:1, 4

Just before he died, my dad was very weak, but tried to continue getting out and around. One morning, as we left a restaurant from breakfast, he had to sit on the curb, too weak to walk 20 feet to the car. I panicked, knowing I wasn't strong enough to pick him up and get him home.

All that summer, I kept trying to be strong for my family, but in the back of my mind, I knew I couldn't do it. I kept asking, "Who will be strong for me? Who will pick me up?"

Mordecai refused to exchange his sackcloth for other clothes because he needed for others to see his pain. So many people today fight to be heard as he did, begging for someone to listen, to let them vent their pain, their grief, their disappointment, their fear. Like me, many people cling to their grief because they need someone to acknowledge the unfairness of it all, to say out loud that the loss of a loved one or a way of life hurts deeply and permanently.

But other people can't really help because they have their own battles to fight. Only God will always listen, acknowledging my pain and then helping me to bear it. Only God can be strong for me. Only God can pick me up.

And only God can carry me home.

HOLY ORDINARY 339

NOVEMBER 11

Personal

Some wanted to seize [Jesus], but no one laid a hand on him. Finally the temple guards went back to the chief priests and Pharisees, who asked them, "Why didn't you bring him in?" "No one ever spoke the way this man does," the guards declared.

JOHN 7:44-46

In Europe, in Asia, and most recently, in the Mideast, young Americans faced torture and death for something antiseptically described as "our country." But really, they died for all of us individual Americans who sit comfortably at home taking that country for granted. When war comes to the world, the fight for freedom is no longer an abstraction from history class; suddenly it is personal.

When Jesus threatened the establishment in His day, the authorities wanted Him arrested, but initially no one would do it. Why? "No one ever spoke the way this man does."

Jesus had gotten personal; He was not just a God, but a human being who spoke as no one ever had, of love and healing, of knowing God in an immediate and life-changing way. No longer a theological or religious debate, the presence of God demanded a change in way of life, and in priorities.

God sent His Son to die so that an ordinary human like me could know Him individually, so that I can know God personally. To do it, Jesus had to submit to torture, abuse, and even death. But Jesus didn't die for religion; He died so that I could directly hear the voice of God.

"No one ever spoke to me the way this Man does." The way this God does.

This is personal.

The best next thing

. . . I do not concern myself with great matters or things too wonderful for me. But I have stilled and quieted my soul. . . .

PSALM 131:1-2

In the movie *Apollo 13,* Jim Lovell cautions his men to focus on tasks at hand rather than worrying about what will happen way down the line. He says, "A thousand things have to happen, in order, for us to get home safe. You're talking about number 876. Right now, we're on number 8."

I worry about events way down the line, and some of the things I worry most about won't even come to pass. I try to play life like a chess game, saying, "If I do this, He'll do that, and then what will I do?"

Too often we think we need to know all of the details before we take the smallest step. But God has the entire course of our lives in His hands, and He may choose not to reveal the entire course to us now.

Using my human judgment, I'd have said, "Don't hurt me. Don't make me change. Don't let me be frightened." But God, knowing that the thing I needed most was a relationship with Him, used those experiences to turn me, to mold me, to teach me. Now I thank Him for using the grief, the growing pains, the fear to show me how small my world is without Him.

It's not my job to see how to get us all the way to the moon and back. It's not my job to discern all the details in the grand scheme of my life.

My only job is to do the best next thing.

NOVEMBER 13

Step here

. . . I lift up my eyes to the hills—where does my help come from? My help comes from the Lord, the Maker of heaven and earth. He will not let your foot slip—he who watches over you will not slumber . . .

PSALM 121:1-3

Mars Hill in Athens, Greece, is a rocky little crown which our group ascended one night in dim moonlight. Coming down the hill is treacherous; on the steep and slippery stone steps, no foothold feels quite sure. As we descended, I went ahead of some others, and called back in the darkness, "Take my hand. Step here next. Lean on this rock. Watch this spot."

Paul traversed the early days of Christianity as we negotiated the hill that night—feeling his way, relying on what he knew to be solid, calling back to guide others' steps. But always, always, he told us that God, the God of Jesus Christ, guards his people, never sleeping, never letting us slip.

As I learn more about the Christian life, I want to call back to help as others have done for me. Lean here, trusting God. Watch this slippery spot of complacency, where you are so grateful to be on solid ground that you forget to help the next soul.

Step here where you begin to know, finally, deeply in your heart, that God holds you in His hands with care and tenderness, every moment of every day. Rest here, my fellow traveler, where you understand that our God never sleeps, so we never slip. Step here, my friend. Step here.

And go with me to our God.

NOVEMBER 14

Lost time

The goat will carry on itself all their sins to a solitary place; and the man shall release it in the desert.

LEVITICUS 16:22

On *NYPD Blue,* when detectives miss work for personal reasons, they call it "lost time." They consider it time lost because they're not doing the work they have sworn to do.

Regrets that we cannot release turn into our lost time as Christians. Our one job on this earth is to love—our God, our neighbors, ourselves. We're not here to judge, or demand, or avenge, or regret, but to love. It is the one job we are sworn to do.

Leviticus says that the man shall release the scapegoat in the desert. God tells me to let go of everything I have ever done to hurt another person, to hurt myself, to hurt Him. All is loaded onto the beast, and the beast remains in the desert. God's Son has died, so my sins have died. I am no longer required to die with them.

God knows that my human instinct is to revisit my sins, to beat myself up over mistakes, refusing forgiveness because I know the depth of what I have done. My instinct is to remain with the beast in the desert. But clinging to sorrow over past failures steals time I should be using to love Him, to love my neighbor, to love myself. Getting past the regrets and accepting total forgiveness, unmerited as it may be, lets me love.

The beast stays in the desert; I turn and go home, to the love of God.

No more lost time.

HOLY ORDINARY

NOVEMBER 15

Seeing a sign

He said, "Go and tell this people: "'Be ever hearing, but never understanding; be ever seeing, but never perceiving.' Make the heart of this people calloused; make their ears dull and close their eyes. Otherwise they might see with their eyes, hear with their ears, understand with their hearts, and turn and be healed."

ISAIAH 6:9-10

Beside a road I often travel stands a large wooden sign, faded and worn, reading, "Jesus wept." Though the sign has probably been there 20 years, I'm so used to seeing it that I no longer "see" it.

If I'm not careful, my Christian life can go that same route, as I become complacent and self-satisfied, failing to remember that I seek God because a Man wept, and suffered, and died for me. In this passage of Isaiah, I hear God weeping, knowing that He continually puts signs before His people, and yet they do not see them. We hear, but we do not understand; we see, but we do not perceive. And so God weeps.

And I don't believe such words are directed only at those who have never heard the voice of God in their lives, but even at those of us who like to think we center our lives on Him. Certain compartments of my life, I fear, remain closed to God. Certain resentments have not yet been healed. Certain people have not heard me speak of my God. And so He weeps.

Still, through it all, God loves me immeasurably, unconditionally. I have seen the signs.

But have I *seen* them?

NOVEMBER 16

A child is missing

Save me, O God. . . . I am forced to restore what I did not steal.
PSALM 69:1,4

A woman surrendered to authorities a few days after she called the parents of a missing girl and claimed to be their daughter, gone for 17 years. At first, I got angry that anyone could be so needy and so hurtful. But then I wondered what legacy of pain the woman carries to need so desperately to be in the news as the long-lost child welcomed home.

As a Christian, I am, in a sense, "forced to restore what I did not steal." I will never meet the grieving parents or the woman who claimed to be their daughter, but I am asked by God to at least try to understand their pain. If I want to embrace God, I have to embrace His people, to become the hand and shoulder and voice of God walking the earth. The pain of all those who ache and make others ache is my pain. "Save me, O God. I am forced to restore what I did not steal."

What can I do in my small corner of the world to salve the Body's pain? I can tell the people I love, today, that I love them, so that they're less likely to feel lost. I can tell those hurting that I hurt with them. I can tell myself that I am a child of God, and a part of God, and need not prove that I'm special.

I can look at people like this woman who hurt so deeply, and I can love her. I can try to understand that she must feel like God's missing child. I can remember that she likely fights the same demon we all fight: wanting to belong.

And longing to be wanted.

NOVEMBER 17

Unfinished work

Create in me a pure heart. . . . The sacrifices of God are a broken spirit; a broken and contrite heart. . . .

PSALM 51:10,17

A highlight of our trip to Italy was, of course, seeing the sculpture of David in the Accademia in Florence. Nearly 18 feet high, muscle rippling from marble, he looks toward the battle God will have him fight. He is magnificent.

But in the hall approaching David is another group of sculpture, unfinished works of Michelangelo called "The Young Slave," "The Awakening Slave," "Atlas," and "The Bearded Slave." Plainly visible on those pieces of marble are the marks left by the master's tools.

Clearly I'm one of those unfinished works. A friend recently suggested that whenever I get hurt, or angry, or prideful, as I so often do, I should say no to the instinct to fight back or carry resentment. Though painful, those blows help form my heart after the heart of Christ. With every bit of chiseling I endure, I learn to ignore the hurt, to love when loving seems impossible, to heal when the I'd rather hurt back.

The message in the Accademia seems clear. When my spirit is wounded or my heart breaks, when contrition reminds me that I am not all that God wants me to be, I remember the way to God's warrior. I must first be His slave—young, awakening, maturing—until I'm ready to take the world on. God is forming me to fight His battles.

He is making me His masterpiece.

Presence

. . . the Lord was with Joseph and gave him success in whatever he did.

GENESIS 39:23

Once a group of friends brought me a gift of a beautiful, hand-painted ceramic cross. It was a gift that came unexpectedly, as many of life's great gifts do. The feeling I had must be like the one Joseph had, trusting, knowing that the Lord is here, knowing that every good gift, and every success, comes from Him.

Material success would be fine, I guess, but more meaningful to me is the deeper, more joyful success of knowing that I am loved. When something good happens to me, I try to remind myself that I didn't cause it, that all good comes directly from Him. And as difficult as it may be, I also try to discern the gifts wrapped in pain, the loss disguising gain. Those trying gifts ultimately turned my life toward God.

God speaks to me in many ways, sometimes, as I have said, in the "voice with no sound." But He also speaks when kind, loving, supportive words come my way from other people. He speaks when an unpredictable turn of events saves the day. He speaks when an unexpected gift arrives.

And He has spoken through all of eternity with the arrival of that one undeserved, unearned, unexpected, joyful and moving gift. Like the gift I received from friends, it was a cross, made by human hands, delivered by human hands, borne by human hands.

But given by the hand of God.

NOVEMBER 19

He rains

Were you angry with the rivers, O Lord? Was your wrath against the streams?... You split the earth with rivers; the mountains saw you and writhed. Torrents of water swept by; the deep roared and lifted its waves on high.

HABAKKUK 3:8-10

Tuvalu is a small Pacific island whose 11,000 inhabitants rely heavily on agriculture. With no streams or rivers, though, rainfall is its only source of fresh water. Cyclones have roiled the seas so much that saltwater seeps into the soil and wells, leaving residents with less and less freshwater.

The voice of God is the rainfall that comes from the heavens—the only pure water—but we store that rainfall in vessels that can become polluted by this world. Self-interest and hunger for power seep in, sending us far from God despite initial good intentions. The waters of "the deep" threaten our search for God and our acceptance of His people.

Religion, set up to catch living water from the sky, can go deeply and widely against His will. Constantly, in church and in all of life, the question must be before us: Is this about God, or is it about me? Has the living water been tainted, or is this a signal from the heavens?

I wonder if these difficult days for churches mean that we need to focus more clearly on God, and less intently on ourselves. It seems that, in the life of the church, the skies look pretty dark right now.

Perhaps they hold the promise of rain.

NOVEMBER 20

Now you can go

The Lord said, "Surely I will deliver you for a good purpose...."
JEREMIAH 15:11

As the war in Iraq wore on, an NPR journalist in Iraq said that the people there seemed grateful for U.S. help, but anxious to begin anew without us. He said it's as if the Iraqis were saying, "Thank you for liberating us. Now you can go." Sons, daughters, loved ones were sacrificed for that freedom, so it seemed a slap in the face to hear, "We no longer need you."

In tragedies, major and minor, we are more likely to seek God, and to somehow believe that He can deliver and restore us. But when the smoke clears, and equilibrium seems to return, we turn away, certain that now we can handle things without Him. "Thank you for saving me, God," we say. "Now you can go."

But God has greater plans for us; He "delivers us for a good purpose," not to plunder this world, but to rebuild it. My freedom came at great cost, and I can only begin to repay that sacrifice by taking the strength God gives me and helping liberate others as I have been liberated.

Being dismissive of God in good times is equivalent to saying to Him, "I'll call you when I need you again." Our gratitude, instead, should bring us to our knees, asking what we can possibly do to pass this gift of liberation on to another. And every time we see the figure of a cross, we should remember why we should stay connected, even when we think we no longer need God.

Freedom came at the cost of His Son.

HOLY ORDINARY

NOVEMBER 21

On thin ice

And we know that in all things God works for the good of those who love him, who have been called according to his purpose.... No, in all these things we are more than conquerors through him who loved us....

ROMANS 8:28-39

I once read a story about a horseman who, in a nighttime winter snowstorm, unknowingly rode across a frozen lake. When he reached the other side and learned what he had done, he realized how close he came to perishing, and broke down in tears.

I cursed the winter not that many years ago, but I look back now and see that those conditions saved my life. God kept me in the cold and dark just long enough to keep the ice firm so I could reach the other side. If circumstances had been any brighter or warmer for me in those years of transition, I wouldn't have turned to Him at all. The thin ice I traversed would have broken, and I would have perished. I came so close.

I know it's overly dramatic, but occasionally I get depressed over my age and mortality, and even imagine the details of my death. Then I look back at a brilliant, charismatic young man in his thirties, who saw every detail of His own demise. I see a man who went willingly to die, even for people who still won't admit that they know Him. To turn away from that fate would've been the easy thing to do. It would've been perfectly human.

Instead, He opened His arms, and pulled me to Him, to save my life. Very often, I can almost feel Him here.

He is so close.

Defining moment

The royal official said, "Sir, come down before my child dies." Jesus replied, "You may go. Your son will live." . . . So he and all his household believed.

JOHN 4:49-50, 53

When I was young, I overheard my dad saying how surprised he was that John Kennedy had been elected President. When I asked why, he told me that many people didn't want a Catholic President. The statement crushed me, because I was Catholic at the time.

If I had been told that prejudice is "opinion adverse to anything without just grounds or before sufficient knowledge," I wouldn't have understood. But when I heard that someone disliked me before they even knew me, I understood in my gut the meaning of the word.

The man in this Scripture passage learned about God, not through others' definitions, but through experience. His dying son recovered when this Jesus told him, "Your son will live." He suddenly understood how it felt to be loved by God because the living, breathing, loving God had stepped directly into his path.

I believe in God not by definition, but by experience. He came to me in my dark and closed-off place and told me gently, "You will live." So I understand the definition of God, a definition to be heard not with the head, but with the heart. God means I will live. God means I am loved, that I have always been loved.

Even before I knew Him.

Armor

While they were still talking about this, Jesus himself stood among them. . . . And while they still did not believe it because of joy and amazement, he asked them, "Do you have anything here to eat?" They gave him a piece of broiled fish, and he took it and ate it in their presence.

LUKE 24:36, 41-43

Archaeologists at the Jamestown colony site have found lightweight, arrow-proof vests the settlers made by chopping up unwieldy armor and weaving it back together. Something that had first been useless, then almost a liability, became useful in the new life.

Jesus' greatest "weakness," if it could be called that, was His humanity: vulnerability to pain and death and the need of physical sustenance and rest. While He lived as a human, those characteristics seemed, indeed, to be nothing more than weakness.

But like chopped up armor that becomes better protection, Jesus' humanity would become His great strength. His disciples had walked the dusty road with Him, and they had seen Him tired and hungry. They had stood by and seen Him abused, tortured, and killed. So when He later stood among them, and did something so human as to ask for something to eat, His humanity became testament that He is, indeed, the Son of Man and the Son of God.

The armor is momentarily destroyed. Its useless dead weight is cut up, woven into strength. God lives as Man, and then as God again.

Weakness turns to strength.

NOVEMBER 24

Snow problem

... should not a people inquire of their God? Why consult the dead on behalf of the living? ... they will look toward the earth and see only distress and darkness and fearful gloom, and they will be thrust into utter darkness.

ISAIAH 8:19, 22

Several years ago, I had to drive in white-out conditions in the Midwest, and I've never been more afraid for my life.

My dad and I were coming home from a nearby town at midday. The weather turned treacherous; it would take an hour and 20 minutes to drive 22 miles. New snow no longer fell, but fine powder filled the air, whipped around by fierce winds approaching 50 miles an hour.

Every inch of air, road, and field blurred together in whiteness, so it was impossible to see where the side of the road ended and the ditch began. I followed a truck ahead very closely, although I knew that driver couldn't see the road any better than I could. It frightened me to realize I was trusting my life to a person I had never even met.

We survived, but I know I risked disaster. Yet, too often, I'm still stupid enough to look at someone else and think, "Well, at least I'm doing better than that person." It's a dangerous tactic—choosing my road based on another person's judgment—unless, of course, that person is the Son of God. He's the one we should follow.

He's the one to bring us safely home.

HOLY ORDINARY 353

NOVEMBER 25

The innermost room

Peter answered him, "We have left everything to follow you! What then will there be for us?"

MATTHEW 19:27

One Thanksgiving weekend, tornadoes with winds of 207 miles per hour blew through part of the metropolitan area where I live. One family crawled out, unhurt, from the remnants of their laundry room, the innermost room of their house and the only part left.

Not one wall of the family's home remained intact. Belongings were strewn across miles of rubble. Every material thing they owned was lost. The mother immediately talked about how blessed they were. She said, "God is good."

People without faith can lose everything when two air masses collide and start their deadly spin. They think they have "the good life," but they emerge to discover they have nothing at all of real value.

When we choose to follow God, storms will still come, and in those storms, some of the old familiar things and places and friends will disappear. The difference is that our faith in God assures us that we are blessed, no matter how devastating the scene around us may appear.

Peter asked Jesus, "What then will there be for us?" After the storm, we Christians will never face that feeling that all is lost. The One we treasure, we carry deep in our hearts, deep in our souls. In our innermost room. Where others see loss, we will see God. That's "what there will be for us."

We will see God.

NOVEMBER 26

The presents of his people

How can I repay the Lord for all his goodness to me? I will lift up the cup of salvation and call upon the name of the Lord. I will fulfill my vows to the Lord in the presence of his people.

PSALM 116:12-14

My friends and I don't exchange Christmas gifts; instead, we simply go out to dinner during the holidays and enjoy a few quiet hours together. We don't like the thought that people we love are fighting maniacal holiday crowds to find the perfect gift. We would rather just spend some time together.

And while I want to give Him the best of everything, God doesn't want me agonizing over gifts, either. After all, what could I get Him that He couldn't get for Himself? The only unique gift I can offer Him is me—my presence.

Like the psalmist, though, I am anxious to thank God for rescuing me from the depths of despair. But what do you get for someone who has everything? Should I get involved in more church activities? Should I study the Bible more? How many souls can I help turn towards Him?

But God loves me as I love my friends, and He knows the love in my heart for Him. He doesn't want me running crazily around, seeking the perfect gift to show Him my love.

He doesn't need presents from His people; He longs for the "presence of His people." So start giving God your best presence right now.

Beat the holiday rush.

NOVEMBER 27

Darkness and Light

. . . do not be distressed and do not be angry with yourselves for selling me here, because it was to save lives that God sent me ahead of you. For two years now there has been famine in the land, and for the next five years there will not be plowing and reaping. But God sent me ahead of you to preserve for you a remnant on earth and to save your lives by a great deliverance.

GENESIS 45:5-7

A local TV weatherman used to rate the forecast for the next day on a scale of 1-10, a 10 requiring absolutely clear skies and warm temperatures. I ignored his ratings, though, because the most aesthetically beautiful days to me are the ones with dark clouds penetrated by rays of sunshine.

The most memorable and breathtaking times of my life have been the moments, days, weeks when the dark and the light were inextricably woven together. Tragedy appears, with triumph sewn carefully inside the lining. I lost my dad, my sister, my self. I found my God, my faith, my life. I lost jobs, but found callings.

God uses the darkness and light, over and over. Darkness and light. The pattern repeats over and over, the threads changing, but the dark and light woven together irrevocably.

Even in the lives of the saints before us, and certainly in the life of Christ, the pattern is there. Profound pain and deep joy. Mourning and celebration. Death and life. Darkness. Then Light.

Forever.

NOVEMBER 28

The power of One Word

. . . before me was a white horse, whose rider is called Faithful and True. . . . He has a name written on him that no one knows but himself. He is dressed in a robe dipped in blood, and his name is the Word of God. . . .

REVELATION 19:11-16

A&E's "Biography of the Millennium" named the 100 most influential people of the past 1,000 years. Johann Gutenberg, inventor of the moveable type printing press, was named the single most influential person of the millennium. Without access to the printed word, other giants in history— Newton, Pasteur, Luther, Einstein— could not have been effectively educated or inspired. Their ideas would not have lived on to influence others.

But proliferation of the printed word gave every person the wisdom of the ages, and gave every person a voice in the world. Jesus offers us a similar gift in our relationship with God. Before He appeared, direct knowledge of God was limited to a few; commoners like me had no access to Him.

But when Christ came—-when the Word appeared—-every human being in all of history, from the most gifted to the most ordinary, gained a direct connection to the wisdom of God. Every person gained a voice in heaven. So Christ gives us the gift of seeing God for ourselves, of seeing God in ourselves. Knowledge of one Word—living, not printed—changed all of history.

". . . and His name is the Word of God."

HOLY ORDINARY

NOVEMBER 29

Right or left

As Paul discoursed on righteousness, self-control and the judgment to come, Felix was afraid and said, "That's enough for now! You may leave. When I find it convenient, I will send for you."

ACTS 24:25

Once I became curious about the definition of the word "right" when it refers to the direction. How could it be defined without saying, "the opposite of left"? The dictionary does it by saying that right is "on the side of the body away from the heart."

Sometimes in my spiritual life I think, "I'm doing better than the next guy, so I'm all right." I keep trying to make right a relative concept, because it makes me uncomfortable to know what is right and not do it. Paul made Felix nervous by talking about righteousness and self-control, so Felix sent him away, saying, "When I find it convenient, I will send for you."

God asks us to choose Him constantly, not to just send for Him when it's convenient. He is the absolute, the reason for and the cause of our existence. In our hearts, we may want something else temporarily, but we know down deep what is really right and what is not.

Today there will be many small forks in the road, many opportunities to choose between what I want to do and what I know God wants me to do. And I will probably find in some cases that what is truly right may be, indeed, "away from my heart."

But it will be closer to His.

NOVEMBER 30

Half empty

The engulfing waters threatened me, the deep surrounded me; seaweed was wrapped around my head. To the roots of the mountains I sank down; the earth beneath barred me in forever. . . ." Those who cling to worthless idols forfeit the grace that could be theirs."

JONAH 2:5-6, 8

In a flood at my apartment complex, every downstairs apartment flooded. For weeks, each one stood open, windows up and ceiling fans running constantly to dry the places out. Half of each building stood vacant.

Human lives are often lived the same way—the physical side of life lit up and active, the spiritual side dark and vacant. Lives without God usually focus on human relationships, material things, earthly success. But other people go away or fail us in their humanness. Material goods wear out, or are destroyed. Jobs disappear. Health can evaporate literally in a heartbeat. Like all low-level places, a life which only emphasizes physical things invites disaster.

God doesn't ask us to forswear the good physical life, but only not to value it above Him. He asks us to cling to Him when the waters are closing in around us, rather than clinging to "worthless idols." Otherwise we forget about God and "forfeit the grace that could be ours."

How foolish we are, to trade the grace of God for a transient physical existence, to vacate voluntarily half of the life God gives us. The lights may be on.

But nobody's home upstairs.

HOLY ORDINARY 359

December

DECEMBER 1

The Gift that keeps on giving

... *"You say, 'I am rich; I have acquired wealth and do not need a thing.' But you do not realize that you are wretched, pitiful, poor, blind, and naked. I counsel you to buy from me gold refined in the fire, so that you can become rich ..."*

REVELATION 3:17-18

It's that wondrous time of year when strangers on television tell you exactly what your life is missing and exactly how they can help you find it. Usually as the holiday season begins, I see commercials that tell me I need gold jewelry, because, "The gift of gold is forever."

When the wise men journeyed to see the Christ child, they brought gold to symbolize His divinity, frankincense to symbolize His humanity, and myrrh, hinting of the suffering He would bear. As I make my journey toward Christ, I can choose to exchange my humanity for His divinity. I can seek God's love, His forgiveness, His righteousness at every turn, or I can focus on myself and wallow in my own humanity. Even when I feel justified in getting angry or hurt, I can have gold or frankincense—divinity or humanity. I can follow my human instincts and try to put myself above other people, or I can forgive them, and myself, instantly. As Christ would do.

As a Christian, it's no longer a matter of fate, but a clear and conscious decision. If I could have the gold, why not take it? God will live in me if I let Him.

And the gift of God is forever.

DECEMBER 2

From on high

I have seen the burden God has laid on men. He has made everything beautiful in its time. He has also set eternity in the hearts of men; yet they cannot fathom what God has done from beginning to end.

ECCLESIASTES 3:10-11

I grew up in the farmland of central Illinois, and I used to think it was the most boring-looking place on the face of the earth. Other states had beaches, trees, mountains. We had acres of flat land and black dirt as far as the eye could see. I never appreciated the place until I flew over it the first time in late summer; it looked like a beautiful patchwork quilt of gold and green and black.

Life with God feels much the same, to me. Places that look the darkest and least promising from my perspective turn out to be fertile ground. And while meaning is not apparent on the surface, patterns develop when all of the pieces are seen from above. Darkness and light work together to bring nourishment and growth.

It's hard to remember amid the darkness, but God has a plan so big for me that I cannot often even glimpse a meaningful piece of it. From His perspective, my life holds great promise, incredible growth and vibrance.

No one piece of life seems to make much sense. But seen from above, all of the squares fit neatly together into a cover God has made to protect, to warm and shelter me.

A quilt to cover all His children.

DECEMBER 3

Hunger

Better a dry crust with peace and quiet than a house full of feasting, with strife.

PROVERBS 17:1

It was a standard joke at our house growing up. Whenever we didn't eat all of our food, my mom would say that there were children in India starving. One of us smart alecks would suggest packing up the broccoli and sending it over.

It's easy to be flippant about nourishment when you're well fed. When hunger pangs—physical or spiritual—have been satisfied in me, it's really difficult for me to remember how many people are still starving.

Once I thrived on chaos, on wondering what would happen next, agonizing over every decision, every circumstance. I didn't know anything better existed.

But then I met people who love God, who are fed constantly by Him and who bear peace and tranquillity and love in His name. No matter what happened around them, they knew peace, because they know God. And their peace came from knowing—absolutely knowing—that they were loved. It's not a luxury item—the certainty that you are loved. It is a necessity; it is life itself. Knowing without a doubt that you are loved makes it possible to see others' hunger, and to help them sate that hunger with the presence of God.

After all, when the peace of God is strengthened and passed along to the next person, we don't just feed my body or your body or the body of a child in India.

We feed the Body of Christ.

DECEMBER 4

Call for price

Do not conform any longer to the pattern of this world, but be transformed by the renewing of your mind. Then you will be able to test and approve what God's will is—his good, pleasing and perfect will.

ROMANS 12:2

One day I hoped to price a product on the internet, but the website said, "Call for price." If they won't tell me the price, I thought, it must cost too much.

I once harbored that same suspicion about Christianity; everyone talked about benefits, but no one mentioned a price. I thought the price must be intimidating: changing my life, following rules, giving up everything that meant anything to me.

Once I encountered, for myself, the presence of God, life did change, but only because I wanted it to. I do "follow the rules" more, but only because I know it pleases the One who gives me life. And once I glimpsed Him, I became less interested in "conforming to the pattern of this world." Now the only thing I want more of is God.

God's will is not to make me miserable, to make me long for things I cannot have, to make me follow a rule to win a spiritual lottery and go to heaven. God's will is for me to be happy, fulfilled, healthy, whole, loving. My discontent with this world tells me that my real fulfillment comes from being with God in His.

Why wouldn't "they" tell me what it costs to know God? Is it because it costs nothing, or because it costs everything?

Or both?

HOLY ORDINARY 365

DECEMBER 5

All good and well

Jesus entered Jericho and was passing through. A man was there by the name of Zacchaeus; he was a chief tax collector and was wealthy. He wanted to see who Jesus was . . . Zacchaeus . . . said to the Lord, "Look, Lord! Here and now I give half of my possessions to the poor, and if I have cheated anybody out of anything, I will pay back four times the amount."

LUKE 19:1-3, 8

I frequently get lazy with spoken language; sometimes when asked how I am, I say, "I'm doing good" when I mean that I'm doing well. But perhaps doing good is better.

Zacchaeus, apparently, was a man who did well; he's described in the Gospel as a wealthy man, so he probably could buy anything he wanted. And yet, he was curious, and made a heroic effort to "see who Jesus was." Once he had met the Son of Man, Zacchaeus gave up half of his possessions and vowed to make fourfold restitution to those he had cheated. In other words, he decided to start doing good.

We all have an insatiable hunger for our God, and we try mightily, as Zacchaeus did, to fill that void with more things, more people, more experiences. Yet nothing fills us until we meet the Son of God, a Man who shows us the insignificance and transience of some of the things we have spent our lives pursuing.

Once we meet God, we do as the wealthy chief tax collector did. We worry much less about doing well.

And we decide to do some good.

DECEMBER 6

I'll be home for Christmas

But when the kindness and love of God our Savior appeared, he saved us, not because of righteous things we had done, but because of his mercy. He saved us through the washing of rebirth and renewal by the Holy Spirit, whom he poured out on us generously through Jesus Christ our Savior, so that, having been justified by his grace, we might become heirs having the hope of eternal life.

TITUS 3:4-7

When I called my nephew early one December to tell him I'd be home for Christmas, I told him that I couldn't bring many presents that year. He said, "We don't care if you come home empty-handed, as long as you come home."

During this season, we celebrate the birth of Jesus Christ, the Man who saved my life. What gift can I possibly offer to repay God for giving me eternal life through—and with—His Son? How do I adequately thank my Father for this gift whose arrival we celebrate in this season?

Sometimes I get a little spiritually neurotic, trying to thank Him for the richness He brings to my life. But down deep, I know that God would prefer that I stop and spend time with Him. More than any "righteous things" (or self-righteousness) I can offer, God He saves me—allows me to be reborn and renewed—purely because He loves me. In fact, if my hands are empty when I come to Him, He will give me more gifts, every day of the year. So it's perfectly fine for me to go home to God empty-handed.

As long as I come home.

HOLY ORDINARY

Join now and save

And when they climbed into the boat, the wind died down. Then those who were in the boat worshiped him, saying, "Truly you are the Son of God."

MATTHEW 14:32-33

At the construction site for a new business, a sign exhorted passersby to "Join now and save." There was no indication of whether I would be joining a health club or a weight loss program or heaven knows what else. But if I "join now, I save."

I wonder if the people we talk to about Christianity feel that same confusion. We exhort them to join us, to seek our God, our way, often with little explanation of what that seeking might mean in everyday life.

People need to understand what they're joining before they care about becoming part of it, about "getting in the boat" with Christ. They need to look at me and you and each Christian and see what joining God has meant to us, to see that we are the first to love, the last to judge, the nearest shoulder, the gentlest touch, the most uplifting word. They need to see the joy, the healing, the depth, the strength that our God brings into our lives every single day.

They need to see, not our joining some club, but our joining God in making this a better place to live. Then they will seek God in earnest, and not just because someone says they should do it. They will heed the words, because they will hear them resonating deeply within their own hearts.

Join now, and be saved.

Forgiving and forgetting

I lift up my eyes to the hills—where does my help come from? My help comes from the Lord, the Maker of heaven and earth.

PSALM 121:1-2

A woman who worked in the same building with me for years never did really know what I was. Whenever she approached, I would wince, thinking, "She doesn't even remember my name."

Often I have congratulated myself on finally "getting past" a difficult, painful, and resentment-filled situation. A friend, struggling with a similar circumstance, may ask, "How did you do it?" and I get all puffed up about telling "my" story.

But saying that I forgave and began putting my life back together means that, like the woman at my office, I fail to remember the name of Someone right in front of me. I didn't forgive the hurt; God did. I didn't find the strength to move on; God gave me the strength. Forgiveness is God's work, not mine.

Long ago when I read the words, "To err is human; to forgive, divine," I thought they meant that my choosing to forgive someone would make me more like God. But now I believe that those words mean that it is God's realm alone to forgive. I don't approach Him by forgiving; I approach Him to hand over the hurt, which can only be taken away and soothed by His hands.

To err is human, but the greater error is forgetting that forgiveness belongs only to God. So when I congratulate myself for it, I know what He must be thinking.

"She doesn't even remember my name."

DECEMBER 9

Letter and Spirit

Then the Lord said to him, "Now then, you Pharisees clean the outside of the cup and dish, but inside you are full of greed and wickedness . . . you give God a tenth of your mint . . . but you neglect justice and the love of God. . . ."

LUKE 11:39, 42

At the height of the Washington sniper attacks in 2002, the lead investigator read in a prepared statement, "You've asked us to say, quote, We have caught the sniper like a duck in a noose, end quote. We understand that having us say this is important to you."

The sniper intended to make the authorities look foolish when he struck again. In fact, though, they complied with the letter of his "law" and ignored its spirit.

God, you've asked me to say, quote, I love my neighbor as myself, end quote, so I will say it. And then I will make decisions based solely on my needs and my desires. You want me to say that I love you first, yet I squeeze you into my schedule when I have time. You want me to say that I worship the one true God, but on my way to worship I bow to other gods, like what I drive, where I live, whom I know.

God wants me to spend less time talking a good game of Christianity and more time living it. He only wants to hear those words—polish on the "outside of the dish"—if they translate into the love of Him and of other human beings. When I live for Him, I won't simply comply with the letter of His law.

Quote, I will live in His Spirit. End quote.

DECEMBER 10

Will someone explain?

The Spirit told Philip, "Go to that chariot and stay near it." Then Philip ran up to the chariot and heard the man reading Isaiah the prophet. "Do you understand what you are reading?" Philip asked. "How can I," he said, "unless someone explains it to me?" So he invited Philip to come up and sit with him.

ACTS 8:29-31

Before I became a Christian, I had lunch with a friend, and out of the blue, she said, "You realize at some point we're going to have to talk about God." We were both astounded when I said, "You know, I've been thinking a lot about that lately."

She felt that God was telling her to start the conversation, and she initially resisted, thinking that the conversation would go exactly nowhere. She never expected that I would be anxious to talk about my spiritual life, probably because she was unaware that I had one.

I love God deeply, but I still think up all sorts of reasons not to talk to people about Him. They'll resent me. They'll laugh. They'll run. They'll say derisively, "Carol done got religion."

But I didn't get religion; I got God, so overwhelmingly that He spills out of my heart and into the lives of others. And it would not have happened if my friend hadn't heeded the message she received. Like Philip, she listened to the Spirit of God, and became the one person near enough to help another human being find Him.

Are you that person for someone else today? Are you listening?

Will you go?

HOLY ORDINARY

DECEMBER 11

Tears in heaven

Before your very eyes Jesus Christ was clearly portrayed as crucified. I would like to learn just one thing from you: Did you receive the Spirit by observing the law, or by believing what you heard? Are you so foolish? After beginning with the Spirit, are you now trying to attain your goal by human effort?

GALATIANS 3:1-3

When I was 20, I had a violent argument with my parents because I wanted to buy a small motorcycle, and they adamantly opposed it. If I had bought it, and had gotten hurt, they would not have disinherited me. But I would have seen them cry over pain I had caused myself, pain I could've avoided if I had only done as they asked. And it would have broken my heart to see my father cry over my needless suffering.

When I became a Christian, I "received the Spirit . . . by believing what I heard" from God. Since that day, I have known that He is always with me, and that I will be with Him in eternity because I accepted the unutterable sacrifice of His Son.

So as I continue to make mistakes, will they eventually reach a total that will keep me out of heaven? If not, then what will be the price for all of the times God's child fails Him?

Perhaps I would pay the same unimaginably painful cost I would have paid if I had gotten injured ignoring my parents' advice. A beloved child is hurt, through her own mistakes. A Father weeps over her needless pain. The cost is unspeakable.

Tears in heaven.

DECEMBER 12

Hearing ghosts

Then Peter remembered the word the Lord had spoken to him: "Before the rooster crows today, you will disown me three times." And he went outside and wept bitterly.

LUKE 22:61-62

As Baghdad fell in the summer of 2003, citizens told Americans that Saddam Hussein held prisoners down in wells. They kept hearing their own voices echoed in the wells, and thought they were the voices of surviving prisoners. But a U.S. soldier said they were only "hearing ghosts."

Most of us hear ghosts, and often just as we have been liberated by the presence of Christ. He tells us that we are forgiven our sins, that He has gone to the cross to pay for them, yet we don't accept His word. We continue to listen at those wells, hearing voices and transgressions and hurts we have done, hurts done to us by others.

And so we deny Christ, though not as overtly as Peter did. We say, "I know God forgives me, but I can't forgive myself." We set ourselves up as judge of what is truly forgivable and what must be heard echoing in our lives. We deny Christ, the meaning of His life, the meaning of His death.

Those wells of forgiveness were made to cleanse us completely, to quench our thirst for God, not to remind us of how far short we fall of Him. God forgives completely, absolutely. The voices we hear are our own. To find God, we have to stop shouting at ourselves. No more echoes in the well. No more ghosts.

No more denying Christ.

DECEMBER 13

For imperfect strangers

Jesus answered them, ". . . what about the one whom the Father set apart as his very own and sent into the world? . . . even though you do not believe me, believe the miracles, that you may know and understand that the Father is in me, and I in the Father."

JOHN 10:34, 38

One evening our local news channel promised that an upcoming news story would feature the mother of a soldier killed in the war in Iraq. Such "news stories" feel to me much more like emotional voyeurism than journalism; after all, what can the poor woman say? What more of a statement can a parent make than to sacrifice a child for perfect strangers? My son has been killed, she could tell us, and it hurts. What's left to ask?

The people in Jesus' time, and even those in our time, on the far side of the cross, continually ask God for signs which will prove His attention, His care, His very existence. It seems a sort of spiritual extortion: God, if you really want me to believe in you, you'll give me this sign that I require. He has already made the ultimate sacrifice, the sacrifice of His Son, and yet we demand more proof that we are loved.

"What about the one whom the Father set apart as his very own and sent into the world?" What more can God say to convince us that He loves us? "My Son has been killed," He could tell us. "I sacrificed Him for imperfect strangers, and it hurts."

What's left to ask?

DECEMBER 14

The site of God

And the twenty-four elders . . . fell on their faces and worshiped God, saying: ". . . The time has come for judging the dead, and for rewarding your servants the prophets and your saints and those who reverence your name, both small and great—and for destroying those who destroy the earth."

REVELATION 11:14-19

When I worked at the state's economic development department, I heard of a German industrial prospect who came to assess a site here for a new manufacturing plant. When he saw litter and overgrown weeds along the highway, he left without seeing the site, as he didn't want to live or work where people took so little pride in tending their own community.

As much as I'd like to point out the inconsistency, the foolishness, the harshness, the failure to love in others' lives, that is not my job as a Christian. I am charged with tending my own spirit, with "reverencing" the name of God with my life. I'm not required to examine and grade others' searches for meaning, but to simply make my life a place where God wants to live.

I find it very liberating that God—and God alone—decides how to reward those of us, small and great, who seek Him in earnest. Judgment is God's work—not mine—so He will deal, in His infinite justice and mercy, with others' faithfulness or unfaithfulness. And in the meantime He asks just one thing of me.

That I tend to my own little piece of the road.

HOLY ORDINARY

DECEMBER 15

Hear, now

[Jesus] said to them, "If anyone has ears to hear, let him hear."

MARK 4:23

Once I rode on the elevator with a man talking on a cell phone. He was talking on it as he walked up, on the elevator ride, and as he went down the hall. Thanks to modern advances—in communication, no less—I felt invisible.

Aren't I smart? I can hear signals from the next room, the next channel, the next car, the next state, the next hemisphere. Even the next planet. Yet the next person becomes anonymous, invisible, mute. I can hear a voice transmitting from outer space, but not the authentic sounds of life with God, and for God. Lost in the noise are the sounds that can be heart-filling and heart rending: the whimper of my abused neighbor, the song of friends, the cry of deep loss, the heartbeat of a child. The voice of God.

Like all humans, I frequently run into unexpected and acute pain. In the midst of it, I try to stop all static, refusing to answer the phone, or e-mail, or voice mail messages until the noise passes. Although I first feel as if I am closing everyone out, I'm actually letting Someone in.

God the Father speaks to me in the hush, in the voice heard only in the quietest reaches of a human heart. His words soothe me, strengthen me, draw me so close to Him that His breath, His voice become part of me.

Stay with me, He says. We're going to be all right.

DECEMBER 16

Run, Forrest! Run!

... all the people had been weeping as they listened to the words of the Law.... Nehemiah said, "Go and enjoy choice food and drinks, and send some to those who have nothing prepared. This day is sacred to our Lord. Do not grieve, for the joy of the Lord is your strength."

NEHEMIAH 8:9-10

In the movie *Forrest Gump*, young Forrest wears leg braces and is tormented by bullies. As he tries to escape in a stiff-legged, odd gait, his friend yells, "Run, Forrest! Run!" Suddenly the leg braces burst apart and he finds that he can run. *Fast*.

How would he have felt, after running like the wind, if someone had told him that the braces had to go back on? He would be like the people who wept when they heard God's law, in agony because they knew how beautiful a life with God could be and how miserably they had failed Him.

But the braces feel comfortingly familiar. So I worry, which is a failure to trust God. I need to control, which is a failure to trust God. I keep certain compartments of my life locked, which is a failure to trust God. I willingly strap on those braces and say, "No more running for me. I'll just limp along on my own." How intelligent is it to refuse the gift of joy?

God knows how often I fail Him, but He also knows how much I love Him. So He asks me to stop weeping, to accept the joy in Him that brings me strength—strength to run.

Fast.

DECEMBER 17

Spirit and Image

. . . we preach Christ crucified: a stumbling block to Jews and foolishness to Gentiles, but to those whom God has called, both Jews and Greeks, Christ the power of God and the wisdom of God.

1 CORINTHIANS 1:23-24

I read that the phrase "spittin' image," describing the uncanny likeness of one person to another, comes from the phrase "spirit and image." " He looks just like his father," the saying went. "He's the spirit and image."

Though I write about God and Jesus every day, I still struggle to see Jesus Christ as a person. I get the "Spirit" part, but have trouble with the "image." Finally, when dealing with some grief issues, the image became clearer.

I was asked to picture Jesus in the living room of my family's home. After "seeing" Him there, I began to see a living Christ throughout the places and times of my life. Not in a painting on the wall, not an ethereal spirit, but a man, up and walking around in my house, in my life.

I have said it before, but now I can really see that Jesus, this Person I just met, is alive, and He accompanies me to places I cannot bear to go alone. When, in my mind, I visit the people I've lost, He is there, and He is here. In an almost physical way, He holds their hands, and mine.

It's not just that Jesus lived once long ago, but that He lives, like me, with me. In my house. In my heart. I can finally see Him there.

He's the Spirit and Image of His Father.

Still Here.

"Seek me and live . . ."

AMOS 5:4

In the sixth grade, I desperately wanted a new bike, but had no expectation to get one. I already had a bike—a dorky, blue, girly looking thing—and I knew my parents couldn't afford to waste money. But when Christmas morning came, I had not only a new bike, but I had the coolest bike in town. I couldn't have dreamed such a gift was possible.

When I came looking for God, I had low expectations of what He would give me. I wanted to feel more peaceful, safer. I wanted to stop feeling guilty. I wanted to stop feeling small. Many mornings I awoke, almost surprised to find, "Well, I'm still here." That's not life—it's only survival.

Then Christmas comes, and God doesn't offer me only what I request, but gives me more than I imagined possible. He gives me a God. But He also gives me a man, one who refuses to save Himself, so that He can save me. A precious Son sent to hang on a cross, humiliated, beaten, destroyed as a man. A precious Son who rises from the grave, gloriously triumphant as a God. Who could've guessed such a gift existed?

All I ask now is to be close to God, and I'm beginning to see that's all He wants of me. It seems so simple, but when I seek only Him, I have a life that is rich, full, breathtakingly beautiful.

All because I started listening for His voice. And to His voice.

I wonder what gift we will open next.

DECEMBER 19

Ascent

I lift up my eyes to you, to you whose throne is in heaven . . .
PSALM 123:1 (A SONG OF ASCENTS.)

By the grace of God, one summer I had the stunning experience of standing beneath the ceiling of the Sistine Chapel in Rome. The part of the work that fascinates me shows the Creation, in which Adam's lifeless hand extends toward God. The initiative, the passion, the life, the energy, are God's. Adam's only role is to incline himself toward God.

Psalm 123, subtitled, "A song of ascents," was sung by persons journeying to the temple, beginning in far-off lands and moving toward God. Most journeys to God, though, begin with something that might better be called "a song of assent," because agreeing to reach toward God is the one step that we control. Once we assent to God's touch, we begin our ascent toward life with Him. We become part of His work of art.

What other explanation but the hand of God could account for magnificent, holy artwork like the Sistine Chapel and the Pietà? What about other "works of art" that we find in our world, like the reaching of one man toward another in charity or care, forgiveness or mercy? What other explanation could there be for a life previously thrown away, yet remarkably saved and given passion, holiness and depth?

Only one explanation suffices: the touch and the voice of God. Will we assent to sing with God?

Will we accept His song of ascent?

DECEMBER 20

Thirst for God

". . . Be strong and very courageous. Be careful to obey all the law my servant Moses gave you; do not turn from it to the right or to the left, that you may be successful wherever you go. . . . Do not be terrified; do not be discouraged, for the Lord your God will be with you wherever you go."

JOSHUA 1:7-9

The last time I got on an airliner, I carried a Styrofoam cup of coffee with me. The security guard asked me to sip the drink in his presence to prove it wasn't something dangerous. He figured that, if I was willing to consume this liquid, it's not going to hurt anyone else.

Perhaps it's a lesson to be taken to heart by every person who talks to another about God. I have seen people use religion and their supposed knowledge of God as a weapon to judge others and justify themselves. They insist that others pursue a relationship with God, though their own lives show no evidence that they understand His commandment to love Him and love others. The power of God is not a weapon, but a way of life which requires commitment, courage, sacrifice and, above all, love.

So instead of just carrying my faith around and expecting others to accept it, I have to let them see God in me, to let them see my thirst for Him. I have to make it clear that this "product" I'm trying to sell is not a weapon to be used against them, but something I am willing to consume myself.

And something I am willing to let consume me.

HOLY ORDINARY 381

DECEMBER 21

Winter's longest night

The people walking in darkness have seen a great light; on those living in the land of the shadow of death a light has dawned.

ISAIAH 9:2

At winter solstice, the sun is at its lowest elevation, with our part of the world tilting away from it. Passage of this day—the year's shortest day and longest night— will mean the days are lengthening, brightening again. To me, this time of year symbolizes hope.

Love shapes our lives when we find God. But before we can express and accept love, we first have to feel hope that we can "get there from here." Love seems almost irrelevant when it takes all of your strength to get through a day.

We've all experienced times that nearly convinced us the light would never come again—walking alone in the "shadow of death," lost in nighttimes that felt inexpressibly dark, long, frightening. But in pitch dark, even a pinpoint of light attracts the eye. Perhaps God tilts our world ever so slightly away from Him so that we'll finally notice His light.

When we do, we edge closer to see that the glow emanates from a stable, where the center of attention is a baby boy. The light around Him is somehow cleaner, brighter, warmer; suddenly we can see our long spell of darkness ending. God has tilted our part of the world closer to the Son.

The difference, when we have hope, is not that "things are looking up."

The difference is that we are.

DECEMBER 22

Bread and water

They did not thirst when he led them through the deserts; he made water flow for them from the rock; he split the rock and water gushed out.

ISAIAH 48:21

On a radio feature program once, I heard the heart-wrenching story of Holocaust survivors who are now aged and less able to close out nightmarish memories. One female patient called an orderly a "murderer" for taking bread from her meal tray because in the concentration camps, bread not only fed, but acted as currency for other privileges. Bread in the camp was water in the desert.

Sometimes we Christians forget that God is infinite, that His ability to sustain is limitless. Like the Holocaust survivor, we hoard our experience of God by constructing barriers and judging in self-righteousness. We insist that people conform to our standards before they can seek "our" God.

Yet manmade ceremonies and theologies and symbols are irrelevant to those who are starving. And those most distant from God will perish if we fail to share the bread and water of His presence with them. To survive long enough to find the God of Jesus Christ, they have to be fed somehow along the way, no matter what they believe or how they live.

God's church should never be a place which hoards the precious Bread of life for the "deserving." It should be a sign pointing to God, a sign speaking of plenty. I am a Christian, my sign should say. I carry the Bread of life.

And there is enough to go around.

DECEMBER 23

Do you see?

Suddenly the fingers of a human hand appeared and wrote on the plaster of the wall. . . . The king watched the hand as it wrote. His face turned pale and he was so frightened that his knees knocked together and his legs gave way.

DANIEL 5:5-6

One year a teacher at my tiny grade school gave preliminary vision tests. We were supposed to look at a large E projected on a screen, then turn a cardboard E to orient it the same way. I not only couldn't tell which way the E faced, I couldn't see it at all. Until that moment, I had no idea that I couldn't see.

Today many people are unable to see God, but, more frighteningly, they are unable to see that they cannot see. Finances, hunger for power and status, and the world's dizzying pace have all obscured the presence of, and the need for, God. Many can't even see the handwriting on the wall, much less translate it. And when the world's transience or their own mortality gets their attention, they are too terrified, like the king, to discern what the writing means.

Someone has to point out the presence of God in this fast, superficial world. Someone has to teach those who think they don't need God that He breathes peace—not terror—into a human heart. Someone has to point to the small moments, and say, "You call that coincidence, or luck, or talent, or the kindness of strangers, but you are standing in the presence of God."

Someone has to make them see that they cannot see.

DECEMBER 24

God bless us, every one

Your love has given me great joy and encouragement, because you, brother, have refreshed the hearts of the saints.

PHILEMON 7

Every Christmas Eve for years, my sister and I camped out in front of the television to watch Alastair Sim in *A Christmas Carol*. We loved that movie as much—or maybe even more—the 20th time as we did the first time we saw it. No surprises remained; we could even recite most of the dialogue by heart. But seeing it each time helped us relive all of our blessed Christmases past.

When I first became a committed Christian, it used to astonish me that longtime, practiced Christians hungered to be around me, someone with new faith. Originally I thought, "Why would they want me in this discussion? I'm sure they already know all about anything I could contribute."

Certainly a new Christian "refreshes the hearts of the saints" by renewing memories of their own conversions. But new believers also remind us that God offers a clean slate in every moment we live. Mistakes are behind us as soon as we ask forgiveness, so a fresh start awaits no matter how many days or weeks or even lifetimes we have already committed to God.

The moment we go to God, the ghosts are gone. He gives us the best of Christmas past, of Christmas present, and of Christmas future every day that we choose the Christian life. It makes sense that we enjoy reminders of that gift.

"God bless us, every one."

DECEMBER 25

The best Christmas ever

Rejoice in the Lord always. . . . Do not be anxious about anything, but in everything, by prayer and petition, with thanksgiving, present your requests to God. And the peace of God, which transcends all understanding, will guard your hearts and your minds in Christ Jesus. . . .
PHILIPPIANS 4:4, 6, 7

One Christmas in the early 1980s, my family was snowed in, with temperatures of 20 below zero, wind chills more than 50 below, and the blowing snow creating "white-out" conditions outside. It was the best Christmas we ever had.

When my sister arrived, she brought bags of groceries, piles of gifts, and her three sons. So we had everything there we could want or need. We spent those few days eating, playing games, and watching television, comfortable in our cocoon of joyful warmth and love.

Conditions outside don't matter at all if you're being fed and warmed and loved inside. No matter how turbulent the outer world may get, I now enjoy such inner peace that I seldom lose my equilibrium, something that used to happen to me routinely. Unkind words which once bumped me off course now hurt less often. Crises no longer double me over in anxiety, as I get better at handing problems over to God. I love living in this warm, safe place.

The weather outside is frightful.

DECEMBER 26

His Word, our flesh

Yet to all who received him, to those who believed in his name, he gave the right to become children of God. . . . The Word became flesh, and made his dwelling among us.

JOHN 1:12, 14

Okay, Christmas Day is past, and Christ is here. Now, what are we going to do about it?

According to John's gospel, with Christ's coming, "the Word became flesh." We finally were able to see how the Word of our omnipotent, omniscient God can go to work in a shabby little human world.

But it's not just that we were given, in Christ, a model of Christian behavior. The staggering commission we received, when we received Christ, is to function as part of his body. So we're not just talking about God's Word becoming incarnate in the person of Jesus. We're talking about the Word of God becoming incarnate in the person of me, and the person of you, and in every person who truly gives himself over to God through Christian worship.

We haven't just acknowledged that we became part of Christ's world through communion with other Christians. We've acknowledged that we are part of the flesh of his body.

We are the body of Christ. We are the Word made flesh.

Now, what are we going to do about it?

DECEMBER 27

Night and Day

... since we have a great priest over the house of God, let us draw near to God with a sincere heart in full assurance of faith. ... Let us hold unswervingly to the hope we profess, for he who promised is faithful. ... let us encourage one another—and all the more as you see the Day approaching.

HEBREWS 10:21, 23, 25

According to Hebrew custom, each day runs from evening to evening; the Sabbath, for example, begins at sundown, not at dawn.

How many people, like me, would never have found God, or even looked for Him, if we hadn't started in the darkness? Only in the abject darkness did I realize that I cannot handle this world.

Even Jesus' life began with darkness—the threat of murder by Herod, life as a mortal, humiliation, torture, death. And then, only after the darkest of nights, the stone rolled away, and the Light appeared.

Yet no one could have convinced me, in the night, that I was learning lessons that would ultimately save my life. One who is depressed or grieving or filled with doubt often can't even hear words of encouragement, because the darkness begins to feel like home. I know. I have been there.

God called to me in that darkest night to tell me to "hold unswervingly" to hope. Then, I couldn't even hear Him, but now I hear Him whispering to the others.

The darkness will not last forever, child of mine. The Light of the world is coming. Hold on one more night.

The Day approaches.

DECEMBER 28

Solving for X

O Lord, by your hand save me from such men, from men of this world whose reward is in this life. You still the hunger of those you cherish; their sons have plenty, and they store up wealth for their children.
PSALM 17:14

On the west coast of Wales is a town whose name is Llanfairpwllgwyngyllgogerychwyrndrobwllllantysiliogogogoch. My spell-checker thinks it's misspelled, and I have no clue how to say it. But then, my computer and I don't speak Welsh.

A similar barrier separates the generations, especially baby boomers from Generation X: we don't share a language, or even the same values. Most of us boomers began our spiritual lives because our parents told us to, and fewer people in their 20s and 30s have that same incentive to begin searching.

So today the value of a relationship with Christ must be clear, intrinsic, showing not just the "how" but also the "why." A seeker who sees no joy, no comfort, no sense of purpose in the Christian life will look elsewhere, thinking the "reward is in this life."

Why would someone choose a life that looks from the outside to be judgmental, joyless, unaccepting? Why?

Ironically, the letter "X" is used as shorthand for the name of Christ, the One they must see lived out in our lives. So perhaps we can show others why they would want to search for the one true God by proving the undeniable formula for happiness.

"X" equals why.

DECEMBER 29

Wholly longing

If anyone considers himself religious and yet does not keep a tight rein on his tongue, he deceives himself and his religion is worthless. Religion that God our Father accepts as pure and faultless is this: to look after orphans and widows in their distress and to keep oneself from being polluted by the world.

JAMES 1:26-27

Rick Bass, a novelist who lives in Montana, works to save pristine acres of roadless land there. He knows that his visibility empowers him; he says that he cannot imagine loving something as deeply as he loves that wilderness, yet having "no voice" to do anything about it.

How many people experience a deep and disquieting longing for God and no way to express it? How many ache for meaning but find no trace of it in their experiences with religion? As James says, failure to live for God makes religion worthless—or worse, as hypocrisy prevents people from seeking a deep relationship with God.

Man—not God—invented religion, and we have allowed too much of that system to become "polluted by the world." Politics, denominational squabbles, and self-righteousness are the noises the unchurched often hear from us more clearly than the voice of God.

Unless every act and moment of our religion is about God, it is worthless. Religion, after all, is nothing more than man's feeble attempt to define God. True spirituality, though, is something else.

It is God defining man.

Solving for why

Suddenly, when they looked around, they no longer saw anyone with them except Jesus.

MARK 9:8

A South Carolina senator who served for over 50 years decided in 2003 not to run for reelection. He said of the Congress, "We are not serious about anything except the next election."

Our world is filled with examples of institutions that forget why they were established. The Congress runs too much on special interest money. Government agencies seem more concerned about retaining turf than about serving the public. Children's soccer games overflow too often with parental anger and pressure.

Like most humans, I get so wrapped up in my life that I fail to remember that I am here for the glory of God. Oddly, I seem to remember Him best when times are worst—in moments of deepest pain, grief, regret. When the world becomes too suffocating for me to handle, I apologize to God for whining about burdens and forgetting blessings. Yet, no matter how unfaithful or ungrateful I have been, I am shocked to see that God is still there. "I look around, and no longer see anyone with me except Jesus."

There are places in my life that no one else can go. Some are regrets or fears so deep that I cannot express them; others are dreams so towering that I'm afraid to even say them out loud. Those are the moments when I need most to remember that God is here for me.

And that I am here for Him.

DECEMBER 31

Be still

"Be still, then, and know that I am God."

PSALM 46:10

Be still. Lay down your armor, in all its forms. Lay down your control; it's an illusion, anyway. Down deep, you're actually thankful that it's an illusion, because you want to rest. I will take care of you. I always have. That will never change.

Lay down your sadness. Give it back to me. That deep and unrelenting sadness over your losses shows only how deeply you have loved, how deeply you are loved. Don't you think I know what it's like to give up someone you love more than anything?

Be still. You know I understand. Your tears are mine. Give them to Me.

Be still. Lay down your weapons. Lay down your need to be right. Lay down your frenzy to know everything. Lay down your urge to bring others down so that you can feel superior. Rise above them by coming to Me.

Be still. Lay down your obsession with being perfect. Being perfect is not your job. It's mine.

Be still. Lay down your anxiety. Being a responsible adult doesn't mean you have to agonize over every detail of life. Lay down your worries before me, so that you can stand up straight and draw closer to me. It's all I want from you.

Be still. Lay down your gifts before me. Bring every talent I have ever given you to the altar so that I can bless it and give it back to you a thousand times over.

Be still. Lay down your praise before me, all the joy in your life. You know it all comes from me. You know it. You may find it through your family or a friend, or through music or nature or laughter. But you know its Source. Be still, and let it flow.

Be still. Lay down your life, your love, your loss, before Me. As my Son did.

Be still, my child, and rest in Me. Know with all of your heart that I am God. Be still. I love you.

Be still.

Index

A
abundant life 10/13
action 2/16, 3/21, 4/8, 6/22
anger 4/12, 4/22, 10/13, 11/17
anger with God 5/27, 8/12
anxiety 5/2
baggage 1/23, 1/24, 6/7

B
Bible 1/3, 1/28, 5/30, 8/5
blessings 3/12
blindness 2/15, 2/28, 4/4, 7/3, 12/23
body of Christ 1/16, 2/25, 3/29, 4/6, 4/11, 4/29, 6/10, 7/24, 7/31, 8/16, 8/21, 11/13, 11/16, 12/2, 12/22, 12/24, 12/26
bondage 1/16, 4/29
burdens 5/26, 6/7

C
change 1/1, 1/11, 1/12, 1/26, 1/31, 2/5, 2/10, 2/20, 3/5, 3/8, 3/19, 3/23, 3/31, 4/13, 4/18, 4/21, 5/5, 5/13, 5/14, 5/15, 5/23, 5/25, 6/8, 6/12, 6/17, 7/15, 7/16, 7/30, 8/19, 8/23, 8/28, 8/31, 9/9, 9/10, 9/11, 9/26, 9/30, 10/10, 10/25, 10/27, 11/4, 11/21, 11/25, 12/16
choices 8/24, 10/6, 10/12, 10/29, 11/5, 11/7, 11/16, 11/24, 11/29, 12/11
Christ as model 2/16, 7/11, 7/19, 8/2, 9/17, 8/30, 9/29, 10/5, 10/25, 11/7, 12/7, 12/26
Christ to the world 1/6, 2/7, 2/16, 2/18, 2/19, 2/25, 3/20, 3/29, 5/6, 5/8,
Christian life 1/8, 2/10, 2/16, 2/19, 2/25, 3/5, 3/20, 3/21, 5/2, 5/30, 6/5, 6/16, 6/22
church 6/15, 8/18
comfort zones 2/5, 2/19, 2/27, 5/13, 5/14
commitment 9/3

community 2/12, 2/18, 2/21, 3/13, 3/29, 4/3, 4/4, 5/6, 5/26, 5/29, 6/10, 6/22, 7/12, 7/15, 7/21, 7/31, 8/1, 11/14, 12/24
compassion 6/24, 6/27, 6/30, 8/21, 9/12, 9/27, 10/26
complacency 8/19, 8/28, 12/16
connections 1/18, 4/20, 6/3
constancy 2/3, 2/6, 3/7, 3/12, 5/2, 5/25, 6/2, 6/3, 6/11, 6/19, 6/21, 7/4, 7/18, 7/20, 7/27, 8/9, 9/3, 9/11, 9/16, 9/26, 11/2, 11/3, 11/17, 11/10, 11/24, 11/29, 12/25, 12/31
control 9/7, 9/30
cosmology 8/7
courage 8/15
creation 8/7
crisis 10/19, 11/25
culture 2/11, 5/17, 6/18, 7/23, 8/31, 9/1, 9/2

D
death 8/13
demons 6/11
denial 10/1, 10/29, 11/15
desires 9/28
despair 8/22
direction 8/22
doctrine 3/1
doubt 1/30, 8/25, 10/27, 11/8

E
ego 4/9, 4/12, 6/12
emptiness 8/3, 8/29, 10/3, 10/4, 10/14, 11/9, 12/29
eternal life 6/14, 10/5, 11/2, 11/30
evangelism 1/13, 1/18, 2/20, 3/1, 3/4, 3/23, 4/17, 4/24, 4/29, 5/16, 5/30, 7/14, 7/23, 8/3, 8/10, 8/15, 9/9, 10/3, 10/4, 10/5, 10/27, 10/28, 11/3, 12/3, 12/7, 12/28
everyday life 2/19
evil 3/30, 4/28
expectations 5/23

INDEX

F
failure 2/4
faith 1/30, 3/2, 3/17, 4/23, 4/28, 8/9, 9/4, 9/30, 10/21, 11/8, 11/22, 11/23
fear 1/30, 3/7, 6/7, 6/8, 6/11, 6/12, 6/18, 6/19, 6/21, 6/28, 7/30, 8/26, 8/29, 9/4, 9/10, 9/21, 10/1, 10/19, 10/25, 10/26, 10/27, 11/24
focus 3/31, 4/14, 5/10, 9/1, 11/12
forgiveness 1/21, 1/23, 2/3, 2/4, 2/24, 3/3, 3/4, 3/10, 3/28, 3/30, 4/1, 4/12, 5/9, 5/19, 6/2, 6/3, 6/7, 6/9, 6/17, 6/26, 7/6, 7/21, 8/6, 8/14, 9/17, 9/23, 9/25, 10/1, 11/14, 12/1, 12/8, 12/12
freedom 1/16, 7/30, 8/29
free will 8/24

G
gifts 7/26, 9/14, 9/22, 9/24, 9/28, 10/11, 10/18, 10/31, 11/4, 11/8, 11/26, 12/18, 12/19, 12/21, 12/24
God first 4/13, 10/7, 10/8, 10/30/ 11/7, 11/26, 12/6, 12/9
God in everything 1/2, 1/17, 12/23
God in others 11/18
God in this world 2/22, 2/27, 3/3
God's desire for us 6/20
God's love 7/5
God's sacrifice 2/1, 2/14, 3/25, 4/7, 4/16, 4/24, 6/6, 12/13
God's will 1/7, 1/15, 2/2, 2/4, 2/5, 2/7, 2/9, 2/10, 2/15, 3/5, 3/11, 3/16, 3/26, 4/15, 4/30, 5/1, 5/11, 5/13, 5/18, 6/8, 6/12, 6/13, 6/30, 7/4, 7/13, 7/18, 7/24, 8/11, 8/22, 8/29, 9/2, 9/6, 9/7, 9/13, 9/18, 11/12, 12/2, 12/10, 12/15
grace 1/2, 1/10, 2/1, 2/13, 3/14, 3/21, 3/25, 3/26, 4/7, 4/16, 4/19, 4/24, 5/9, 5/31, 6/2, 6/3, 6/6, 6/19, 6/20, 7/6, 7/20, 7/21, 10/2, 10/16, 10/23
gratification 2/1
gratitude 1/21, 4/15, 4/16, 7/10, 7/14, 9/22, 10/31, 11/4, 11/20, 11/25, 11/26, 12/8, 12/13, 12/18, 12/21, 12/24
grief 3/24, 4/3, 5/21, 6/27, 7/15, 7/26, 8/13, 9/11, 11/10, 11/27
growth 3/31
grudges 4/1
guidance 2/18, 5/1, 6/13

H
healing 4/10, 5/19, 6/4, 6/7, 6/10, 7/26, 8/14, 9/17, 9/20, 10/26, 11/2, 11/15, 11/22, 12/4, 12/12
heaven 2/8, 6/18
holiness 1/2, 7/11
hope 8/22, 9/19, 12/21
humanity 10/2, 11/1, 11/11, 11/23, 12/1, 12/17
hunger for God 5/29, 6/4/ 7/3, 7/8, 8/3, 9/9, 9/12, 10/14, 11/6, 11/19, 12/3, 12/4, 12/5, 12/29
hypocrisy 1/3, 1/14, 4/6, 5/3, 6/15, 6/26, 6/28, 7/1, 8/3, 8/5, 8/30, 10/28, 11/6, 11/15, 12/7, 12/9, 12/14, 12/20, 12/28, 12/29, 12/30

I
idols 5/29
image of God 1/5
imitation of Christ 2/16
immensity of God 3/15, 4/23, 8/27, 10/24, 5/11
inclusion 2/23
intellect 4/2, 4/23, 5/12, 6/11, 8/7, 9/24, 11/8

J
joy 6/16, 7/10
judgmentalism 1/14, 1/23/ 3/28, 4/10, 4/24, 10/28, 12/1, 12/14, 12/22, 12/28
justice 1/7

K
kingdom of God 6/23, 7/30, 8/20, 8/27, 10/7
knowing God 5/7, 5/22
knowledge 9/24

L
law 4/27, 6/1, 7/25, 8/1, 9/15, 10/30, 11/5, 12/9, 12/16

INDEX

legalism 1/7/ 2/12, 4/19, 4/27, 5/2, 5/4, 5/17, 6/1, 6/17
lessons 1/26, 7/22, 8/6, 8/25, 8/27, 9/11, 9/20, 9/21, 11/17, 11/21, 11/23, 11/27, 12/2, 12/27
limitations 1/11
listening 4/25, 12/15
living for God 2/16, 4/22, 5/8, 5/22, 5/28, 7/1, 7/23, 7/31, 8/8, 8/20, 8/31, 9/6, 9/8, 9/14, 10/3, 10/4, 10/9, 10/10, 10/12, 10/15, 10/17, 10/22, 10/23, 11/1, 11/5, 11/30, 12/5, 12/7, 12/11
loneliness 1/18
loss 3/16, 3/19, 4/3, 4/18, 5/5, 5/14, 5/15, 5/21, 5/23, 6/14, 6/18, 6/24, 6/27, 7/16, 8/13, 8/28, 9/10, 9/11, 9/12, 9/21, 11/10, 11/27
love your neighbor 1/4, 2/7, 2/23, 2/25, 3/6, 3/27, 4/6, 4/8, 4/12, 4/22, 4/26, 4/29, 5/2, 5/6, 5/30, 6/15, 6/22, 6/24, 6/29, 7/2, 7/4, 7/12, 7/26, 8/16, 8/18, 8/21, 8/30, 9/15, 9/29, 10/4, 10/5, 10/11, 10/15, 10/20, 11/16, 12/9
loving God 5/31, 7/2, 8/12

M

manipulation 10/20
materialism 1/25, 1/27, 3/12, 3/18, 3/22, 4/13, 4/17, 9/26, 9/28, 10/3, 10/9, 11/9, 11/30, 12/5
meaninglessness 5/29
meditation 4/5, 4/25
mercy 6/2, 6/3, 6/9, 7/6, 9/19, 9/25, 11/14
miracles 9/23, 9/28
mistakes 8/6, 9/25, 12/11
morality 10/12
mourning 1/26, 4/3
mystery 8/25

N

new start 1/1

O

obedience 12/10, 12/19
other gods 7/28

P

pain 4/3, 11/17, 11/27
passion 5/18, 6/24
patience 2/12
peace 4/27, 5/7, 5/15, 5/24, 6/10, 6/14, 6/20, 8/3, 8/13, 9/21, 10/6, 10/29, 11/4, 11/7, 12/3, 12/4, 12/15
personal relationship with God 8/19, 9/2, 10/7, 10/10, 10/17, 11/11, 11/22, 11/28, 12/17
piety 1/5, 2/18, 3/8
potential 2/2, 2/5, 3/11, 3/26, 4/21, 5/17
power 8/27
prayer 1/14, 1/22, 2/17, 2/21, 3/13, 4/5, 4/20, 4/25, 5/1, 5/11, 5/15, 5/26, 5/27, 6/10, 6/30, 7/7, 7/9, 7/10, 7/18, 8/13, 8/21, 9/8, 12/15, 12/31
prejudice 3/9
presence of God 5/8, 9/16
priorities 1/1, 1/5, 1/20, 1/29, 2/10, 2/15, 2/22, 3/1, 3/5, 3/18, 3/22, 3/24, 3/27, 3/31, 4/9, 4/13, 4/14, 4/15, 4/17, 4/18, 4/22, 4/30, 5/2, 5/4, 5/10, 5/15, 5/18, 5/28, 5/29, 6/1, 6/7, 7/2, 7/8, 7/10, 7/16, 7/24, 8/4, 8/8, 8/24, 8/26, 8/30, 9/1, 9/2, 9/8, 9/22, 9/30, 10/6, 10/7, 10/8, 10/10, 10/11, 10/17, 10/22, 10/29, 10/30, 11/9, 11/20, 11/29, 12/1, 12/11, 12/20, 12/25, 12/29
prisons 1/16, 1/25, 3/11, 4/29, 6/23
protection 9/5

Q

quiet time 2/17, 4/5, 4/25, 7/7, 12/15, 12/31

R

rationalization 10/12, 11/5
reason 4/2, 4/22, 5/12, 8/7, 11/8
redemption 3/14, 3/21, 7/11, 7/29, 8/23, 9/19, 9/20, 9/27, 10/18
regret 2/23, 2/24, 3/3, 3/4, 6/25, 8/6, 8/14, 9/19, 9/20, 9/28, 10/1, 11/14, 12/12

INDEX

religion 1/9, 3/1, 3/8, 3/31, 4/19, 4/27, 5/3, 5/4, 5/7, 5/12, 5/31, 6/1, 6/15, 6/28, 8/18, 8/29, 10/2, 10/15, 10/24, 11/16, 11/19, 12/20, 12/29, 12/30
repentance 6/29
resentment 1/23, 3/10, 5/19, 6/17, 7/6, 9/6, 10/13, 11/17
rest 7/7, 9/5
resurrection 1/6
righteousness 1/7, 1/14, 1/30
ritual 1/28, 11/6

S

Sabbath 7/7
sacrifice 4/1, 4/19, 6/27, 7/10, 7/22, 8/22, 9/3, 9/14, 9/27, 10/31, 11/18, 11/21, 11/28, 12/4, 12/13, 12/18
safety 9/1, 9/5
science 8/7
seeking God 2/28, 4/4, 5/4, 8/25, 10/19, 12/6
self, loss of 9/13
selfishness 11/20, 12/22
self-esteem 1/19, 8/8, 9/24, 11/16
self-interest 11/19, 11/20
self-justification 10/15
self-reliance 10/21, 11/2, 12/8
self-righteousness 10/13, 10/15, 10/24, 12/14, 12/22, 12/28
service 2/7, 4/8, 4/11, 4/24, 6/22, 7/12, 7/31, 8/1, 8/16
sin 12/11
small things 1/17, 2/26, 3/20, 4/8, 4/11, 4/15, 4/22, 4/26, 5/21, 6/5, 6/23, 7/17, 7/19, 8/17, 9/14, 9/29, 10/11, 10/16, 11/1
spiritual disciplines 3/31
stillness 2/17, 4/5, 4/25, 7/7, 12/15, 12/31

stubbornness 7/13
study 8/25
success 10/9
suffering 11/27, 12/2, 12/21, 12/27

T

time 4/30, 11/26
timing 1/15
tolerance 3/9, 10/28
transformation 2/13, 2/21
transience 9/26, 11/3, 11/25, 11/29, 12/5, 12/28
trials 10/18
trust 1/7, 1/26, 1/31, 2/2, 2/8, 2/9, 3/7, 4/23, 5/13, 5/24, 5/25, 6/11, 6/21, 7/9, 7/18, 7/20, 7/25, 8/2, 8/9, 8/11, 8/12, 8/18, 9/4, 9/5, 9/8, 10/6, 10/21, 11/8, 11/12
truth 2/6, 7/4
turning to God 1/12, 1/24, 1/27, 2/4, 3/21, 4/2, 4/18, 4/21, 5/5, 5/12, 5/16, 5/21, 6/3, 6/5, 6/13, 6/16, 6/17, 7/5, 7/13, 7/14, 7/21, 7/27, 8/17, 8/26, 9/10, 9/21, 10/16, 10/21, 12/1, 12/10, 12/19, 12/23, 12/27

U

urgency 9/9

W

weakness 10/27, 11/10, 11/23
wholeness 4/10
will 3/24, 8/19
wisdom 9/20
witness 2/20
work 2/19, 2/22, 5/17
worry 5/12
worship 1/28
worthiness 1/10, 1/21, 1/24, 2/12

Holy Ordinary

The book *Holy Ordinary* is the outgrowth of a writing ministry that began in August of 2000. I had hoped to write for several monthly devotional publications, and, to sharpen my writing skills, I began sending out "practice" messages by e-mail to a few friends. God has taken that humble beginning and multiplied its effects in His hands.

I grew up as a member of the Roman Catholic Church, but for whatever reason, I did not really connect with God until I was in my early 40s. I knew, through all of those decades, that the longing I felt was spiritual, but I had no idea how to find God, or even how to begin looking. I read all the right books and attended church sporadically, but I still didn't "get" God.

Then, one friend invited me to her little Episcopal church, and I started seeing God's work through other people and through the breathtaking Episcopal liturgy. Another friend told me a story which made me realize that God was ready when I was. I clearly remember the moment, the day, the place where that revelation sank in: God wants me near Him, and all I have to do is turn to Him.

Now, over 15 years since I started actively seeking God, I must thank God for all of you who have shared the search with me. The encouragement you have offered has helped sustain me through some difficult times in my life. The feedback and insight you have shared with me have given me new ways of seeing God in my own life. I hope that you will continue to stay in touch with me so that my relationship with you and with God can continue to grow and deepen. I thank you all for allowing me to walk this spiritual journey with you. May God bless you as richly as God blesses me.

Carol Mead

Holy Ordinary
Finding God in the Everyday

by Carol Mead

More information on the book and the "Holy Ordinary" ministry is available at the following website:

holyordinary.com

Thank you for your support!